Understanding Mental Objects

The ways in which an individual relates to and perceives other people (his or her 'objects') has always been a preoccupation of psychoanalysis and in recent years a plethora of concepts has grown up in the literature. In this groundbreaking study, Meir Perlow traces the major theoretical developments regarding mental objects and sets out to clarify the changing meanings of different concepts from context to context.

The book begins with an historical survey of how mental objects have been understood in the various schools of psychoanalysis. These include Freud and his associates, the object-relations approaches of Klein, Fairbairn and Bion, orientations derived from ego psychology such as those of Schafer and Kernberg, and the self-object orientation of Kohut. In Part Two the author discusses the conceptual and clinical issues involved in the major differences between the concepts. Finally, he delineates three basic meanings of the concepts as they have emerged in the literature and shows how they relate to ongoing debates in contemporary psychoanalysis.

This long overdue clarification of a complex area, with its wide-ranging and imaginative grasp of the different theories about objects, will be an invaluable reference for all psychoanalysts and psychologists.

Meir Perlow Ph.D., is Senior Clinical Psychologist at Eitanim Psychiatric Hospital, Jerusalem. He was formerly a lecturer in psychoanalytic theory at the Hebrew University, Jerusalem, and now conducts a variety of seminars on psychoanalytic subjects.

THE NEW LIBRARY OF PSYCHOANALYSIS

The New Library of Psychoanalysis was launched in 1987 in association with the Institute of Psycho-Analysis, London. Its purpose is to facilitate a greater and more widespread appreciation of what psychoanalysis is really about and to provide a forum for increasing mutual understanding between psychoanalysts and those working in other disciplines such as history, linguistics, literature, medicine, philosophy, psychology and the social sciences. It is intended that the titles selected for publication in the series should deepen and develop psychoanalytic thinking and technique, contribute to psychoanalysis from outside or contribute to other disciplines from a psychoanalytical perspective.

The Institute, together with the British Psycho-Analytical Society, runs a low-fee psychoanalytic clinic, organizes lectures and scientific events concerned with psychoanalysis, publishes the *International Journal of Psycho-Analysis* and the *International Review of Psycho-Analysis*, and runs the only training course in the UK in psychoanalysis leading to membership of the International Psychoanalytical Association – the body which preserves internationally agreed standards of training, of professional entry, and of professional ethics and practice for psychoanalysis as initiated and developed by Sigmund Freud. Distinguished members of the Institute have included Michael Balint, Wilfred Bion, Ronald Fairbairn, Anna Freud, Ernest Jones, Melanie Klein, John Rickman and Donald Winnicott.

Volumes 1–11 in the series have been prepared under the general editorship of David Tuckett, with Ronald Britton and Eglé Laufer as associate editors. Subsequent volumes are under the general editorship of Elizabeth Bott Spillius, with, from Volume 17, Donald Campbell, Michael Parsons, Rosine Jozef Perelberg and David Taylor as associate editors.

ALSO IN THIS SERIES

NEW LIBRARY OF PSYCHOANALYSIS
—— 22 ——

General editor: Elizabeth Bott Spillius

Understanding
Mental Objects

Meir Perlow

London and New York

First published 1995
by Routledge
11 New Fetter Lane, London EC4P 4EE

Simultaneously published in the USA and Canada
by Routledge
29 West 35th Street, New York, NY 10001

© 1995 Meir Perlow

Typeset in Bembo by LaserScript, Mitcham, Surrey
Printed and bound in Great Britain by
Mackays of Chatham PLC, Chatham, Kent

British Library Cataloguing in Publication Data
A catalogue record for this book is available from the British Library

Library of Congress Cataloguing in Publication Data
A catalogue record for this book has been requested

ISBN 0−415−12178−7 (hbk)
0−415−12179−5 (pbk)

Contents

Preface

In this outstanding work Dr Perlow uses the term 'mental objects' to refer to a whole group of concepts. These include memories of other people and relationships to them, so-called internal objects, part-objects, introjects, objects identified with, and the like. There is tremendous confusion in this field, and in his approach to organizing the concept Perlow has approached the topic appropriately and usefully under the umbrella heading of 'mental objects', before going on to delineate differences in the various conceptions in the psychoanalytic literature.

The method of the research has been to undertake a thorough historical review of the concept and to develop theoretical formulations following this. The careful dissection of literature is in itself a major piece of clarification and shows particularly well the problems of defining the boundaries of each of the ideas considered. All of this lays the ground for Perlow's later theoretical elaboration.

Perlow sees a number of concepts, generally labelled 'internal objects', as referring to specific phantasies regarding an object. He makes the distinction between representations, which refer to constructs postulated as existing outside the realm of subjective experience, and phantasy, referring to a subjectively experienced phenomenon, conscious or unconscious. This is an important step in clarifying a confused area. Further, in considering mental representations Perlow draws attention to affective as well as cognitive aspects. He discusses the notion of mental objects in regard to developmental capacities and deficits, as represented by the relation between self and object representations, and, here again, Perlow takes a step towards clarifying a confused area.

Perlow considers Ferenczi's concept of introjection, which was taken over by Freud and has come to play an extremely important part in psychoanalytic theorizing. He shows how there has been disagreement over the nature of the process, as well as about the timing of its occurrence. He then discusses the important contributions of Karl Abraham, which influenced both Freud and Melanie Klein. This is followed by a discussion

ix

of Klein's concept of the internal object, and Perlow has made a significant contribution in exploring this Kleinian notion and tracing its links to the ideas of non-Kleinian psychoanalytic theoreticians. He appropriately devotes attention to the Controversial Discussion of the 1940s in the British Society, in which the Kleinian and Freudian theorists aired their disagreements.

Fairbairn's work in this area is extremely important and is well and critically discussed by Perlow. Like Melanie Klein, Fairbairn has provided the basis for the development of a growing trend in psychoanalytic thinking, based predominantly on an object-relational perspective. Then Perlow goes on to discuss the work of Bion, which represents an elaboration of Melanie Klein's views. Bion is difficult to understand, and Perlow has done outstanding work in delineating Bionian formulations and assessing their relation to the various notions subsumed under the heading of 'mental objects'. He pays attention to writers who have contributed to this area, such as Bychowski, Spitz, Edith Jacobson (whose work is appropriately discussed in detail) and Grotstein.

Perlow goes on to discuss what he calls 'the representational theorists', namely, Novey, Beres and myself. His discussion here is extremely informative, and the way he has managed to tease out various common threads in the contributions of these authors is impressive; moreover, he also considers the more recent criticisms of the representational viewpoint. Perlow is clear about his own criticism of the concept of representation, and puts his case forcefully and convincingly. He dissects the work of Roy Schafer, who has written extensively on the process of internalization, and goes on to examine the contributions of Kernberg, who has been greatly influenced by Edith Jacobson and by Kleinian thinkers. He brings in the work of Stierlin, who took the approach that inner objects should be considered in terms of the various functions they fulfil. Still within the rubric of ego-psychological orientations, Perlow discusses the difficult concept of object constancy in the psychoanalytic sense. Here his clarification of the issues is extremely useful.

In the final part of the historical survey, the contributions of Winnicott and Heinz Kohut are looked at. Both these authors are extremely important in this particular field, although their theoretical formulations are rather blurred at the edges. Nevertheless, their ideas have had a major impact, and Perlow has been able to grasp and discuss them in a clear and useful way.

The second part of Perlow's work is devoted to considering problems which have arisen as a result of his analysis of the literature. He considers the following five issues: the origins of the mental object; the status of the mental object; the mental object in relation to motivation; the mental object as a developmental capacity; and the mental object's position in relation to the self. He treats the question of origin in terms of the relative influence of internal and external factors in development, a major issue in past and current psychoanalytic theory. He takes up the question of the relation between phantasy and realistic perception, and links this with the problem of mental representation. He then discusses the whole issue of whether mental objects – or rather, of *which* mental objects – should be considered to be in the realm of subjective experience, or outside it.

The understanding of motivation is central to psychoanalytic thinking, and important in relation to mental objects. Perlow tackles this difficult area exceptionally well, and his discussion of the mental object as a developmental capacity presents a fresh and extremely interesting viewpoint. His consideration of the position of the mental object in relation to the self is thorough and extensive.

In addition to the points mentioned above, Perlow writes on what he refers to as the clinical issue of responsibility. This has always been a difficult problem when one comes to consider the concept of unconscious intentionality. He pays particular attention to Melanie Klein's and Kohut's views, as well as to more recent work by Merton Gill, and this section is of particular interest.

The concluding part of this remarkable work is a conceptual analysis of mental objects, and here Perlow adopts a three-fold approach, first considering mental objects as representations, then as phantasies, and finally as developmental capacities – that is, as basic structures of the personality. He comes down firmly on the side of viewing representations as being outside the realm of subjective experience, and in doing this he takes a stand against the ambiguity which has bedevilled this particular concept. In regard to the idea of mental objects as phantasies, he distinguishes between the two, in an attempt to deal with the current confusion in regard both objects and phantasy. He proposes to distinguish between concepts of mental objects that refer to phantasy on the one hand, and those relating to representations or capacities on the other, and places phantasies firmly in the experiential realm, in contrast to representations and schemata.

Perlow traces the far-reaching implications of the developmental approach in regard to mental objects and mental representations at different levels of development. He makes the interesting point that 'The highest level of personality organization is that at which the individual's representations have achieved their full structural development and they are both differentiated and integrated'. Finally, he concludes that the aim of his research has been to 'further our understanding of the plethora of terms and concepts that have developed in the psychoanalytic literature to describe and explain the ways in which the mind structures its interactions with other people'. In my view he has certainly fulfilled his task extremely well and has produced an admirable work. He has delineated and refined a great many previously confusing issues in the area of 'mental objects', and there is little doubt that his study represents a major contribution to the field.

Joseph Sandler
London
October 1994

Introduction

Psychoanalytic theory has in recent years tended to shift from a drive-orientated approach to an interest in the role of an individual's interpersonal relationships in the formation and patterning of his mental organizations, processes and capacities. Greenberg and Mitchell (1983) have recently described this shift in terms of a growing interest in a 'relational model',[1] which serves as an alternative to, and is sometimes integrated with, the original drive model. It is the purpose of this book to examine the major concepts used in the psychoanalytic literature to conceptualize those mental organizations considered to be related to, and often originating in, the individual's relationships with others; these are the concepts which have played an important part in the shift of interest described by Greenberg and Mitchell (1983). There is a need for such an examination because psychoanalytic literature has presented a plethora of concepts which are related to such mental organizations, and which have not been adequately delineated from one another or defined in the context of the different trends in psychoanalytic theory extant today.

First, a note in regard to the general term I have coined for use in the present study: 'mental objects'. I am using this term to refer to a group of concepts which have been used in the psychoanalytic literature to refer to various mental organizations, structures, processes and capacities in an individual which relate his or her perception, attitude, relationship with and memories of other people (commonly referred to, in the psycho-analytic literature, as 'objects').[2] Some of the prominent members of this group are: object images, internal objects, part-objects, object representations, introjects, identifications, transitional objects, selfobjects, psychic presences and object constancy.

Each of these concepts (and others discussed in this study under the rubric of 'mental objects') is embedded in a theory of mental functioning, and although they all derive from psychoanalytic theory it is not uncommon for these theories to differ from one another. Therefore it is not

1

enough to define each concept and delineate it from its cognates. Rather it is necessary to examine each concept in the context of the theory (and often, theories) within which it developed, with an eye to the changing meanings of different concepts from context to context. In addition to such an examination, there is a need to discuss some of the basic theoretical and conceptual issues lying at the base of the plethora of concepts, prior to a delineation of the basic dimensions of meanings implied by the various concepts of mental objects. Such a delineation will constitute the contribution of the present study to a more coherent conceptualization of the meanings of concepts of mental objects.

This book is in three parts. Part One is a historical survey, in which the major concepts of mental objects that have been used in the psychoanalytic literature will be examined in the context of the theories within which they were developed. This will provide the basic material for the following two parts: Part Two discusses the conceptual (and also clinical) issues involved in the major differences among the concepts examined in Part One; Part Three offers a conceptual delineation of three basic meanings of the concepts of mental objects as they have developed in the psychoanalytic literature. In this last part I will also provide examples of how these three basic concepts are related to various ongoing issues in the psychoanalytic literature.

Although the basic concepts discussed in Part Three are actually the outcome of the whole of this study, I will present a brief preview of these in this introduction. This preview will lighten the task of entering into the intricacies of the historical survey, providing the reader with an idea of where we are headed. All the points noted here will be further elaborated in the chapter on conceptual delineation.

I have distinguished three basic meanings to which concepts of mental objects in the psychoanalytic literature refer:

1 representations (or schemas),
2 phantasies,
3 developmental capacities and deficits.

First, the concept of representation as used in this study, refers to an amalgamation of memories regarding an object, which functions as an anticipatory set for future interaction. As such, a mental representation of an object refers to a 'schema' which organizes experience and provides a context both for present perceptions and phantasies, and for the recall of past memories.

A number of clarifications must be made regarding the meaning of these terms in the context of psychoanalytic theory. In contrast to the representations (and schemas) of cognitive psychology, the emphasis in psychoanalytic theory is on the *emotional* aspects of the interaction with the object, and representations are conceived of as having an emotional-cognitive character. For example, objects may be represented as angry, loving, intrusive, demanding, exciting, disappointing and so on. It should be noted that this is more complex than merely stating that the individual tends to think of the object as angry, loving and so forth, because the implication is often made that the individual's own emotional state is closely involved in the emotional state attributed to the object.

Another important distinction between the psychoanalytic concept of representation and that of cognitive psychology is in regard to the degree to which representations are considered to represent reality. The basic interest of cognitive psychology (in regard to representation) is how a person represents reality, the difficulties in such tasks and how the capacity to represent reality in a fully developed fashion develops. In contrast, psychoanalytic theory started from a conception according to which the mental apparatus functions primarily in reaction to sexual (and aggressive) drives and wishes. While different trends in psychoanalytic theory emphasize to different extents the influence of the drives and wishes on representations of objects, a basic assumption common to all is that representations are heavily influenced by such drives and wishes. This assumption constitutes such a basic difference *vis-à-vis* the conception of cognitive psychology regarding representation that the use of the same word for both is highly confusing, and this difference must constantly be taken into consideration.

Another clarification regarding the psychoanalytic concept of representation is that it does not necessarily have the connotation of 'the capacity to represent an object in its absence' which characterizes Piaget's concept of representation. While some psychoanalytic theoreticians have suggested that the psychoanalytic concept of representation be used to refer to that capacity (for example, Beres and Joseph 1970; Grotstein 1981), by and large psychoanalytic theory has not made the same strict distinction between sensorimotor schemas and representations that was crucial to Piaget's theory. This point will be discussed further in Part Three.

Second, the concept of phantasy is a very basic one in psychoanalytic theory. Like other concepts, it has taken on different meanings according to the different theoretical contexts in which it appears. These differences will be further clarified following the historical survey. At this point it is sufficient to note that concepts of mental objects, especially concepts such as 'internal objects', 'introjects' and 'psychic presences', have been used to refer to specific *phantasies* regarding an object (whether conscious or unconscious). Thus, for example, the statement that 'the introjected penis continued to threaten her from the inside' (Fenichel 1925: 56) refers to the patient's *phantasy* of a threatening penis inside her.

It is important to distinguish between the concepts of phantasy and of

3

representation, although the two are closely linked. In psychoanalytic theory, phantasy is considered to be a motivated behaviour, fulfilling (as do all behaviours) a function (or a number of functions). The basic function considered to be fulfilled by phantasy is that of wish-fulfilment (Freud 1911b; Sandler and Nagera 1963). Representation differs from phantasy in two important ways. As defined in this study, representation refers to an anticipatory set based on past experience – not to an experience itself. Thus, following the distinction between theoretical constructs (the non-experiential realm – Sandler and Joffe 1969) and subjectively experienced phenomena, representations refer to theoretical constructs. In contrast, phantasy refers to a subjectively experienced phenomenon – whether conscious or unconscious. The fact that psychoanalytic theory postulates unconscious experiences makes the distinction between theoretical constructs and (unconscious) experience less clear than in other areas of psychological theory, but the distinction is certainly important for a conceptual analysis. Thus even the unconscious phantasy is (by and large) considered by psychoanalytic theory to refer to a subjectively experienced phenomenon.

The second distinction between phantasy and representation is related to the function(s) of phantasy in mental life. As noted, phantasy has, by and large, been considered to be related to wish-fulfilment. Whether in the frame of reference of the theory of sexual drives, or in a wider frame of reference referring to other sources of motivation (for example, Fairbairn's object-directed motivation or Sandler's affective homeostasis), phantasy has been conceived as part of attempts by the mental apparatus to attain a wished-for state. Phantasies of objects thus fulfil a role in the process of wish-fulfilment, and may be considered to be motivated behaviour. In contrast, representations of objects are not considered to be behaviour, and are not considered to be motivated. Although psychoanalytic theory does postulate that representations are influenced by drives, wishes and phantasies – that is, their 'shape' (or content) is affected – representations are not considered to be constructed in order to provide wish-fulfilment. As we shall see, this difference is an important one.

The third meaning associated with concepts of mental objects in the psychoanalytic literature is that of a mental object as a developmental capacity and deficit. Concepts such as the fusion of self and object representations (as developed by E. Jacobson, and further by Kernberg), and object constancy, refer to more than an amalgam of memories serving as an anticipatory set for the perception and phantasying of interpersonal interactions (which is how I have defined representation in the present study). These concepts imply a view of representaions as basic structures of the personality, the structural characteristics of which (for instance, their degree of differentiation and integration) determine the level of organization of

4

the personality as a whole (psychotic, borderline and neurotic). According to these views, these structural characteristics are developmental achievements, which may be disturbed to various degrees, in which case they constitute developmental defects affecting the level of functioning of the personality in many areas. This view of the structural and developmental aspects of concepts of mental objects also tends to have clinical implications for treatment, which will be further discussed in Parts Two and Three.

These three basic meanings – representations, phantasies and developmental capacities and deficits – are not commonly distinguished in the psychoanalytic literature. It is my contention – upon which I will elaborate further in the conceptual analysis – that the distinction between these three aspects contributes to an understanding of the divergent trends and usages of concepts of mental objects in the psychoanalytic literature.

PART ONE

Historical survey

The historical survey will deal with three main groups of psychoanalytic theoreticians, roughly reflecting the main lines of historical development of concepts of mental objects in the psychoanalytic literature. The first group established the basis for most of the concepts which later developed – Freud, and his close associates, Ferenczi and Abraham.

Following this group came Melanie Klein, whose development of the concept of internal objects made that concept a central one in psycho-analytic theory. Closely influenced by Melanie Klein was Fairbairn, who made use of Klein's concept of internal objects, but who developed a theory of motivation so different from that of Klein that his concept of internal objects came to have very different meanings from those of Klein. Grouped with the Kleinians are two other theoreticians, one of whom gave Klein's concepts an interesting twist without officially changing them (Bion), and another, more recent, writer who has attempted a combination of Kleinian and other concepts (Grotstein).

The third group comprises theoreticians working out of an ego psychology orientation. These theoreticians may be seen as furthering the development of ego psychological concepts of mental objects, both in response to the challenges of Klein's and Fairbairn's concepts (Jacobson, Kernberg, Stierlin) and in response to the growing interest in concepts that reflect the influences of early childhood experience on development (Spitz, the representational theorists – Novey, Beres, Sandler and also Schafer – and a section on the concept of object constancy). (I have included a short survey of some of Bychowski's work at the beginning of the ego psychology group, not so much because he was an ego psychology orientated theoretician, but because of a specific connection of his concepts to the development of the ego psychology concepts.)

The historical survey ends with a chapter on the specific concepts of two theoreticians who have developed theoretical frameworks and concepts of mental objects which extend beyond the strict framework here presented

– Winnicott's concept of transitional objects and Kohut's concept of self-object. As will be seen, these two concepts differ in essence from all the other concepts of mental objects surveyed here.

1

Freud and his associates

Freud

In this chapter I will trace the development of Freud's major ideas regarding the mental structures related to objects, that group of concepts which have been termed here 'mental objects'. Freud himself did not write about the mental representations of objects (as that concept has been defined in this study, see the Introduction), although some of the ideas he discussed and developed provided the basis for the later development of that concept. Especially difficult in regard to Freud's writings, from the perspective from which we are now viewing them, was his use of the term 'object' without explicitly distinguishing between the real people who were the 'objects' of an individual's love and so on, and that individual's mental images of those people.

While Freud began his theoretical writings with a rather simplistic conception of the percept as a distinct 'idea', leaving as its impression a 'mnemonic trace' which corresponded directly to the realistic percept,[1] his ideas regarding the mental processes and structures related to objects gained greatly in complexity. In this chapter I will describe four stages of this development:

1 the idea that the early childhood 'picture' (i.e., mental image) of the parent continues to exert an influence on later choice of an object;
2 the role of mental images in the libidinal economy, and especially in phantasy and the process of 'introversion';
3 the idea that an object may be 'set up in the ego' (introjected), which led to a view of its having an active function in the mental apparatus; and
4 the concept of the superego.

These ideas present a line of thought in which there is an increasing emphasis on the role played by object-related structures: beginning with the ongoing effects of a 'static' mental image, to the active functions of introjected objects to which Freud attributed such feelings as anxiety, guilt and shame. When Freud presented the concept of the superego (1923b), he brought together a number of the aspects of the earlier ideas. In this chapter I will present the stages of development of this line of thought in Freud's writings, which served as the basis for later views (especially of Melanie Klein) of a mind 'populated' by objects, and which has played such an important role in later psychoanalytic theory.

Freud's theory of memory

Before entering into that line of thought which will be described in this chapter, note must be taken of some of Freud's basic ideas on memory and perception, that constitute the basis of the processes which will be described later. Freud's early conception of perception and memory draws on the psychology of J. F. Herbart,[2] which was popular at the time. According to this theory, 'mind' is considered to consist of basic discrete units of thought – ideas (*Vorstellung*),[3] each possessed of a force. This force determines the relative clarity or intensity of the idea to which it is attached, and whether that idea will succeed in passing the threshold, or *limen*, of consciousness. In addition, ideas may be opposed to one another, leading to the mutual diminution of their respective intensities – Herbart developed mathematical formulae to compute these interactions – and to the inhibition of the weaker by the stronger. Another important concept in Herbart's psychology was that of apperception. According to Herbart, for an idea to attain consciousness, for it to be apperceived, it had to be assimilated to a totality of conscious ideas – the 'apperceiving mass'.[4]

Freud's conception of memory and perception was similar to that of Herbart. Freud too used the term *Vorstellung*[5] as the basic discrete unit of thought to which psychic energy was attached.[6] His early childhood seduction theory of pathogenesis emphasized the memory trace of a single traumatic event as a pathogenic factor. The event itself was preserved as an 'idea', and it was considered to become[7] invested with psychic energy in the form of affect.[8] With the introduction of his theory of drives in 1905 (1905d),[9] Freud substituted the concept of 'instinctual' energy for his earlier concept of affect as the basic psychic energy. Ideas and energies were considered throughout Freud's work as separate entities – ideas could be invested and disinvested with energy (cathected and decathected), and both could undergo various vicissitudes (especially repression) either separately or together. Freud's theory of the drives constituted a powerful theory of motivation, one which greatly changed his whole theory of mind, but he did continue to use the basic concepts of ideas and energies as the basic units as he had previously. In addition, he continued to view the memory traces of images of objects connected with pleasurable experiences as having an ongoing influence, serving as models of pleasurable experience to which the individual would continue to be attracted at later times (and conversely in cases of unpleasure). Thus the images of objects were considered to play an important role in the mental economy. The first explicit and distinct application of this view may be seen in relation to Freud's ideas about the influence of mental images from childhood on later object choice, to which we will now turn.

Mental images of objects and object choice

With the introduction of his theory of the sexual instincts, Freud distinguished between the aim of the instinct and its object: 'Let us call the person from whom the sexual attraction proceeds the *sexual object* and the act towards which the instinct tends the *sexual aim*' (1905d: 135–6). This definition was later reaffirmed in his 1915 study on the instincts: 'The object of the instinct is the thing in regard to which or through which the instinct is able to achieve its aim' (Freud 1915c: 122). While these definitions of the concept of object refer only to the object of the drive, and may seem to refer to the actual object and not to the mental image of that object, Freud's use of the concept of object quickly expanded to include many other aspects in addition to the drive aspect,[10] and also was used by him to refer to the mental images of objects.[11]

One of the ideas introduced in the original version of Freud's (1905d) 'Three essays on sexuality'[12] was related to the mental image of the object (rather than to the actual object) – a short section titled 'The after-effects of infantile object-choice'. There Freud introduced the idea that the mental image (which Freud called the 'picture') of the parents, as it was preserved in the mind of the individual from childhood into adulthood, exerts an influence on his later choice of a love-object – 'A man, especially, looks for someone who can represent his picture of his mother, as it has dominated his mind from his earliest childhood' (Freud 1905d: 228). As an example of this influence Freud mentioned the love of a young person for an older partner of the opposite sex.

In later writings Freud repeated and further developed this idea. In the first two of his 'Contributions to the psychology of love' (Freud 1910h, 1912d), he repeatedly emphasized the role of the *unconscious* aspects of the mental images of the parents (especially the mother) in determining later object choice. These mental images were considered to function both in directing the adult towards certain choices (1910h) and in directing him away from certain choices (1912d).

These later elaborations constitute a much more complex view of the functions of the enduring mental images. These are no longer simply an early 'picture' of the mother, a more or less accurate representation of external reality, but rather a complex structure in which drives and phantasies have added to, and distorted, the realistic basis. As such, it is composed of both conscious and unconscious components. Specifically, Freud discussed the influence of the child's Oedipal wishes towards the mother and aggressive wishes against the father, in the development of the unconscious component of the child's mental image of the mother. This view of the mental image as a complex structure is of great importance as a step in the development of Freud's views regarding the functions of mental images of objects. Of course, Freud's notions at this point are still limited to a specific function of the object image – that of choosing, in a positive or a negative manner, an object – and do not extend to other aspects of the object beyond the sexual (and aggressive) aspects. As such, it does not, of course, constitute a general theory of mental representation as will later develop in the psychoanalytic literature. It does constitute an important development beyond the simple trace theory of memory which we discussed above.

Phantasy and introversion

A crucial step in the development of Freud's ideas regarding the functions of object images was related to the development of his thinking on the subject of phantasy. After exploring phenomena such as dreams (1900a), parapraxes (1901b) and humour (1905c), Freud turned to explore phantasies. In contrast to the subjects mentioned above, phantasy was very closely related for Freud to the central question which interested him – the development of neurosis. After the presentation of his theory of libido and its role in the development of neurosis (1905d), Freud turned to the concept of phantasy to account for the connection between libido and its frustration on the one hand, and neurotic symptoms on the other (Freud 1908a, 1910j). He further developed a general view of mental functioning according to which phantasy constituted an alternative to the engagement of reality, an area of mental life still under the sway of the pleasure principle, which guided the functioning of the drives, and was not yet controlled by the reality principle (Freud 1911b, 1916x). In the context of his theory of pathogenesis he came to consider phantasy as constituting an intermediate stage between the frustration of discharge of libido and the outbreak of neurotic symptoms, and adopted Jung's term 'introversion' for this process:

the portion of libido which is capable of becoming conscious and is directed towards reality is diminished, and the portion which is directed away from reality and is unconscious, and which, though it may still feed the subject's phantasies, nevertheless belongs to the unconscious, is proportionately increased. The libido (whether wholly or in part) has entered on a regressive course and has revived the subject's infantile imagos.

(Freud 1912b: 102)

Thus, via these concepts of phantasy and introversion, Freud's views regarding object images (which he frequently called 'imagos') and their functions gained greatly in complexity. Infantile images of objects were considered to play an important role both in the temporary satisfaction of wishes in phantasy, and in the process of the production of neurotic symptoms. These phantasies were considered to have persisted from child-hood on, eventually serving as a template for neurotic symptoms in the case of the intensification of libido due to frustration. This contrasting of satisfaction and discharge in reality on the one hand, and in phantasy on the other, was an important step in Freud's theorizing, one which would be further developed in the concept of the superego.

Closely related, both historically and conceptually, to the concept of introversion, was the theory of the withdrawal of libido from the external world in psychoses (Freud 1911c). Freud (1914c) noted that this process differed from that of introversion in neurosis[13] – in the case of introversion the libido recathects infantile images of the object in phantasy, while in the withdrawal in psychosis even object images are abandoned and the libido withdraws to a cathexis of the ego – or, as Hartmann (1950) would later clarify, of the self. Thus the regression in psychosis is considered deeper than in neurosis, and object-related phantasy is abandoned in favour of a regression to narcissism. These two notions regarding the regression of libido (to infantile images of objects, in the case of neurotic introversion, and to the ego, in the case of psychosis) were closely related to the further concepts developed by Freud. The next step in the development of this line of thought will be the idea that the ego may be conceived of as containing within itself relationships with its different parts.

Ego ideal and introjection

The idea of the existence of internal relationships between 'parts' of the ego developed with the introduction of two important concepts – the ego ideal and introjection.

Freud introduced the concept of the ego ideal in his paper 'On narcissism'

(1914c: 93–7). There he discussed two different entities: an ego ideal, possessing 'every perfection that is of value' (ibid.: 94); and a critical agency that measures the ego in light of that ideal. Freud was not consistent in maintaining this distinction, sometimes combining these two into one agency (for example, 1921c: 109–10).

Regarding the critical agency, two points are of interest: its origin in 'the admonitions of others' (Freud 1914c: 94) and its clinical expression by the paranoiac in the delusions of being watched and criticized (ibid.: 95). A short while afterwards, Freud (1917e)[14] was able to extend the concept of the critical agency to another area of pathology – the (often delusional) self-criticisms of the melancholic. Regarding these, Freud discerned that they were not all applicable to the patient himself; rather, they seemed to apply to the patient's love-object, the loss of whom had triggered the melancholic process. To account for this discrepancy Freud suggested that the patient was identifying with the love-object and criticizing it via himself.[15] He formulated this condition as 'a cleavage between the critical activity of the ego and the ego as altered by identification' (Freud 1917e: 249). This formulation suggests, in a much more explicit and direct manner than in the 'Narcissism' paper, that self-criticism may be conceived as an intrapsychic relationship between two parts of the ego, one attacking (criticizing) the other.

Freud originally referred to the process whereby the melancholic identified with his lost love-object, thereby 'setting it up' within his ego, as 'narcissistic identification' (1917e: 249–51; 1916x: 227–8). He distinguished between narcissistic and hysterical identifications, on a basis similar to that used in his distinction between narcissism and introversion (as described above): narcissistic identification was considered to involve the withdrawal of object cathexis, including the cathexis of object images in phantasy, and a regression to the narcissistic cathexis of the ego. In contrast, cathexis of object images in phantasy was considered to continue in the case of hysterical identification. Freud soon abandoned the term 'narcissistic identification' and began referring to this process as 'introjection' (1921c). This term had originally been introduced by Ferenczi (1909), and the history of Ferenczi's use of it and his contacts with Freud regarding it are presented below in the chapter on Ferenczi.

Freud did not strictly distinguish between the terms 'introjection' and 'identification', and used both to refer to the intrapsychic process whereby the object is considered to be 'set up in the ego', as in melancholia.[16] By 1921 Freud was ready to apply this idea not only to melancholia, but also to the functioning of the ego ideal in psychoses: 'the ego . . . enters into the relation of an object to the ego-ideal . . . all the interplay between the external object and the ego as a whole . . . may possibly be repeated upon this new scene of action within the ego' (1921c: 130).

14

Here Freud was already giving expression to the idea that would have such influence on later psychoanalytic thought – that interpersonal relationships (relationships with the external object) are transposed to the intrapsychic realm, leading to intrapsychic relationships between the different 'parts' of the ego.[17] This idea will be further elaborated in connection with Freud's theory of the superego, to which we shall now turn.

The concept of the superego

Freud's theory of the superego provides us with his most complex formulations regarding mental structures considered to be related to objects. It is beyond the scope of this study to review Freud's theory of the superego in its entirety.[18] In this section I will note those aspects of the superego concept that served as a basis for the later development of concepts of mental objects. Four such points are relevant:

1 the formation of the superego (introjection);
2 drives versus reality as the origin of the superego's severity;
3 later development of the superego; and
4 the superego as an 'internal object'.

1. THE FORMATION OF THE SUPEREGO

In constructing his theory of the formation of the superego, Freud (1923b) drew on his earlier formulations regarding introjection in melancholia and identification in the formation of the ego ideal. He discussed two stages in the formation of the superego: early identification with the parents, and later identification at the time of the solution of the Oedipal complex.

In 'Group psychology and the analysis of the ego' Freud (1921c) distinguished between identification as it originally took place in the child, and a later regression to identification. He considered identification to be 'the earliest expression of an emotional tie with another person' (p.105). It is clear from his discussion there that he meant more than imitation when he spoke of identification, although the behavioural outcome of identification was often imitation. Identification also referred to an emotional attitude towards the object. Freud formulated the distinction between the emotional attitude in identification and that of object choice as 'what one would like to *be*' as opposed to 'what one would like to *have*' (p.106). This was closely related to his concept of the ego ideal. When he formulated his views on the formation of the superego he stated that this early identification was 'the origin of the ego-ideal' (Freud 1923b: 31). He stated the same in terms of the role of the mental image of the object in *New Introductory Lectures* (Freud 1933a), where he described the ego ideal as 'the precipitate of the old picture of the parents, the expression of admiration for the perfection which the child then attributed to them' (p.65). Thus the mental image of the idealized parents was considered to continue to exert an influence on the ego ideal in later life.

This early identification was considered by Freud to serve as a basis for a later intensification of identifications which occurred during the period of the solution of the Oedipal complex. Such intensified identifications were considered to affect a 'part' of the ego, such that it became differentiated from the rest of the ego – the superego.[19]

While it was clear from his presentation that Freud considered this stage of the formation of the superego to be similar to the process of introjection as he described it in melancholia, in 1923 Freud had not yet worked out the details of the connection between the two processes. The problem in applying the process of introjection (on the model of melancholia) to the formation of the superego was that in introjection the object that is considered to be introjected is the lost love-object. In the case of the Oedipal boy, this would mean an introjection of the image of the mother. This view of the formation of the superego is in contrast to another view expressed by Freud (1923b: 32), that the superego (of the boy) is based on an identification with the father. Freud was aware of this incongruence,[20] and shortly after (1924c, 1924d) suggested a solution to this problem according to which the images of both parents were introjected in the formation of the superego. This proposition was based on the view that both parents could constitute love-objects for the child, and that in both cases the fear of castration would lead to the abandonment of the Oedipal wishes and to the introjection of the images of the lost love-objects (1924d: 176–7). This view, that the superego was formed on the basis of the introjection of both parental images, became Freud's accepted view (for example, Freud 1926d: 139; 1933a: 64).

2. DRIVES VERSUS REALITY AS THE ORIGIN OF THE SUPEREGO'S SEVERITY

Clinical observations, involving unconscious guilt and an unconscious need for punishment, led Freud to his formulation of the concept of the superego (1923b).[21] One of the outstanding characteristics of these phenomena was considered to be the severity and harshness of the guilt and need for punishment, especially in cases of obsessional neuroses and melancholia. But Freud's theory of the formation of the superego, based on the introjection of (or identification with) the parents, did not seem adequately to account for this harshness, as Freud noted: 'Experience shows . . . that the severity of the superego which the child develops in no way corresponds to the severity of treatment which he himself has met with' (1930a: 130).

To account for the discrepancy (between the superego we would expect to find, on the basis of the process of introjection, and between the clinical findings of harsh and severe superegos), Freud made a number of suggestions to correct the theory of superego formation. In this section I will present his major proposals, leading eventually to the solution at which he arrived in *Civilization and its Discontents* (Freud 1930a), which constituted a major revision of the theory of superego formation. These proposals, and Freud's eventual solution, played an important role *vis-à-vis* the issue of drives versus reality in the origin of the superego, and thereby set the stage for later deliberations on this issue.

Three major proposals may be discerned regarding the origin of the severity of the superego:

(a) Introjection of the parental images emphasizes, or selects, certain aspects of the parents' behaviour;
(b) The process of identification with the parents involves the defusion of instincts and a release of aggression;
(c) Aggression originally directed towards the external world is redirected, via the superego, onto the self.

One line of thought that Freud pursued in his attempt to account for the severity of the superego was that the introjection of the parental images at the time of the solution of the Oedipal complex involved not all the aspects of their images, but only the harsher aspects: 'The superego retained essential features of the introjected person – their strength, their severity, their inclination to supervise and to punish' (Freud 1924c: 167). Freud suggested that the reason for this selection was the part played by the process of introjection in the dissolution of the Oedipal complex. This was considered to involve the desexualization of the child's relationship with his Oedipal objects, and it seems that Freud considered that this desexualization would strip the parental images of their 'softer' qualities, leaving them harsh and severe (ibid.). Another similar suggestion that might help account for the superego's severity[22] was that 'a child's superego . . . is constructed on the model not of its parents but of its parents' superego' (Freud 1933a: 67). The reason for this selection was considered to be in the parents' own behaviour towards the child, in which they displayed their own identifications with their own parental restrictions (ibid.). Common to both suggestions was the idea that superego formation was indeed based on the introjection of the parental images, and that a certain extent of one-sided distortion of these images accounted for the discrepancy between actual parental behaviour and the severity of the images introjected.

17

The second line of thought that Freud proposed was based on the economic point of view.[23] Having established that the formation of the superego came about via a process of introjection, Freud turned to view the energic aspects of this process. He suggested that the regression from object cathexis to the narcissistic level of identification (or introjection) involved a 'transformation of object-libido into narcissistic libido' and that this 'obviously implies an abandonment of sexual aims, a desexualization – a kind of sublimation, therefore' (Freud 1923b: 30). As a result: 'After sublimation the erotic component no longer has the power to bind the whole of the destructiveness that was combined with it and this is released in the form of an inclination to aggression and destruction. This defusion would be the source of the general character of harshness and cruelty exhibited by the ideal' (ibid.: 54–5) – that is, by the superego. Thus Freud considered there to be an economic aspect of the process of identification (or introjection) whereby the superego is formed and that this economic aspect contributes a quality of harshness and aggression not present in the original images of the parents.[24]

The third line of thought that Freud proposed (closely related to the other two) is that as a result of the suppression of aggressive impulses, due to social restrictions, aggression is 'turned round upon the self'. This turning round of aggression upon the self is considered to occur via the superego – 'the more a man checks his aggressiveness towards the exterior the more severe – that is aggressive – he becomes in his ego ideal' (Freud 1923b: 54); that is, his superego. Thus the superego is continually being 'fuelled' with aggression as a consequence of the ongoing suppression of aggression, which finds its outlet in attacks on the ego via the superego.

The solution that Freud eventually proposed in *Civilization and its Discontents* (1930a) throws light on the problematics involved in the whole question. In a lengthy discussion, Freud (1930a: 129–30) noted the discrepancy between two of the lines of thought that he had earlier proposed – the first (selective introjection) and the third (redirection of aggression). His solution consisted of a reformulation of the role of aggression in the process of the introjection of the parental images. Instead of trying to understand the origin of the superego's severity in terms of the (educational) aggression of the parents towards the child, Freud reversed the relationship; he stated that the superego's harshness may be seen as a vicissitude of the child's own aggressive impulses towards the parents. 'By means of identification he [the child] takes the unattackable authority [the parents] into himself. The authority now turns into his superego and enters into possession of all the aggressiveness which a child would have liked to exercise against it' (ibid.). This formulation brings the theory of the formation of the superego more into line with the conception of introjection in melancholia: the aggression of the superego is considered to be the individual's own aggression, redirected. Introjection is thus conceived of as the formation of a mental structure which redirects the individual's aggression onto the self. Thus Freud solved the question of the severity of the superego, which was not in proportion to the behaviour of the parents whose images were supposed to have been introjected; the severity of the superego is an expression of the individual's own aggressive impulses, not a reflection of the parents' behaviour.[25]

The question of the origins of the superego's severity leads to an issue that was to become a very crucial one in psychoanalytic theory: the origins of mental objects, internal or external. This issue was not new to Freud's thought, if we recall the decisive move he took in abandoning his early theory of childhood seduction as the pathogenic factor in neurosis (Freud 1896b) in favour of a view of internal factors – drives, wishes and intra-psychic conflict – as the processes leading to pathology. Although that move had been taken at a very early point in his career, the issue itself did not disappear, and continued to crop up in later writings (for example, Freud 1918b). Furthermore, Freud's close friend and collaborator, Ferenczi (1933), had to a certain extent revived and elaborated Freud's earlier view regarding the far-reaching effects of traumatic experiences on the formation of personality,[26] and had applied these ideas to the concept of the superego. Freud's (1930a) solution to the question of the origin of the superego's severity was arrived at after a long period of deliberations, not only by Freud but also by many other analysts. Freud (1930a) himself noted that the view of the superego as independent of actual parental behaviour was one held 'by Melanie Klein and other English writers' (p. 130, n. 1). In fact, Ferenczi seems to have written to Freud expressly to oppose the latter's adoption of Melanie Klein's view on the question of the origin of the superego's severity, suggesting instead that external factors were of greater importance (Grosskurth 1987: 189).[27] Thus we see that the issue of internal versus external factors in the origins of the superego was a very live issue for Freud and other analysts at the time, and we shall see in later chapters how this issue further developed in psychoanalytic theory in regard to other concepts of mental objects.

While it would seem that his 1930 formulation placed the superego much closer to the drives than to reality, Freud did not want to divorce the superego completely from reality (as Melanie Klein seemed to have done; Klein, 1927a).

> But it would also be wrong to exaggerate this independence [of the severity of the superego from the severity of the treatment the child experienced] . . . . What it amounts to is that in the formation of the superego . . . innate constitutional factors and influences from the real environment act in combination. This is not at all surprising;

on the contrary, it is a universal aetiological condition for all such processes:

(Freud 1930a: 130)

Freud's reservations regarding the extent of his agreement with the 'Kleinian'[28] view of the origins of the superego's severity appear again in his *New Introductory Lectures* (Freud 1933a: 62).[29] It would seem that Freud did find it difficult to regard the superego as so completely under the influence of the drives, and found it more compatible to view the superego as based on reality but distorted by the drives. We shall see how this tension continues to play itself out in psychoanalytic theory.

3. LATER DEVELOPMENT OF THE SUPEREGO

We have seen that Freud considered the superego to originate in the introjection of (or identification with) the parental figures. But the introjected parental figures were not, in Freud's opinion, the end of the development of the superego, which he considered to continue beyond its original formation.

Freud (1926d)[30] considered the 'introjected parental agency' to be the 'nucleus' of the superego (p.139), and he indicated that two processes were involved in its further development: (1) later social figures were added to those of the parents (Freud 1933a: 64); (2) the fear of castration, originally attached to the parental figures, developed into social anxiety (Freud 1926d: 128, 139).

Freud referred to this development of the superego as a 'depersonalization' of the parental agency which was the nucleus of the superego (ibid.), or as a 'detachment [of the superego] from the figures of whom it was originally the psychic representative' (Freud 1931b: 229). He thus expressed the idea that the fully developed superego was no longer identical with the introjected parental figures, and that in the process of development it acquired a more 'impersonal' quality (Freud 1933a: 64). This idea becomes important in later psychoanalytic writings, especially in relation to such questions as the distinction between concepts such as superego and internal objects,[31] in regard to concepts of 'structure' and the experiential and non-experiential realms,[32] and the idea of the regression of the superego. These subjects were not expressly discussed by Freud himself,[33] and it seems that beyond the mention of this developmental aspect of the superego he did not apply it to any specific topic.[34]

4. THE SUPEREGO AS AN 'INTERNAL OBJECT'

Freud's views on the relationship of the ego and superego are stated in general terms in the last, and incomplete, chapter of *An Outline of Psychoanalysis* (Freud 1940a). His statement there opened up an important aspect of the conception of the superego – the superego as an 'internal object':

> A portion of the external world has, at least partially, been abandoned as an object and has instead, by identification, been taken into the ego and thus become an integral part of the internal world. This new psychical agency continues to carry on the functions which have hitherto been performed by the people (the abandoned objects) in the external world: it observes the ego, gives it orders, judges it and threatens it with punishments, exactly like the parents whose place it has taken . . . if the ego has successfully resisted a temptation to do something which would be objectionable to the superego, it feels raised in its self-esteem and strengthened in its pride. . . . In this way the superego continues to play the part of an external world for the ego, although it has become a portion of the internal world.
>
> (Freud 1940a: 205–6)

Two aspects of Freud's conception of the superego and its relationship with the ego, illustrated in the above statement, should be noted: (1) the superego is conceived of as an active agency, an internal counterpart to external objects; (2) the relationship of the ego and superego is described as an active interrelationship, with mutual demands and responses,[35] very similar to an interpersonal relationship.

Freud, of course, usually emphasized the hostile and critical activities of the superego, which were specifically prominent in melancholia and obsessional neurosis. In his comparison of the two he emphasized the importance of the reaction of the ego to the attacks of the superego as a distinguishing feature. Whereas in obsessional neurosis the ego 'rebels against the imputation of guilt' made by the superego (Freud 1923b: 51), in melancholia 'the ego ventures no objection; it admits its guilt and submits to the punishment' (ibid.).[36] Freud's elaboration of the ego's response in melancholia gives us an idea of the emotional complexity which he attributed to the relationship between the ego and superego: 'in melancholia . . . the ego gives itself up because it feels itself hated and persecuted by the superego, instead of loved. To the ego, therefore, living means the same as being loved – being loved by the superego' (ibid.: 58). He conceived of the ego and superego as engaging in a complex ongoing relationship that was a continuation of the earlier relationship between child and parents.

21

Summary

We have seen the development of Freud's ideas regarding the functions of the mental images of objects in the personality, beginning with the simple notion of the mental image of the parents as serving as a guide to later object choice, via the more complex functions of mental images of objects in the processes of phantasy and introversion, to the both complex and concrete descriptions of the functions of the superego, both as a structure and as an 'internal object'. This development constitutes a radical change in the place of the concept of 'object' in Freud's theories; as noted, Freud used the term 'object' both in reference to a person in the external world and to the mental image of the object. It has been widely noted that the role of the 'object' was relatively minor in Freud's theory of the drives, as merely an aspect of the drive it was considered to be the aspect that was least important (Freud 1915c: 122). However, as Freud progressed from a theory of the drives to a more general theory of the structure of the personality, especially in the structural model (Freud 1923b), the concept of the 'object', especially as it is embedded in the concept of the superego as an 'internal object', became a major aspect of personality.

This development was not without its difficulties, although these were not apparent at once. The concept of the superego is not easily integrated into the drive-defence psychology that is emphasized in the id–ego part of the structural model. The emphasis on a drive-defence view of personality has led North American ego psychology to ignore (to a certain extent) the concept of the superego.[37] As opposed to 'scientific' and abstract concepts such as psychic energy, mechanisms of defence and ego functions, the concept of the superego readily lends itself to anthropomorphization, and in fact it is difficult to account for it otherwise.[38] A model of the mind based on a view of the intrapsychic relationship of the ego and superego (as a continuation of the interpersonal relationship with the parents – Freud 1940a) is very different from a model of the mind based on the neutraliz-ation of id-energies by the ego.[39] This divergence of two models from what Freud originally presented as one tripartite model became one of the most powerful cleavages in psychoanalytic theory – between ego psychology (especially as developed in North America) on the one hand, and Melanie Klein's theory of 'internal objects' (and the object-relations theories influenced by her) on the other.[40] Closely related to this development is the expansion of the concept of 'object', from a very specific and restricted use as the object of a drive (Freud 1915c: 122) to a much wider use in which the object refers to another person with whom an interpersonal rela-tionship exists.

To return to other issues raised by Freud in his writings, one is especially important for later developments in psychoanalytic theory: the question of the origin of the superego's severity. This question is one aspect of a more general issue regarding the influences of internal versus external factors in the formation of mental objects. This issue is relevant not only to the concept of the superego, but may also be seen to be at work in Freud's (1910h, 1912d) earlier discussions of the unconscious aspects of the mental image of the object, aspects influenced by the drives and unconscious wishes. Here we already see Freud emphasizing that aspect of the psychoanalytic concept of mental objects (in this case the mental images of objects) that would so vividly distinguish it from the more cognitive conceptions of mental representations of objects (such as Piaget's) – the influence of the drives (and possibly other internal factors) on the mental structures that organize perception of reality. This will be further discussed at length in Chapter 11.

Ferenczi

The concept of introjection

The concept of introjection was first put forward by Ferenczi in one of his earliest psychoanalytic papers (1909). The concept, as defined by him at that time, included a number of different aspects that Ferenczi considered to be part of one general process. He further explained his 1909 definition of introjection in a paper specifically devoted to that subject a few years later (Ferenczi, 1912). There he defined introjection as

> an extension to the external world of the original autoerotic interests, by including its objects in the ego. I put the emphasis on this 'including' and wanted to show thereby that I considered every sort of object love (or transference) both in neurotic and normal people . . . as an extension of the ego, that is, as introjection.
>
> (1912: 316)

Ferenczi's definition of introjection was thus a very wide one, including in it all emotional attachments and interests in other people. He considered introjection to be the basic process whereby attachments to objects in the (external) world are established (1909: 48–9). Furthermore, he distinguished between two stages of development – the stage of introjection and the stage of projection, relating introjection to the earlier stage of omnipotent thought, and projection to the later development of reality-orientated thought (Ferenczi 1913).

Ferenczi also considered introjection to be the basis for the later phenomena of transference and of displacement, inasmuch as the mechanism of introjection may be used for defensive purposes. Thus, he considered the mechanism of introjection, when 'unconsciously exaggerated', to be the hallmark of the neurotic, as opposed to projection, which characterized the paranoiac. The neurotic 'lavishes his affects on all possible objects that do not concern him' in order to 'keep unconscious various connections that concern him nearly' (Ferenczi 1909: 50). His clinical examples of these processes illustrate that he also included in the definition of introjection phenomena such as phobic avoidance, whereby the object of the avoidance became included within the ego's sphere of interest.

It is important at this point to note the connection between Ferenczi's concept of introjection and some of Freud's concepts. While already at this very early time Ferenczi was discussing the processes whereby the ego is established in terms of introjection, Freud during this same period was establishing the distinction between processes related to the cathexis of (external) objects and processes related to the cathexis of the ego – narcissism (Freud 1905d: 145, in a note added in 1910; 1910c: 100; and more extensively in 1914c). Although Ferenczi too referred to this view of Freud's (for example, 1914: 297–8), it is not compatible with his own views on introjection and projection as the basic developmental stages. This is so because for Ferenczi, attachment to the object takes place at the earlier stage (introjection), while the projective mechanism serves to differentiate between inner and outer, self and non-self, as a later development. In contrast, Freud considered the relationship with the object to be a later development, and paranoiac projection to constitute a regression to an earlier, pre-object-love (narcissistic) stage.[41]

Ferenczi did not seem to realize the implications of this difference between his views and those of Freud. That this was so is borne out in Ferenczi's letters to Freud in regard to the concept of introjection. As noted above, although Ferenczi introduced this concept as early as 1909, Freud did not make mention of it in his paper on melancholia (Freud 1917e) in spite of Ferenczi's suggestion to Freud (in a letter dated 22 February 1915, in Ferenczi 1949) that the term was appropriate for the processes described by Freud in relation to melancholia. Ferenczi (in a second letter, dated 25 February 1915, ibid.) suggested that the process described by Freud in terms of 'the shadow of the object [falling] upon the ego' (Freud 1917e: 249),[42] would be better described in terms of the 'introjection' of the object. Freud did not accept this suggestion and did not use the concept 'introjection' in 'Mourning and melancholia'. Indeed, it seems that Freud correctly realized that Ferenczi's concept of introjection implied processes which contradicted those that Freud was proposing in regard to melancholia. This contradiction was especially important in regard to Freud's view that the narcissistic identification of the ego with the object in melancholia was a result of the loss of, and consequent withdrawal of libido from, the object (Freud 1917e: 250). Ferenczi's concept of introjection did not imply such a process of the abandonment of object-love in favour of narcissism. Rather, it emphasized the possibility of an ongoing attachment to the object. Thus it would seem that Freud was right in his opinion (to which Ferenczi responded in the letter of 25 February 1915) that Ferenczi did not wholly comprehend Freud's views on melancholia, suggesting as he did the term 'introjection' for a process for which it was clearly not appropriate. It is of interest to note that Freud did refer to Ferenczi's concept of introjection in another paper appearing the same year as the above-mentioned correspondence (Freud 1915c) in a context more appropriate to Ferenczi's definition of the term. Also of interest is that Freud eventually did adopt the term 'introjection', using it in conformity with his own views on the relation between object loss and 'introjection' (Freud 1921c). The concept of introjection later came to be used by Freud to describe the process whereby the superego was formed, a process which Freud considered also to be related to the abandonment of the object-choice of the Oedipal phase (Freud 1923b, 1924c).

Ferenczi, on his part, accepted Freud's views regarding the distinction between identification (a term which both Freud and Ferenczi used synonymously with 'introjection') and object-love, and the idea that identification constituted a regression from object-love (Ferenczi 1922). But in spite of the fact that he propounded this view of Freud's, his formulations continued subtly to reflect his original view, according to which object-love was an aspect of introjection and not a later, and contrasted, stage. Thus, in 1922 he stated that the stage of identification 'is simultaneously the building of a bridge between the self and the outer world' (Ferenczi 1922: 374), and in his last paper he states in regard to the stage of identification that 'I should like to call this the stage of passive object-love, or tenderness' (1933: 163). This latter statement, although made in reference to Freud's view of identification preceding object-love, constitutes an interpretation of identification rather different than that usually implied by Freud, one very much in keeping with Ferenczi's own earlier ideas.

Here a note in regard to the general context of Ferenczi's concept of introjection is relevant, and the theoretical (and therapeutic) issues involved. Ferenczi, in spite of being for many years Freud's closest associate, one who remained faithful to Freud, both personally and in theoretical matters, did eventually develop ideas differing from some of Freud's major tenets. Much was made at the time of Ferenczi's death (1933) of his 'experiments of technique', of which Freud disapproved (Jones 1957: 162–5). These experiments were so bitterly criticized at the time that his last paper, presented in the year of his death, was not published in English for more than fifteen years.[43] But beyond questions of technique, which were undoubtedly very meaningful to Ferenczi himself, the theoretical issues with which he was struggling were also of great importance, and of relevance to the present study.

The central idea that Ferenczi was exploring was the influence of trauma on the development of personality, and his immersion in this idea was so great that his views led him to a return to Freud's pre-1897 views[44] on the role of trauma as the pathogenic agent in the development of the neuroses. But Ferenczi was going beyond Freud's original ideas, which were limited to the effects of a specific traumatic event (or events) on the development of neurotic symptoms. Ferenczi was discussing the development of personality as a whole, and the effects of traumatizing relationships with objects (mainly parents) on this development (or, as Ferenczi originally called his paper, 'The passions of adults and their influence on the sexual and character development of children').

This exploration was thus a further step forward from Freud's original views, in the direction, later to be continued in the writings of object relations and developmental theorists, of the influence of the personalities and behaviours of the parents on the development of the child's personality as a whole (not restricted to traumatizing relationships). In this context he developed the concept of the 'introjection of the aggressor',[45] whereby children may 'subordinate themselves to the will of the aggressor, to divine each one of his desires and to gratify these' (Ferenczi 1933). Ferenczi described how this process influenced the inner world of the child, and thereby allowed the child to deny the occurrence of the aggression in relation to external reality, and to continue 'maintaining the previous situation of tenderness' (ibid.: 162). This concept of Ferenczi's is strikingly similar to ideas on internalization which were later developed by Fairbairn (1952), and which would constitute the basis for the latter's object-relations theory of personality.

It is also of interest to note that these views of Ferenczi in regard to the important role played by the parents in the development of the child's personality also led him to a difference of opinion with Freud in regard to the concept of the superego. When Freud (1930a: 130) eventually accepted Melanie Klein's view regarding the internal origin of the severity of the superego, Ferenczi wrote to Freud (on 11 November 1930 – Grosskurth 1987: 189), opposing this opinion. Ferenczi emphasized that it was the nature of the relationship with the parents that should be considered to be the origin of the superego's severity – 'the consequence of a treatment that was relatively speaking too strict'. Of course, Ferenczi was more in accordance with the idea that it was introjection that led to the formation of the superego.

The differences of opinion between Ferenczi and Freud discussed above, although very muted, eventually came to be a major subject of debate in the British Psycho-Analytical Society, in regard to the the concept of 'primary narcissism'. In the context of the differences between Freud and Ferenczi, it is especially interesting to note Michael Balint's concept of 'primary object-love', which he rightly considered to be an extension of the line of thought developed by his analyst and teacher, Ferenczi (Balint 1949a). Thus, in spite of Ferenczi's personal efforts to adopt Freud's point of view over his own thinking (poignantly visible in his letters to Freud and in his recently published clinical diary (Dupont 1988), his own views did eventually come to full expression in the work of his student, Balint, and via Balint came to exert an important influence on the views of the 'Independent group' in the British Society, and on object-relations theories.

To summarize: Ferenczi's concept of introjection (1909, 1912) may be seen to express some of the deep theoretical differences that eventually developed between himself and Freud. Of special interest in the context of the present study is the way in which from the beginning, it expressed Ferenczi's interest in the earliest stages of the infant's emotional attachment with the world. Thus, rather than emphasizing intrapsychic processes, a characteristic of Freud's theoretical concepts, Ferenczi's concept of introjection may be considered to emphasize an interpersonal aspect, laying stress on the external influences on aspects of the inner world.[46]

Abraham

As with Ferenczi, Abraham's contributions to the development of ideas regarding mental objects are closely intertwined with those of Freud, to the extent that many ideas seem to have developed in the dialogue between them. This is especially true of the theory of melancholia, to which both Abraham (1911, 1924) and Freud (1917e) made major contributions, and which was much discussed between them in their correspondence (Abraham and Freud 1965). In this section I will focus on a number of ideas regarding the concepts of mental objects which were developed by Abraham and which exerted a lasting influence on later developments in the psychoanalytic literature.

Freud (1917e) based his theory of melancholia on the mechanism of narcissistic identification.[47] In Freud's view, this mechanism led to the establishment of the lost love-object within the ego, and to intrapsychic interplay between the introjected object and the rest of the ego. One of the important aspects of this interplay, in Freud's view, was the ambivalence towards the love-object – that is, the object was not only loved, it was also hated.

Abraham's contribution focused on the aggressive attitude towards the love-object, and especially the connection of this attitude to the oral impulses. In Abraham's (1924) view, the aggressive oral impulse to devour the love-object underlies the narcissistic identification with the object. Thus the melancholic imagines himself as having done tremendous damage to his object in the process of identifying with it, damage for which he deserves to be punished. The masochistic self-punishment of the melancholic is the outcome of that need for punishment. Abraham suggested this view to Freud prior to the publication of Freud's paper on melancholia (Abraham and Freud 1965: 215–18), and Freud incorporated it into the published version, acknowledging Abraham's contribution (ibid.: 220; Editor's note in Freud 1917e). This view of Abraham's later became part of his well-known distinction between the later (biting) and earlier (sucking) oral stages (Abraham 1924).

In this context it is important to note that Abraham emphasized the 'spatial' aspects of instinctual processes. Phantasies involving 'being inside' or 'taking in' and 'being outside' or 'ejecting' were considered to be direct expressions of oral and anal impulses, respectively. This emphasis on the 'place' of the object (namely, whether it was phantasied as being inside the body of the individual, or outside) later came to acquire a central importance in the work of Melanie Klein (who had been an analysand of Abraham's), according to which the processes of 'ejecting' (projection) and 'taking in' (introjection) were considered to be those that constituted mental life.

Another of Abraham's ideas that was to play an important role in the development of concepts of mental objects was that of a relationship between introjected objects. Freud, in his paper on melancholia (1917e) and further in the concept of the superego (for example, Freud 1923b), conceptualized certain mental occurrences in terms of an intrapsychic relationship between the ego and an introjected object (the superego). In developing this idea, Freud thought of the interpersonal relationship between the individual and his object as transposed to the intrapsychic realm. Abraham (1924: 462; 1925: 318) further extended this idea, conceptualizing certain mental processes in terms of a relationship between two introjected objects – the introjected mother and father.

This view, while appearing at first glance to be but a modest extension of Freud's original idea, differed from it in an important way: the ego (or self) was not part of the interaction. There is nothing especially difficult in this, if by 'introjected object' Abraham meant no more than a phantasy regarding an object. In that case, as many objects as we want can be phantasied, interacting in unending variations. But Abraham, following Freud's lead in regard to the superego, was not merely describing the contents of a phantasy – he was using the concept of 'introjected object' as explanatory in regard to certain other phenomena, as referring to structures of the personality. (Abraham himself, of course, did not mention the concept of structure; this is how his ideas would have to be understood in terms of the basic concepts being used in this study. See the Introduction for these concepts.) This extension of Freud's description of personality as constituted of a part which is (experienced as) the self and a part which is related to the object (the superego), to a description in terms of the interactions of various objects among themselves, was a shift that would later come to constitute a major divergence from Freud's theory of the structure of personality, in the views developed by Melanie Klein.

One of Abraham's most original and influential contributions to concepts of mental objects was the concept of 'partial object-love' as a stage in the development of object love (Abraham 1924). Although certain ideas appearing in Freud's writings may be considered to foreshadow this concept, Abraham's elaboration of these ideas into an integrated concept justifies a discussion of his contribution.

Freud's interest in the development from autoerotism to object-love may be traced back to his early attempts to integrate the 'choice of neurosis' with a theory of the development of the libido. Within that framework he suggested that autoerotism be considered 'the lowest sexual stratum', which is succeeded by alloerotism (Freud 1950a: Letter 125). To this early contradistinction between auto- and alloerotism Freud (1911c) later added narcissism as an intermediary stage. In spite of this seemingly clear progression, according to which the individual is considered to progress from a state of objectlessness (autoerotism), to a stage in which the self is the object of the drives (narcissism), to a relationship with another person (alloerotism or object-love), others of Freud's ideas did not fit in with this linear progression. One of those ideas (Freud 1905d: 200, 222, 234; 1914c: 87–8) in regard to the earliest relationship with an object, was that there is a developmental progression from a relationship with the mother's breast, to a relationship with the whole person of the mother. This same idea was also mentioned elsewhere in terms of a regression from a relationship with a whole person to a relationship with a part of that person's body (Freud 1917c: 130).

Abraham's concept of 'partial object-love' may thus be seen as an expansion of these ideas of Freud's. But in elaboration these ideas took on new meaning and importance. Abraham considered partial object-love to be the beginning of a new attitude towards the object – that of 'having some care for the object' (Abraham 1924: 488). Previously, the infant paid no attention to the needs of his objects, being fully willing to destroy the object in the satisfaction of his own impulses (for example, by incorporation). When the infant begins to display care for the object, an interest in the continued existence of the object and a willingness to restrict his own impulses to this end, this may be considered to constitute the beginning of object-love. But the transition from a narcissistic attitude, oblivious of the interests and needs of the object, to object love in which there is care for the object, has an intermediary stage – that of partial love, or partial introjection. At this stage, the infant attempts to preserve the object by restricting his introjection of it to a part of the object, so that the major part of the object may continue to exist. A further step in this development is the individual's giving up of the impulse to incorporate even a part of the object, which is replaced by a wish to possess the object. This replacement of possession for incorporation signifies the individual's growing concern for the continued existence of the object, which constitutes a compromise in terms of the satisfaction of the early wishes. The next stage, that of object-love, at which the object is loved as a whole and not destroyed in the interests of the satisfaction of the impulses (Abraham 1924: 494–6), adds yet another intermediary stage of 'object-love with the exclusion of the genitals'.

Thus, the concept of partial object-love (and the part-object which Abraham considered to represent such an attitude) implied a very important distinction in regard to the development of the individual's attitude towards the object. Not merely reflecting the perceptual capacity of the infant to integrate the image of the mother as a (perceptual) whole, the concept of the part-object implied a developing capacity for concern for the object, in the form of the capacity to renounce instinctual aims in the interest of preserving the object. This conception of a line of development of concern for the object (which is considered to be in contrast to the satisfaction of impulses via the object) was to influence many later developments in psychoanalytic thought regarding mental objects, both in the writings of Melanie Klein and in views orientated towards more ego psychology. Unfortunately, Abraham himself died at the age of 60 in the year after the publication of his 1924 paper so that he himself did not further develop these ideas, which held so much promise.

2

Object-related orientations

Melanie Klein

The concept of the internal object

Undoubtedly it was the work of Melanie Klein that put the concept of internal objects into the centre of the conceptual map of psychoanalysis. This concept was also one of the major Kleinian concepts that aroused a great deal of misunderstanding and controversy. As such, it received a good deal of attention from Kleinian writers who devoted papers specifically to the aim of clarifying it (Heimann 1942a; Riviere 1952b; Segal 1972), without, it would seem, achieving much in the way of understanding in the non-Kleinian psychoanalytic world.[1] One of the major reasons for this seems to be that it is not enough to explain, and provide examples of a concept, without elaborating the general theoretical framework within which it is embedded, and without comparing it to and distinguishing it from other similar concepts belonging to different theoretical frameworks. Thus it is important not only to relate the concept of internal objects to the other central Kleinian concepts which constitute Kleinian metapsychology (such as phantasy, instinct and the relation between psychic and external realities), but also to compare it to similar concepts, and especially to that of mental-representation, as used in the non-Kleinian psychoanalytic literature. This chapter will deal specifically with the Kleinian framework, while the comparison with other theoretical concepts will be reserved for the discussion in Part Two of this study.

In reviewing Melanie Klein's concept of internal objects, I will show how it developed in her writings (it did not spring fully developed at the beginning of her work!) and the many ambiguities and conceptual problems which appeared during this development. Melanie Klein, of course, did not develop her ideas in a vacuum, and in addition to the influences of earlier psychoanalysts (especially Freud, Ferenczi and Abraham), it is important to note the contributions of her co-workers. These, especially Joan

Riviere, Paula Heimann, Susan Isaacs, Herbert Rosenfeld and Hanna Segal, contributed greatly to the clarification and application of Melanie Klein's ideas. As far as the concept of internal objects is concerned, this contribution was mainly one of clarification and application, and little has been added to the concept as Melanie Klein developed it. I will therefore include the contributions of these writers in this chapter on Melanie Klein, using them to supply elaboration where Klein has relied on the implicit meanings of the term, and pointing out where they have chosen certain emphases where Klein has left more than one possible meaning.

Beginning with her earliest writings following Freud's (1923b) introduction of the concept of the superego, Melanie Klein was impressed by the disparity between the real-life parents and the child's image of these parents. She came to conceive of the image the child has of his parents as an (almost) separate, autonomous entity – not a realistic image of the parents. Melanie Klein considered that it was with this image (or internal object, as she later came to call it) that the child had a relationship, as well as with the real-life parents. Much of her work was dedicated to exploring the vicissitudes of this relationship, and her changing views on the subject may be seen as a reflection of the growing complexities she encountered in these explorations. She eventually came to view these internal objects as the product of the intertwining and meshing of aspects of the self, on the one hand, and (what we would today call) the representations of the real-life people (objects), on the other hand. From this point of view, she considered development (from the paranoid-schizoid to the depressive position) to consist (among other things) of the assimilation of these internal objects into the self, leading to a more realistic experience of both object and self.

Melanie Klein herself did not discuss her work in these terms. Her terminology, indeed her concepts themselves, are of a much more concrete nature. Thus her descriptions, for example, of projection into objects, and of internal objects being expelled into the outside world, present a serious obstacle to theoretic conceptualization. This tendency has come under continuous criticism from non-Kleinian analysts (for example, Brierley 1939, 1942, 1943, 1944; Glover 1945; Joffe 1969; Kernberg 1969) and has been valiantly defended by Kleinians (such as Riviere 1936; Isaacs 1952; Meltzer 1967; Segal 1978). This topic is no doubt one of interest, but it seems to have diverted attention from serious study and discussion of the processes which Melanie Klein has described.

In this section I will present the development of Melanie Klein's ideas related to the concept of internal objects. The presentation will be ordered chronologically, with an emphasis on the development of three distinct themes:

1 Until 1932 – from imago to internal object;
2 1932–1945 – internal objects and the instincts;
3 1946 onwards – self and objects.

The chronological and thematic divisions are, of course, not as clear-cut as it might seem from the above, for themes often overlap. But I think that this division allows a presentation which both remains faithful to the complexity of the material, and, on the other hand, allows a conceptual overview of the development of the themes both explicit and implicit in Melanie Klein's writings.

A note on Melanie Klein's use of the concept 'object'

Before beginning a review of the development of Melanie Klein's ideas, a word is needed about her use of the term 'object', both internal and external. Like Freud, Melanie Klein did not devote herself to systematic definitions of the terms she used, relying rather on an implicit tradition within psychoanalytic circles as to the various meanings of her terms. This tendency is, of course, problematic, especially because the theories propounded by Melanie Klein are very different from many others in the psychoanalytic literature, leading to new meanings for old terms. The fact that the newness of these meanings is not always acknowledged leads to a certain extent of conceptual confusion.

As will be seen in this section, Melanie Klein's concepts are of a very concrete nature. The Kleinian rationale for the concrete nature of their concepts was presented most systematically in Susan Isaacs' and Paula Heimann's respective papers in the 1943 Controversial Discussions in the British Psycho-Analytical Society (Isaacs 1952; Heimann 1952). There they argued that their concepts reflect the concrete, sensual nature of the infant's earliest experiences, before the development of verbal and abstract thought. Accordingly, all later concepts were considered by them to be derivatives of the original infantile experiences. They considered later experience and thought to owe their force and emotional influence to ongoing connections with the original infantile experiences.

For this reason they considered it justified to ignore many of the distinctions developed in later life: ultimately these distinct processes are considered to derive from the same basic processes, and their common derivation is considered more important than their later manifest differences. This attitude is, of course, similar to Freud's basic insight that very different manifest thoughts, behaviours, phantasies and so on may be affected by the same underlying unconscious processes. The difference between the Kleinian attitude and that of other psychoanalytic trends of thought is one of degree; that is, the extent to which differing manifest processes and content are considered to be derived from the same underlying processes. To much of the psychoanalytic world, the Kleinian tendency in this repect is outright absurd.

In relation to the concept 'object', especially in Melanie Klein's usage of this term to refer to the basic constituents of the mind, the range of phenomena referred to by the Kleinians under this term is enormous. Based on the view that all later distinctions derive from the earliest infantile experiences, Kleinians bunch such diverse phenomena as perceptions, memories, thoughts, phantasies and feelings together. The infant is considered to live in a basic psychic reality of sensation. Another difficulty in reading Melanie Klein is that, like Freud, she often referred both to the mother and to the child's phantasies, memories and perceptions of the mother, by the same term, 'object'. This is especially confusing because in other contexts Melanie Klein writes of 'external' and 'internal' objects, where it is clear beyond any doubt that both concepts refer to mental images and not to the mother herself.

From imago to internal object

Melanie Klein did not use the concept of internal objects in her earliest papers, and her view that the child has phantasies about objects (people) being physically inside him or her, and that these phantasies are of central importance, developed gradually. Shortly after Freud introduced the concept of the superego as an introjection of, and identification with, the parental figures (Freud 1923b, 1924c), we find Melanie Klein discussing her clinical material in these terms (M. Klein 1926). She described her patient's inhibitions in play (Rita was 2¾), which in analysis were shown to be related to guilt felt towards her mother. Melanie Klein emphasized that 'the prohibition of the childish wish (to take her brother for her own child) no longer emanated from the *real* mother, but from an introjected mother'. Further on she used the term 'identification' to refer to this same process, following Freud, who used the two terms 'introjection' and 'identification' almost interchangeably. Melanie Klein was also very sensitive to the clinical fact that the figure with which the child identified was not a realistic figure. She emphasized that Rita's 'introjected mother . . . exercised a harsher and more cruel influence upon her than her mother had ever done'. She considered this excessive harshness to be connected with her patient's Oedipal wishes to 'usurp her mother's place with her father, to steal from her mother the child with which she was pregnant and to injure and castrate the parents'.[2]

This emphasis on the concept of imago, as opposed to the realistic

34

images of the objects, and her view that the child's behaviour should be understood as involving and reflecting its phantasied relationships with these imagos (perhaps to a greater extent than with realistically viewed objects), constituted one of the early differences between Melanie Klein's approach and that of Anna Freud (M. Klein 1927a). Melanie Klein considered the small child's phantasies regarding interaction with fantastic figures (witches, fairies, animals and so on) to reflect the child's various superegos (or the various aspects of its superego) – this, at a period in the child's life well before that considered by Freud (and Anna Freud) to be the beginning of superego formation. Her identification of these phantasy figures with the superego lent to these phantasies a certain permanence which they might not otherwise have been considered as having; phantasies may come and go, but superegos *are*. This is a good example of the criticism directed at Kleinian theory for not distinguishing between structure (as quasi-permanent configurations) and phantasy (Fairbairn 1943; Kernberg 1969). Whereas Anna Freud distinguished much more strictly between phantasies and a 'proper superego' (A. Freud 1928), Melanie Klein considered all phantasies to reflect the superego (or introjected objects).

This difference in use of the concept of 'superego' was related to an important difference regarding the conceptualization of object-relations. Freud had originally (1917e, 1921c) emphasized, regarding melancholia, that introjection of (or identification with) the object came to take the place of a relationship with an external object. When he later (1923b, 1924c, 1924d) advanced the concept of the superego as an introjection of the parental figures, he linked this process, too, to the abandonment of the Oedipal object-relationships which were replaced by a new (internal) relationship with the superego. This idea, of the relationship with the superego as a substitute for the relationship with the external objects, became an important point of divergence between the views of Melanie Klein and Anna Freud. Anna Freud understood this as implying that a 'proper superego' could only be considered to exist when there was a lessening of the intensity of the tie between the child and his parents. As long as the child was completely emotionally dependent on his parents, a superego could not be considered to be present as an important factor in the child's emotional make-up. In contrast to this view, Melanie Klein seems to have interpreted Freud's view as definitive: inasmuch as a super-ego existed, it could be considered to function as a substitute for the relationship with external objects. Thus the phantasy figures ('imagos'), which Melanie Klein considered to be superegos, could be considered to be functioning as substitutes for external objects. In other words, the child's most important relationships could be conceived of as being with his imagos, rather than with his real parents.

It is beyond the scope of this study to explore the important differences in technique that were related to these different theoretical approaches, differences which served as the topic of the 1927 Symposium on Child Analysis in the British Psycho-Analytical Society. In relation to our discussion of Melanie Klein's concept of internal objects, two points are of importance. First, Melanie Klein's emphasis on the fantastic nature of the child's phantasy objects. Joan Riviere referred to this explicitly at the 1927 Symposium (Riviere 1927): 'The objects of unconscious phantasies are imagos formed to some extent after the pattern of real people, but not to a material extent on real experience.' This emphasis was to become one of the hallmarks of the Kleinian approach. The second point relates to the function of these imagos: Melanie Klein tended to consider the child's relationships with these fantastic imagos as his basic object-relationships, with reality taking a decidedly second place. It was this aspect of her early approach that eventually grew into the conceptualization of internal objects as entities in their own right.

At this early date (1926) Melanie Klein was already referring to the idea that the introjected parental figure was *inside* the child, 'tormenting it inwardly' and susceptible to 'expulsion' (especially in play). This idea was later to become a very central characteristic of the Kleinian concept of internal objects, but at this point is just mentioned in passing. It is interesting to note the difference between Melanie Klein's conception of the introjected object at this time (1926) and her later concept of internal objects. Whereas in 1926 the emphasis is on the introjected objects being an introjection of a *distorted* (representation of the) object, in her later concept of internal object the issue of the location of the object (that is, its being internal, experienced as inside the individual's body) is of much greater importance. In a later discussion of the same clinical material, she noted

> I would now go further in my interpretation. To the phantasied attacks on her [Rita's] body by her parents as external figures, corresponded fear of inner attacks by the internalized persecuting parent-figures who formed the cruel part of her superego.
>
> (M. Klein 1945)

In Melanie Klein's earlier works she did not yet emphasize the importance of the phantasy of the object being inside the individual's body (or outside it), and her usage of the term 'introjected objects' resembled Freud's to a much greater extent than later.

The growing emphasis on the location of the object (namely, the phantasy of its being inside the child's body) is related to Melanie Klein's growing interest in the oral stages of development and its derivatives in her patients' material. Her interest in the oral stages may be traced to the influence of her analyst and teacher, Karl Abraham, who greatly emphasized the oral stages, especially in relation to melancholia. It was

36

Abraham who introduced the distinction between the oral-sucking and oral-biting stages (Abraham 1924), a distinction which Melanie Klein often referred to in her early writings.

As she came to view the introjection of objects as occurring in the oral stages, she emphasized the influence of the oral impulses on the qualities of the introjected objects. The rationale given for this influence was that the phantasy of taking in the object is determined by the instincts manifested at the time (oral-sucking, or oral-biting), and this leads to phantasies about the introjected object's actions inside the child's body after the introjection.

> The child himself desires to destroy the libidinal object by biting, devouring and cutting it, which leads to anxiety, since awakening of the Oedipal tendencies is followed by introjection of the object, which then becomes one from which punishment is to be expected . . . the superego becomes something which bites, devours and cuts.
>
> (M. Klein 1928: 187)

This idea, that the nature of the introjected object (or superego, as Melanie Klein often referred to it)[3] depended on the libidinal stage at which it was formed, also served as the basis for her explanation of the gradual moderation of the superego. The development of the superego was thus considered to be dependent on libidinal development. Fixation to the oral-biting stage would lead to fixation of the superego in its 'terrible, menacing' character, while advance to the genital phase was considered to be dependent on 'a sufficiently strong fixation to the oral-sucking phase', in which the introjected object was that of 'a mother who provides oral gratification' (M. Klein 1929a: 203–4).

Another line of thought which contributed to the development of Melanie Klein's concept of internal objects is related to her growing awareness of the centrality of infantile phantasies regarding the inside of the mother's body. She considered these phantasies to be of a predominantly sadistic nature, originally attributing them to the anal-sadistic phase (M. Klein 1928). Shortly afterwards, she concluded that the impulse to attack the contents of the mother's body preceded even the anal-sadistic phase, and that its origins were to be found in the oral-sadistic phase (M. Klein 1929b, 1930):

> At the period of which I am speaking (oral-sadistic), the subject's dominant aim is to possess himself of the contents of the mother's body and to destroy her by means of every weapon which sadism can command.
>
> (Klein 1930: 219)

In this paper Melanie Klein described the analysis of a psychotic child (Dick),[4] and in it she develops many of the ideas which were later to be

37

organized in her theory of the paranoid-schizoid position (M. Klein 1946). The themes of attacking, damaging and robbing the contents of the mother's body (especially the father's penis within the mother's body) were predominant in the clinical material. These were expressed in play by attacks on toy trains and carts, in anxiety towards and interest in door-handles and doors (that is, entrances to rooms), opening and shutting them, and other objects symbolizing the mother's body. The material of this case led Melanie Klein to the view that 'The sadistic phantasies directed against the inside of her [the mother's] body constitute the first and basic relation to the outside world and to reality' (M. Klein 1930: 221). Under the sway of these sadistic phantasies, the contents of the mother's body (faeces, urine and the father's penis, which Dick phantasied as located in his mother's womb) became dangerous enemies, threatening to attack Dick, especially after they had been introjected into his body. Thus the objects of his sadistic attacks came themselves to represent the sadistic impulses which he projected onto them.

In regard to another patient, Melanie Klein writes:

> The father's penis, which from the sucking oral point of view is equated with the breast, and so becomes an object of desire, is thus incorporated and in the boy's phantasy, very rapidly transforms itself, in consequence of his sadistic attacks against it, into a terrifying internal aggressor and becomes equated with dangerous murderous animals or weapons.
>
> (M. Klein 1931)

The following passage illustrates Melanie Klein's growing emphasis on the influence of the internal world on emotional experience, to the extent that it may be considered to determine the nature of relations with the external world:

> In those cases in which the significance of reality and real objects as reflections of the dreaded internal world and imagos has retained its preponderance, the stimuli from the external world may be felt to be nearly as alarming as the phantasied domination of the internalized objects, which have taken possession of all initiative and to which the ego feels compulsively bound to surrender the execution of all activities and intellectual operations, together of course with the responsibility for them.
>
> (M. Klein 1931: 245)

This view would later form the basis for Melanie Klein's theory of the early relationship between internal and external worlds, in relation to the paranoid-schizoid position.

We have seen the gradual development of Melanie Klein's concept of

internal objects from its Freudian beginnings as a distorted representation
of the object (imago). Under the influence of Abraham's emphasis on
orality and the growing clinical material pointing to the centrality of
oral-sadistic wishes to possess the contents of the mother's body (and
consequent anxieties related to these contents), Melanie Klein gradually
formulated her own view of the internal object, which eventually emphasized the phantasy of the object being physically present within the
individual's body. She considered this phantasy to be a basic aspect of all
oral impulses and wishes. She emphasized that later, genital-level developments were dependent upon and reflected the earlier oral stages, and that
aspects of development seen by Freud to occur at those later stages (such as
Oedipal conflict and superego formation) should be recognized as early as
at the oral phase.

This emphasis on the oral-stage infant's experience as the basis for later
experience helps to account for the concrete nature of the Kleinian
concept of internal objects. We shall encounter the various criticisms and
explanations put forward in the framework of the Controversial Discussions of the British Psycho-Analytical Society in 1943. It should be
noted, though, that the development of Melanie Klein's concepts (as
reflected in her writings) constitute an organic development; justification,
explanation and systematization were left to others, and came after the
development of the concepts themselves. Although the demands of chronological order necessitate reserving an examination of the Discussions till
after a review of the developments of the 1930s, it appears appropriate to
extract from these Discussions at this point what is relevant to the concept
of the internal object as a phantasy of the object inside the body.

The 'object within' – rationales and criticisms (Controversial Discussions, 1943)

Melanie Klein arrived in London in 1926, leaving Berlin following the
death of her analyst and sponsor, Karl Abraham. As we have seen, the
discrepancies between her views and those of Freud became more marked
in the 1930s, and the differences are generally considered to have reached
a head in 1935 when she published her paper on 'A contribution to the
psychogenesis of manic-depressive states' (Segal 1978). It seems to have
been that paper especially that triggered opposition to her views in the
British Society, with Edward Glover playing a central role in this
opposition. The basic differences in approach to both theory *and* technique, which had earlier surfaced in the Symposium on Child Analysis,
between the views of Melanie Klein and Anna Freud, received further
expression in 1935–36 in a series of exchange lectures between the Viennese
and British Societies. These differences further exacerbated tension within

the British Society when the Viennese Society was moved, almost *en bloc*, to London in 1938 (because of the Nazi threat in Vienna). This (and other tensions – Gillespie 1980; King 1983; Grosskurth 1987) led, eventually, to a series of Scientific Meetings dedicated to the discussion of certain aspects of the Kleinian point of view. These meetings came to be known as the 'Controversial Discussions', and the written comments of the participants on the papers presented remain today a rich source for the understanding of the 'real' issues at stake between the Kleinian and Freudian[5] points of view.

The concept of the internal object as presented above, implying the phantasy of the physical presence of the object (breast, penis, mother, father and so on) within the individual's body, quickly became a focus of conflict in the Discussions. It was further elaborated in the Kleinian presentations at the Discussions, especially in the first two by Susan Isaacs and Paula Heimann ('The nature and function of phantasy' and 'Some aspects of the role of introjection and projection in early development', respectively),[6] and became the linchpin of Isaacs' paper, in her statement that 'the primary content of all mental processes are unconscious phantasies' which she viewed as 'the mental corollary, the psychic representation of instinct'. She went on to defend this view on the basis of the fact that,

> in the infant, experience and mental process must be primarily, perhaps at first entirely, sensorial . . . *in the unconscious mind*, where everything remains concrete, sensorial or imaginal, introjection (earlier referred to as the abstract concept) is always experienced as incorporation – although not, of course, always by the mouth.

At a later meeting[7] she elaborated this view specifically with regard to internal objects. Emphasizing the fact that the infant had no *concept* of an object, only *bodily sensations* (smell, touch and so on) related primarily to 'taking things in (sucking and swallowing)', she considered infantile phantasies to have

> a concrete bodily quality, a 'me-ness'. They are experienced *in* the body, and on this level, IMAGES are scarcely, if at all, distinguishable from actual sensations and external perceptions. They refer to the inside. Perceiving is introjection.

> (ibid.)

She continued to describe the development from this infantile level, to a stage at which objects are recognized to be outside the body, and their images are recognized to be 'in the mind'. But – and this is the crucial point of difference between the Kleinian and Freudian views – there remains a very close connection between the conscious and unconscious levels, between images and internal objects. In Susan Isaacs' words:

40

Such IMAGES, however, *draw their power to affect the mind* by being 'in it', their influence upon feelings, behaviour, character and personality, upon the mind as a whole, *from their repressed unconscious visceral and kinaesthetic associates,* the unconscious world of phantasy[8] which *form the link with the id*; and which do mean, in UCS phantasy, that the objects to which they refer are[9] inside the body, are incorporated.

This point – the extent to which cognitive processes and contents are considered to be in close proximity to instinctual ones – led to heavy criticism. Numerous analysts, such as E. Glover, D. Burlingham, E. Sharpe, S. H. Foulkes, M. Schmideberg and M. Brierley and others, all emphasized the need to distinguish between cognitive processes (especially perception, memory and phantasy imagery) and instinctual or somatic or hallucinatory processes. The Kleinians, in the opinion of these analysts, did not do so sufficiently.

It is interesting to note the difference between a paper by J. Strachey (1930) on the oral impulses involved in reading, and Melanie Klein's (1931) ideas regarding the origins of mental inhibition (each quotes the other and considers their views to be compatible). Whereas both investigate the instinctual processes involved in cognitive processes, Strachey restricts his discussion to cases in which sublimation breaks down.

Insofar as those (unconscious) trends are sublimated, the reading can proceed without meeting with any obstacles raised by other mental forces; if, however, and insofar as, they retain any of their original unsublimated character the reading will meet with the hindrances which would have been put in the way of the unmodified trends.

(J. Strachey 1930)

This delimitation, so important to the non-Kleinians, (almost) does not exist in the Kleinian scheme. Thus therapy (in Melanie Klein's (1931) treatment of John) consisted in the mitigation of the persecuting nature of the internal objects and not (as might be the case in the non-Kleinian point of view) in loosening the connection between the cognitive process and the unrealistic emotional investment it acquired. These differences have, of course, far-reaching clinical implications regarding the analyst's attitude towards material not overtly involved in instinctual conflict. The insistence of the Kleinians on the principle that *all* mental processes are anchored in phantasy and instinctual impulses justifies quicker interpretation at the deep level on the basis of less evidence than is justified in the opinion of non-Kleinians.

To summarize: Melanie Klein's concept of internal objects as the phantasy of the object being physically present within the individual's body was a serious point of divergence between Kleinian and non-Kleinian

views. Implications of this difference extended both to clinical interpretations and to the whole conception of the relation of higher levels of
mental processes to primitive and instinctual ones. We have seen that in
spite of the charges that Kleinian analysts were guilty of 'concrete'
thinking, the Kleinians themselves (especially Susan Isaacs) provided clear
rationales for the Kleinian view. Thus it seems that the differences between
the camps was based (at least partially) on different theoretical perspectives,
rather than only on confusion on one side. (This, of course, implies
nothing in regard to the question, which point of view is correct?) This is
an important point, because subsequent discussions and development of
the Kleinian concept of the internal object rely on this basic bodily-based
phantasy aspect of it. On the other hand, it is also important to note that
the Kleinian view tended to blur the distinctions between perception,
memories, imagery and representations, on the one hand, and the bodily-
based phantasy of internal objects, on the other.

Melanie Klein's conception of the internal object as a body-phantasy
and her tendency to blur the distinctions between internal objects on the
one hand, and perceptions, memories and realistic images, on the other, led
to an interesting difficulty. On the one hand, the internal object is experienced as part of, or belonging to, the individual's body, as being part
of himself. The following passage emphasizes this view:

> The essential difference between infantile and mature object-
> relations is that, whereas the adult conceives of the object as existing
> independently of himself, for the infant it *always refers in some way to
> himself.* It exists only by virtue of its function for the infant, and only
> in the world bounded by his own experiences. Whilst in reality the
> infant is utterly helpless and depends for the maintenance of his life
> completely on his mother (or her substitute), in phantasy he assumes
> an omnipotent position to his objects; they belong to him, are part of
> him, live only through and for him – he continues the pre-natal
> oneness with his mother.
>
> (Heimann 1952)

But, as Heimann herself recognizes in the same paper, the internal object
is also related to as an object. This is borne out in all the descriptions of the
dynamics of relations with internal objects, where it is the self (or ego)
which is interacting with the internal objects, relating to them as to objects.
The following statement by Melanie Klein also illustrates this view.

> The baby, having incorporated his parents, feels them to be live
> people inside his body in the concrete way in which deep uncon-
> scious phantasies are experienced – they are, in his mind, 'internal' or
> 'inner' objects, as I have termed them . . . . In the baby's mind, the

'internal' mother is bound up with the 'external' one, of whom she is 'double' . . . The visible mother provides continuous proofs of what the 'internal' mother is like, whether she is loving or angry, helpful or revengeful.

(Klein 1940: 345–6)

This ambiguity regarding the place of the internal object in relation to self and object is not merely confusion on the part of Kleinians. The dual nature of internal objects, combining aspects of both self and object, is a persistent characteristic of that concept, expressing an important insight of Kleinian psychology. This insight – that self and object are not as simply differentiated in the mind as had been thought – receives its most explicit expression in the concept of projective identification (Klein 1946). But before turning to that concept, another important aspect of the internal object concept must be discussed: the internal object as deeply influenced by the instincts.

Internal objects and the instincts

We have seen how the body-phantasy conception of the internal objects became a central one in the Kleinian theory. Another central issue regarding Melanie Klein's concept of internal objects, which I will present in this section, is that of the close connection of the internal objects with the instincts.

Freud's deliberations regarding the disparity between the severity of the superego, on the one hand, and the (relatively) benign behaviour of the real-life parents (of whom the superego was considered to be an intro-jection), on the other, eventually led him to a formulation (Freud 1930a) in regard to which he continued to entertain reservations. That formu-lation emphasized the influence of the drives (especially the aggressive drive) on the character of the superego. Freud considered the superego to be 'in possession of all the aggressiveness which the child would have liked to exercise against [the parent]' (1930a). This formulation was influenced by, among others, the work of Melanie Klein.[10] As we saw above, Melanie Klein emphasized early on the distorted nature of the child's view of his parents (the 'imago' rather than the real-life image). She considered this distortion to be directly related to the instincts, especially to the oral-sadistic and anal-sadistic drives of early infancy:

As we know, the parents are the source of the superego, in that their commands, prohibitions, and so on become absorbed by the child itself. But this superego is not identical with the parents; it is partly formed upon the child's own sadistic phantasies.

(M. Klein 1927b)

The super-ego is of a phantastic severity. On account of the well-known formula which prevails in the Ucs this child anticipates, by reason of his own cannibalistic and sadistic impulses, such punishments as castration, being cut to pieces, eaten up, etc., and lives in perpetual dread of them. The contrast between his tender and loving mother and the punishment threatened by the child's super-ego is actually grotesque and is an illustration of the fact that we must on no account identify the real objects with those which children introject.

(M. Klein 1927a: 155)

With Klein's growing emphasis on the phantasy of the object-inside-the-body, her tendency to view internal objects as reflecting the instincts became more pronounced. As she came to realize that the formation of the superego (namely, internal objects) could be traced as far back as the oral phases, the relationship between the instinctual impulses and the internal objects became more pronounced. Eventually (Klein 1929b), it became clear that the dynamics of the process of introjection itself, which she considered to be responsible for the establishment of the internal objects, determined their nature. 'For, when the objects are introjected, the attack launched upon them with all the weapons of sadism rouses the subject's dread of an analogous attack upon himself from the external and internalized objects' (Klein 1929b).[11] The idea that the internal object was deeply influenced by the child's instinctual phantasies regarding the object emphasized the close connection between the internal object and the instincts, as opposed to (external) reality. Thus Melanie Klein could note, in describing the effects of treatment, that 'the child's ferocious and phantastic superego – ultimately, that is, his own sadism – was diminished' (1931). The superego is thus considered to reflect the individual's own instinctual impulses, a view far removed from that which considered the superego to be, primarily, related to the parental figures.

This view was further strengthened due to the major change of Melanie Klein's metapsychological orientation, introduced in her book *The Psychoanalysis of Children* in 1932. There she adopted Freud's later dual-instinct theory – the concepts of life and death instinct. Melanie Klein did not specify what led her to make this change. In her clinical work she had come to a growing realization of the centrality of aggressive (or 'sadistic') impulses as *the* pathogenic factor. Freud's interest in the vicissitudes of the libido and the part they played in determining pathology receded to the background. Melanie Klein came to see psychic conflict in terms of the battle between hate and love, between the sadistic impulses to destroy the object and the reparative tendencies to preserve and revive it. It seems reasonable to assume that Freud's life/death instinct concept appeared to her very compatible with her own recently developed views.

But the death instinct was not synonymous with aggression; it implied an aggression which was directed towards the self, in danger of destroying it. And it was this aspect which seems to have been especially compatible with the clinical views that Melanie Klein was developing. According to these views, aggression was not primarily directed outwards, towards the object, and only later, due to various processes of introjection, redirected towards the self. This had been one of the main thrusts of *Freud*'s (1930a) view of the formation of the superego. Melanie Klein had been increasingly moving towards the view that the individual's sadism was threatening the individual from within (in the form of sadistic internal objects).[12] As we have seen, she had formulated her view that the individual felt that attacks would be made upon him by the introjected object in retaliation for sadistic introjections. This complicated formulation was more simply and directly expressed in terms of the death instinct. The death instinct threatened to destroy the individual from within if no outlet were found for it. Persecutory anxiety could now be seen as a direct derivative of the death instinct; the organism's reaction to the death instinct felt to be at work within it was *anxiety*.

This revision made possible a new perspective on the concept of internal objects. What had previously been recognized as the close connection between the instincts (especially the sadistic ones) and the internal objects could now be more directly expressed. The 'new' instincts (that is, the life–death instincts) were obviously constructs at a high level of abstraction. What then were the clinical, subjective expressions of these instincts? Melanie Klein's answer – which was later elaborated by Susan Isaacs (1952) – was that the instincts were experienced as phantasies (as internal objects); attacking the individual (death instinct) or loving and giving life (life instinct) from within. This aspect of Melanie Klein's views on the close connection between the instincts and internal objects may be lost under the fascinating complexities of projection and introjection, reprojection and re-introjection, which constitute the interplay between internal forces (instincts) and external influences. But, beyond these complexities, there appears to be a very basic emphasis in Klein's thought on the close connection of the world of internal objects with the instincts, from which the internal objects seem to derive their ultimate qualities.

The following is a clinical example of the view that phantasies (of internal objects) could be seen as representing the instincts:

A five-year-old boy used to pretend that he had all sorts of wild animals, such as elephants, leopards, hyenas and wolves, to help him against his enemies. Each animal had a specific function. The elephants were to stamp the foe to a pulp, the leopards to tear him to bits and the hyenas and wolves to eat him up. He sometimes

45

imagined that these wild animals who were in his service would turn against him, and this idea used to arouse very great anxiety in him. It turned out that the animals stood in his unconscious for the various sources of his sadism – the elephant being his muscular sadism; the animals that tore, his teeth and nails; and the wolves, his excrements. His fear that those dangerous animals which he had tamed would themselves exterminate him was referrable to his fear of his own sadism as a dangerous internal enemy.

(Klein 1932: 127, n. 4)

Although in general terms both life and death instincts were considered to be similarly expressed by internal objects, Melanie Klein's main clinical interest at this point was in the relationship between the individual's sadistic tendencies, internal objects and persecutory anxiety. The formulation that the death instinct is experienced in phantasy in the form of internal objects which are felt to be persecuting the individual from within, giving rise to severe anxiety, expressed this relationship very succinctly. According to this view, mental life entails complex dynamics developing out of this basic situation; for example, the deflection outwards of the death instinct onto the breast, consequent introjection of the breast as a bad internal object, similar processes involving the life instinct, and the interactions between the life and death instincts. Thus the introduction of the concept of the death (and life) instincts did not reduce Melanie Klein's theories to these terms, but rather served as a succinct theoretical framework within which these theories could be developed.

This view of phantasy (and internal objects) as reflecting the (life/death) instincts had important implications for the question of external versus internal influences in the development of pathology (and personality in general). This is so especially in view of the very wide definition of phantasy in the Kleinian framework (Isaacs 1952). The formulation directly relating phantasy (and internal objects) directly related to the instincts implied that all emotional and cognitive processes could be seen as ultimately derived from the instincts. It provided the theoretical framework for the Kleinian clinical approach which greatly emphasized the close connection between the manifest content of the patient's dreams, phantasies and so on and the instincts. In comparison with other approaches within psychoanalytic theory, relatively little emphasis was placed on (external) reality as a major factor in the determination of subjective experience.

Although Melanie Klein repeatedly emphasized that external and internal factors interact continuously, it seems that her tendency (both at the clinical level and in her discussion of theory) was to view internal factors (namely, the instincts) as somehow more basic. The following statement illustrates this tendency:

46

Whether feelings of frustration or gratification predominate in the infant's relation to the breast is no doubt largely infuenced by external circumstances but there is little doubt that constitutional factors, influencing from the beginning the strength of the ego, have to be taken into account. I formerly made the suggestion that the ego's capacity to bear tension and anxiety, and therefore in some measure to tolerate frustration, is a constitutional factor. This greater inborn capacity to bear anxiety seems ultimately to depend on the prevalence of libido over aggressive impulses, that is to say, on the part which the life instinct plays from the outset in the fusion of the two instincts.

(M. Klein 1952c)

Although this tendency appears clear, Melanie Klein was engaged in an ongoing attempt to formulate the interaction of internal (that is, instinctual) and external (especially, gratifying and frustrating) factors. We will see below the roles that the concepts of part/whole objects and Melanie Klein's theory of development (from the paranoid-schizoid to the depressive position) played in this attempt.

To summarize: we have seen how the concept of internal objects grew and developed, gaining additional meanings. Three major aspects have been noted: (1) internal objects as phantasies of an object physically present inside the individual's body; (2) other contents of the mind considered as derivatives of such body-phantasies, and (3) the far-reaching influence of the instincts on the internal objects.

The convergence of these three aspects into one concept (which was often referred to simply as 'object' without specifying it as being internal, which was implicitly understood) made the concept a very central one in the theory. Non-Kleinians were (and are to the present day) confused by clinical and theoretical discussions in which 'objects' – good and bad, part and whole, internal and external – seemed to constitute the mind and be responsible for all thoughts, feelings and behaviour.

The tendency to discuss everything in terms of the interactions of (internal) objects among themselves and with the ego is, no doubt, confusing. It becomes impossible to distinguish among the vast array of meanings in which the concept 'object' is being used. This difficulty is not simply the product of confusion on the part of the Kleinians or of ignorance on the part of non-Kleinians. Rather, it seems to be related to a basic difference of outlook. The Kleinians considered the phantasy world of internal objects interacting between themselves and with the ego to constitute psychic reality. Their (almost) exclusive interest in this basic psychic reality, and their view that most thought and behaviour could be derived from that level of basic psychic reality, led them to elaborate their discussions in terms of the basic dynamics[13] of the ego and its (internal) objects. Distinctions such

47

as instinct-derived vs. reality-derived, inside vs. outside, 'me' vs. 'not-me' were considered to be less relevant at this level. According to Melanie Klein's theory of development, these distinctions become increasingly applicable at later stages of development; that is, they are viewed as the outcomes of (normal) development. As such they may be considered to play a relatively minor part in the understanding of the basics of psychic reality. Therefore, it often happens that little effort is made to preserve these distinctions even in theoretical discussion.

This approach is illustrated in the following statement by Paula Heimann:

> It must be understood that a description of these most primitive psychic processes, these unconscious phantasies, can be no more than an approximation. In a sense all our descriptions are artificial, because we have to use words for experiences which take place at a more primitive level before verbalization (which probably involves a progressive modification) has been achieved . . . . The phantasies about the inner world are inseparable from the infant's relation with the outer world and real people. It is only a limitation in our means of description which makes it appear as if there were two distinct entities which influence one another, instead of one whole, one multi-faceted interacting experience. In a similar way it is a descriptive artefact to distinguish instinctual impulses and unconscious phantasy. We must be aware that we are merely following another aspect of the same experience when we now turn to a discussion of instinctual impulses.
>
> (Heimann 1952)

Stating the Kleinian case in such a clear-cut manner is an exaggeration. Melanie Klein did not completely ignore these distinctions or consider them to be later developments irrelevant to the important formative processes. She sometimes explored the very distinctions that at other times she ignored. The theoretical justification for ignoring such distinctions as cited above, although an important aspect of the Kleinian framework, does not provide a blanket excuse for all the instances in which these distinctions are ignored. There is room within the Kleinian theory for greater specification as to when these distinctions are applicable and when they are not. But beyond this criticism, it is important to understand that the tendency to blur distinctions between concepts is part of a specific theory of mind in which these distinctions are regarded as by-products of more basic processes. It is the explication of those basic processes, of 'psychic reality', that Kleinian theory emphasizes as its major task.

The Kleinian theory of development

We have seen some of the problems involved in the Kleinian conception of internal objects as reflecting the instincts, especially as regards the questions of internal vs. external factors and of differentiations in mental life. The focus of Melanie Klein's attempt to deal with these questions was her theory of development. The basics of this theory were proposed in 1935 when she introduced the concepts of the depressive and paranoid positions, and further elaborated them in subsequent papers (Klein 1940, 1946) in which she eventually formulated the concept of the paranoid-schizoid position. The development of this theory occurred together with, and constituted an integral part of, the conceptual elaboration of the implications of the life/death instinct concept.

Melanie Klein's concept of the depressive position involved the idea that depression constituted a developmental achievement, and was not present in early infancy. It was considered to be dependent on the development of the capacity to relate to the object as whole-object rather than as a part-object. By this, Melanie Klein meant two things. She considered the small infant (under 6 months) to be incapable of perceiving the mother as a whole person. Rather, the infant was considered to be capable of perceiving only a part of the mother, namely, her breast.[14] In addition, the infant was also considered to be incapable of integrating the good and bad aspects of its objects, experiencing these aspects as separate objects rather than as different aspects of the same object. These two tendencies of the infant – to perceive parts of objects and to experience the goodness and badness of objects as separate objects – were considered to be characteristic of that level of development of the infant at which he could relate only to part-objects.[15] The transition to the level of whole-objects involved development in these two areas: the capacity to perceive the mother as a whole person, and the capacity to experience her as both good and bad. Melanie Klein considered this achievement to be a precondition for the capacity to experience depression for two closely related reasons. First, she states that only when the self is capable of experiencing a whole person, rather than a part, is it possible for the self to identify with the object, and feel depressed at the loss of the loved object.[16] Second, with the integration of good and bad aspects into one whole-object, 'Feelings both of a destructive and of a loving nature are experienced towards one and the same object and this gives rise to deep and disturbing conflicts in the child's mind' (Klein 1935). Depression and guilt are experienced due to the (phantasied) destruction of the loved object (that is, the whole-object, both bad and good).

The achievement of the level of whole-object relations brings with it important implications as regards the nature of the internal objects in relation to the self. One of the important implications of the ability to experience the object as a whole-object is that objects can be experienced more realistically. Rather than being limited by the emotional restriction of splitting the object into good and bad, the infant at the whole-object level is capable of experiencing the object more as it really is – both good and bad. A precondition of this level of experiencing is the ability to cope with the anxieties engendered by this level of integration – especially depression and guilt. Melanie Klein emphasized the frequency of regression from this level due to these anxieties, and a renewal of the splitting (of the object into good and bad).

But goodness and badness of the object do not simply reflect realistic characteristics (gratifying and frustrating). As we have seen, an important aspect of internal objects is that they are deeply influenced by the instincts – good and bad objects influenced by the life and death instincts, respectively. Melanie Klein repeatedly emphasized the fantastic (exaggerated) nature of the goodness and badness of the good and bad objects (1940). She expressed the interrelation of reality and instinctual factors in the following statement:

> From the beginning the ego introjects objects 'good' and 'bad', for both of which the mother's breast is the prototype – for good objects when the child obtains it, for bad ones when it fails him. But it is because the baby projects its own aggression onto the objects that it feels them to be 'bad' and not only in that they frustrate its desires: the child conceives of them as actually dangerous.
>
> (Klein 1935: 262)

In the light of this view, the integration of good and bad aspects of the object is more than just the ability to integrate differing aspects of reality. Melanie Klein considered this integration to reflect also a change in the internal dynamics of the instincts:

> The fear of phantastically 'bad' persecutors and the belief in phantastically 'good' objects are bound up with each other. Idealization is an essential process in the young child's mind, since he cannot yet cope in any other way with his fears of persecution (a result of his own hatred). Not until early anxieties have been sufficiently relieved owing to experiences which increase love and trust, is it possible to establish the all-important process of bringing together more closely the various aspect of objects (external, internal, 'good' and 'bad', loved and hated), and thus for hatred to become actually mitigated by love – which means a decrease of ambivalence. While the separation of these contrasting aspects – felt in the unconscious as contrasting objects – operates strongly, feelings of hatred and love are also so much divorced from each other that love cannot mitigate hatred.
>
> (Klein 1940: 349, n. 2)

This change – the mitigation of hate by love (often referred to as 'fusion of the instincts') – results in a loosening of the close tie between internal objects and instincts. The objects are thus considered to be less deeply influenced by the instincts, and to reflect external reality to a greater degree. Objects can be experienced as separate from the self (differentiation of internal from external objects), with attributes of their own which are (to a certain extent) perceived as such without being determined by the instinctual trends in the individual. This development is of utmost importance in the Kleinian view, as it makes possible the beginning of a benign circle in which benign reality serves to reinforce the life instinct (love), which can then lead to further mitigation of hate, and so on.

The conclusion from these details of Melanie Klein's theory of development seems to be that no single definition regarding the place of internal objects *vis-à-vis* the self and reality will be enough. She did not see internal objects as clearly defined entities such that the relationship between them and external reality and the instincts could be strictly specified. Rather, this relationship is considered to be in a state of flux, changing in accordance with the specific dynamics of the immediate psychic reality. Thus, part-objects are considered to be more strongly influenced by the instincts than by external reality, and whole-objects are considered to reflect reality to a greater degree. The statement that the infant in the depressive position is capable of distinguishing between internal objects and external objects must be understood as meaning that those aspects of the self which are experienced as internal objects are not confused with the perceptions of real people. Accordingly, external objects (which refers to reality-orientated mental representations of objects) are experienced as (relatively) distinct from the feelings and instincts of the individual.

This view complicates even further attempts to tease out the different threads which make up the concept of internal objects The status of internal objects *vis-à-vis* the instincts and reality is thus complicated not only by the conceptual question discussed in the previous section, but also by specific ideas constituting the Kleinian theory of development. Melanie Klein's theory of the development from part- to whole-object relations may be seen as part of the process of coping with the conceptual problems involved in the concept of internal objects. By conceptualizing internal objects as being in a state of flux *vis-à-vis* the instincts and reality, Melanie Klein steered between the Scylla and Charybdis of instincts and (external) reality, of self and external object. This conceptualization leaves room both for the view of internal objects (including perceptions, memories and phantasies of objects, conscious and unconscious) as aspects of the self, reflecting its loving and aggressive aspects (namely, the instincts), and as reflections of the gratifying and frustrating aspects of the external world. Furthermore, it proposes a developmental process whereby the earlier instinct-laden psychic reality is transformed into a more reality-orientated experience.

Self and objects

We have seen the development of the concept of internal objects and some of the major issues to which it was related. The basic aspects discussed – the core meaning of internal objects as 'body-phantasies', the generalization from that core meaning to include other mental contents, and the view of the close connection between internal objects and the instincts – constitute the major meanings of the concept of internal objects. Melanie Klein's later works change little in the meaning of the concept; it seems that the concept of internal objects itself had attained its full conceptual development, and the important developments in her later works build on this concept. Reviewing these later works we can see the role that the concept of internal objects played in the further development of her views. Of special interest will be the vicissitudes of the issue of self–object differentiation as related to the concept of internal objects.

It is important here to note that Melanie Klein used the term 'ego' where we today would probably use the term 'self'. But, in addition, it is important to distinguish between two meanings of these terms. 'Self' may be used to refer to the person, or the personality as a whole. It also may be used to refer to those aspects that a person feels to be 'himself' or 'herself', in contrast to others. This would be closer to the meaning of self-representation, and often 'ego' is used by Melanie Klein thus, especially when she describes the interactions of the ego with the internal objects. Of course, such simple distinctions become complicated when discussing those areas of the personality which we are discussing in this study, as we have seen. Melanie Klein's concept of the 'assimilation' of internal objects and the idea of projective identification address these issues.

Assimilation of internal objects

Melanie Klein (1946) referred to Paula Heimann's (1942b) discussion of the idea of the assimilation of internal objects, which does not seem to have been much discussed by Kleinian analysts.[17] In Heimann's discussion of successful sublimation she emphasized the experience of 'internal freedom and independence' as an essential element of successful sublimation. In contrast to this feeling of independence she described the feeling of compulsion which characterizes the person dominated by internal objects. From this distinction she arrived at the formulation that the feeling of internal independence cannot exist as long as the individual experiences their internal objects as foreign bodies. Only when these internal objects are assimilated into the ego can the individual feel themselves to be free. This can occur when there is a lessening of the destructive impulses, which allows the individual to experience their internal objects as 'more human, less like monsters, less like saints'. This in turn lessens the impulse greedily to attack the internal objects, as a result of which the individual 'acquires the right to absorb their good qualities'.

In Heimann's discussion we can see the developing awareness of the distinction between internal objects as experiences of 'foreign bodies' within the self as opposed to experiences of 'me-ness'. This aspect of the concept of internal objects, the phenomenological status as 'me' and/or 'not-me' was further discussed by Heimann in her presentation in the 1943 Controversial Discussions (Heimann 1952). It was no doubt one of the problematic aspects of this concept, as is illustrated in the papers of Brierley (1939) and Matte-Blanco (1941). The growing interest in this aspect of the concept of internal objects probably played a part in the development of the 'me-ness' aspect of the process of projective identification, to which we shall now turn.

Projective identification

Melanie Klein introduced the concept of projective identification in 1946. In this concept she expressed directly the idea that the object was not experienced as separate from the self, but rather as being, or containing, aspects of the self:

> In so far as the mother comes to contain the bad parts of the self, she is not felt to be a separate individual but is felt to be *the* bad self . . . . In psychotic disorders this identification of an object with the hated parts of the self contributes to the intensity of the hatred directed against other people.
>
> (M. Klein 1946)

She considered this to be one of the basic processes whereby a relationship with an object was established. Any cathexis of an object with either libidinal or aggressive feelings was considered to be a projection of those feelings; that is, the object cathected was by definition both loved (or hated) and experienced as loving (or hating).[18] This idea was now given more concrete form, with the introduction of the concept of projective identification: the object was considered to *contain* parts of the self – those parts which were projected. According to this view, the loved object was felt to be loving because it contained parts of the loving self. 'The projection of good feelings and good parts of the self into the mother is essential for the infant's ability to develop good object relations and to integrate his ego' (ibid.). 'The projection of love-feelings – underlying the process of attaching libido to the object – is . . . a precondition for finding a good object' (M. Klein 1952c).

One major aspect of the concept of projective identification which constitutes an innovation in Melanie Klein's thinking[19] is the idea that in some way a feeling of self, of 'me-ness', is retained in regard to the part of the self projected in projective identification. In this the process of projective identification may be considered to differ from processes discussed earlier under the title 'projection'.

In addition to her description of the individual's experiences of the object as a part, or a representative, of the self, Melanie Klein also discussed the consequent feelings of impoverishment and weakening of the self resulting from the feeling that important parts of the self are missing and are no longer at its disposal. These feelings are considered to develop whether the projected parts of the self are good parts or bad parts. She also mentions feelings that the 'ego has no life and no value of its own' (M. Klein 1946) as related to this process.

The emphasis on the feeling of selfness in relation to both internal and external objects is part of Melanie Klein's growing interest in the early structure of the ego (self).[20] This interest is reflected in her adoption (in 1952) of Fairbairn's term 'schizoid position' together with her previously proposed term 'paranoid position'. Fairbairn's emphasis had been on the splits (schisms) within the ego, brought about in conjunction with the splitting of the object. Melanie Klein accepted this idea, and the idea of the splitting-off of parts of the self, and their projection into objects, is an elaboration of this idea. She considered projective identification to be at the basis of all object-relations (M. Klein 1952c), with both projection of good and of bad parts of the self into the object.

Projective identification is considered to be pathological when it is exaggerated, when it interferes with later processes of differentiation. These later processes do not rule out the ongoing 'ebb and flow' between the different 'positions', which the Kleinians see as a much more ubiquitous and normal process than do non-Kleinians.[21] Klein adopted Heimann's (1942b) idea of the assimilation of internal objects by the ego (for example, M. Klein 1946, 1952c, 1957) and considered it to be an important aspect of the infant's growing sense of reality. She considered the growing differentiation (in the individual's mind) between the individual's own impulses and those of its objects to be closely related to the assimilation of the internal object into the ego. To the extent that the self can be accepted as such, with its good and bad parts, there is less of a need for intermediary entities combining aspects of self and object, and assimilation of the internal objects by the ego can take place. Melanie Klein herself seems to have had doubts as to whether such a complete integration of the self, and consequently differentiation of self and object, could be achieved.

In one of her last papers (1958) she reversed her position regarding this issue, suggesting that in addition to the good and bad internal objects that constitute the superego, extremely terrifying figures are split off from the ego 'in a different manner'. Unlike the good and bad aspects of the superego, which can eventually be integrated and assimilated by the ego, these other terrifying figures 'are not accepted by the ego . . . and are constantly rejected by it'. These figures continue to exist 'in the deep layers of the unconscious' and may intrude into consciousness due to extreme pressures, whether internal or external.

> People who are on the whole stable – and that means that they have firmly established their good object and therefore are closely identi-fied with it – can overcome this intrusion of the deeper unconscious into their ego and regain their stability. In neurotic, and still more in psychotic individuals, the struggle against such dangers threatening from the deeper layers of the unconscious is to some extent constant and part of their instability or their illness.
>
> (Klein 1958: 243)

While it is beyond the scope of this study to speculate on the factors which led Melanie Klein to this sudden change of view – about which the editors of her collected *Writings* (see Klein 1975: 331–2) expressed their surprise – it clearly expresses her doubts surrounding the question of the assimilation of internal objects. The assertion, towards the end of her life, that terrifying aspects of the self ('defused instincts') continued to remain split off and experienced as (internal) objects, implied that the self could never be completely integrated.

Summary

We have seen the development of a number of aspects of Melanie Klein's concept of internal objects. The main ones have been:

1 *Internal objects as body-phantasies.* This refers both to the phantasy of another person (or part of a person) physically inside the individual's body and to the bodily sensations which are experienced as objects.
2 *Internal objects as referring to all contents of the mind—phantasies, memories and perceptions of objects.* The higher-level cognitive contents are considered to be rooted in the deep unconscious levels at which internal objects are experienced concretely (as in 1).

3 *Internal objects as deeply influenced by the instincts.* This is especially important in relation to the death instinct, which gives rise to experiences of
dangerous and annihilating internal objects.

The concept of internal objects has played an interesting role on the border
between self and object in Melanie Klein's theory. In a paradoxical manner
it appears to belong to both realms – to both 'me' and 'not me'. As such it
expresses a basic insight of Kleinian psychology – that self–object differentiation is a complex process and not a one-time, clear-cut achievement.
Internal objects combine aspects of self and object – both by combining
qualities of self with qualities of the object (loving, hating, angry, reposing
and so on) and by combining the basic feeling of 'me-ness' with 'not-me-
ness'. Melanie Klein considered there to be a developmental process in
which the confusion of self with object was gradually sorted out, in the
progress from the paranoid-schizoid to the depressive position.

Fairbairn

Fairbairn's theory of 'endopsychic structure' and object relations (Fairbairn
1944) was developed under the influence of his work with schizoid patients
and his view of schizoid phenomena (or 'the schizoid position') as the basic
organization of the personality.[22]

The first of that series of papers in which Fairbairn developed his own
theory of object relations was devoted to the 'Schizoid factors in the
personality' (1940). Although this paper did not include any of the open
disagreement with Freud's theories which characterized the papers that
followed, his views regarding schizoid phenomena constituted the clinical
background for his consequent rejection of Freud's theory of the drives.[23]
What most impressed Fairbairn in his schizoid patients was their withdrawal from interpersonal relationships in favour of an inner reality.
Fairbairn discussed various schizoid phenomena in relation to this replacement by inner instead of outer realities: feelings of omnipotence; the
de-emotionalization of interpersonal relationships, an attitude towards
other people as 'need-satisfiers' rather than as people with inherent value;
exhibitionistic trends; and others. Following Abraham's (1924) stages of
object-love, Fairbairn considered schizoid phenomena to be closely related
to the libidinal attitude of incorporation and internalization (which were
considered to be very primitive, oral tendencies).

Thus Fairbairn viewed the schizoid's transfer of interest from interpersonal relationships to internal reality as constituting a very deep
regression to the oral attitude of internalization. He considered the basis for
this regression to be emotional frustration in the very early relationship

with the mother. His definition of 'emotional frustration' was the child's feeling '(a) that he is not really loved for himself as a person by his mother, and (b) that his own love for his mother is not really valued and accepted by her' (Fairbairn 1940: 17). This emphasis on emotional rather than instinctual frustration expresses Fairbairn's dissatisfaction with Freud's theory of drives, which he would openly discuss in his next paper (Fairbairn 1941). But even more significant is the development of Fairbairn's basic view that the process of internalization, leading to the establishment of internalized objects, occurs 'under the influence of situations of frustration during the early oral phase' (ibid.).

Two points are important to note in these early ideas of Fairbairn. The first is the emphasis on the distinction between internal and external object-relationships, with the former serving as a defensive substitute for the latter. While building on Freud's view of the superego as an internalized object substituting for external object-relationships (of the parents, at the Oedipal stage), Fairbairn took this idea much further, viewing it as *the basic fact* of mental life, rather than as a specific process leading to a specific outcome. Furthermore, Fairbairn divorced this process from the context of instinctual wishes and defences, and related it to much more general processes of emotional satisfaction and frustration, thereby further turning it into the basic process of mental life.

The second point is that Fairbairn considered this process of internalization to be a result of frustration. Internalized objects are thus considered to reflect (basically) frustrating aspects of experience, and are not considered realistically to represent experience as a whole. Closely related to this view is Fairbairn's concept of 'splits in the ego' (or 'schisms'). While Fairbairn did not exactly define this concept in his 1940 paper – a concept that would serve as a basis for his theory of endopsychic structure – he did mention various phenomena which he considered to be related to it: depersonalization, derealization, *déjà vu*, and even dreams – 'the fact that the dreamer is characteristically represented in the dream by more than one figure is capable of no other interpretation except that . . . the ego of the dreamer is split' (1941: 9). He considered such splits in the ego to be characteristic of schizoid phenomena.

However, the schizoid position, which is the outcome of the process of internalization, was not considered by Fairbairn to be normative, although he did consider it to be widespread, and even universal ('some measure of splitting of the ego is invariably present at the deepest mental level').

Fairbairn, in 1940, may be seen as struggling to integrate his two major insights regarding the schizoid personality into a single theory. He felt that the two insights embodied in the concepts of 'internalization' – the construction of an inner world, in favour of which external relationships are abandoned, and 'splits in the ego' – were not compatible with Freud's emphasis on 'drives seeking discharge'. In his attempt to bring his two basic concepts together into an integral theory of personality, he rejected Freud's theory of the drives in favour of a theory emphasizing the object-seeking nature of the individual, and the consequences of the frustration of this seeking.

Fairbairn's concept of 'structure'

In 1944, Fairbairn introduced his concept of 'endopsychic structure', which provided the conceptual integration he sought for the ideas of 'internalization' and 'splits in the ego', and provided him with an alternative for Freud's view of psychic energy as the basis on which a theory of personality might be organized.

Fairbairn rejected Freud's theory of the drives both for theoretical and clinical reasons. At the level of theory, he rejected Freud's distinction between energy and structure as belonging to a nineteenth-century view of the relation between energy and matter. In relation to his clinical findings, Fairbairn rejected the idea of energy seeking discharge, with the pleasure principle as the basic regulatory principle. Instead, he suggested that 'dynamic structure' was the basic motivation. According to this view, personality was described as constituted of different dynamic structures motivating behaviour in different directions, under the overall principle that the individual seeks to be in close, emotionally satisfying relationships with other people. These dynamic stuctures, active aspects of the personality, are not normative phenomena, but rather are 'split off' (from the 'central ego') and repressed, because of experiences of emotional frustration in interpersonal relationships. It is frustration which leads to the establishment of the basic structures of personality, and as a result these structures constitute a (more or less) rigid organization. (It is interesting to note that Fairbairn was so involved in this aspect of the basically pathological organization of personality that he felt no need to develop concepts relating to the healthy aspects of personality, and in fact did not even seem to recognize the absence of concepts relating to such aspects in his theory.)

Inasmuch as this conception of dynamic structures was the basis of Fairbairn's theory of personality, I will describe some of the details of his views. Fairbairn considered there to be two basic frustrating aspects of the object that are internalized and established as structures within the personality: the exciting aspect and the rejecting aspect. As these aspects are internalized and established as internalized objects (which Fairbairn emphasized as structures, in contrast to Melanie Klein's emphasis on phantasy), complementary aspects of the self are split off from the core-self. Fairbairn called these the 'libidinal ego' and the 'anti-libidinal ego' (corresponding to the 'exciting object' and the 'rejecting object'; the 'anti-libidinal ego' is considered to be that aspect of the self that aggressively attacks the love-dependent 'libidinal ego'). Thus the basic organization of the personality is built on two sub-systems which are split off and repressed – a libidinal sub-system and an anti-libidinal (or aggressive) one. Each sub-system consists of an object structure and an ego (or self) structure. Repression of internalized objects takes place in conjunction with the repression of the complementary ego (self) structure. These structures, and the 'central' object and self structures, are all considered to be engaged in interactions between themselves. The dynamics of the personality are considered to be definable in terms of the interactions of these structures, and in this Fairbairn's approach is closely similar to Melanie Klein's descriptions of the interactions of the ego and the various internal objects.[24]

At this point it is important to note that Fairbairn's usage of the concept of structure was a central issue in his theory of personality and that he considered it to be a major conceptual innovation in psychoanalytic theory. He did not claim this innovation for himself, but rather considered Freud to have already made use of the idea of dynamic structure in conceptualizing of the superego. Fairbairn saw himself as extending Freud's idea and following it to its logical end – the replacement of the concept of psychic energy with that of dynamic structures. He also considered the concept of structure to be more appropriate than Melanie Klein's idea of internal objects as 'phantasy'. Fairbairn emphasized that the internal objects that he was describing were not to be thought of as 'mere figments of phantasy' (Fairbairn 1949: 154), 'mere images' (Fairbairn 1955: 148), or simple memories (Fairbairn 1954: 107). Rather, he conceived of them as basic organizations of the personality, stable and persistent over time. His criticism of Melanie Klein's conceptualization of internal objects in terms of phantasy was related to his view that phantasy did not sufficiently emphasize their 'realness' – 'These internal objects should be regarded as having an organised structure, an identity of their own, an endopsychic existence and an activity as real within the inner world as those of any object within the outer world' (Fairbairn, quoted in Grosskurth 1987: 320). Furthermore, he stated that the process whereby such structures are established within the personality cannot be conceived of 'as simply a manifestation of that general perpetuation of experience which is described as 'memory'' (Fairbairn 1954: 107).[25] He emphasized that it is specifically the defensive process of internalization (or introjection – Fairbairn did not tend to distinguish between the two) that accounts for the establishment of such structures.

Origins of the internal objects

Following Freud's (1923b, 1924c, 1930a) deliberations in regard to the question of the orgins of the severity of the superego – whether to relate it to the personality of the parents (as implied by the use of the concept of introjection or identification), or to relate it to internal factors, such as the individual's own aggressive tendencies – Melanie Klein developed a theory emphasizing the internal origins.[26] This approach was closely related to her view of the infant's personality as struggling to come to terms with the death instinct and the anxieties to which it gives rise. The early internal objects (which were conceived of as part-objects) were conceived as representing the death and life instincts and the struggle between them within the infant's personality. Only at a later stage was reality considered to have a (hopefully) benign influence on this struggle, allowing the infant to introject good objects and thus overcome and mitigate the destructiveness of the death instinct.

Fairbairn, in clear opposition to Melanie Klein's views on this matter, rejected the concept of a death instinct or of an inherent aggressive instinct, and considered aggression to be a reactive phenomenon, in response to emotional frustration (Fairbairn 1943, 1944, 1963). Fairbairn emphasized that the nature of the basic internal objects as 'bad' objects was due not to the influence of inborn instincts, but rather to the nature of the interpersonal interaction with emotionally significant people (especially the mother) which led to their formation. Thus it was the nature of the real object (in interaction with the individual) as rejecting and as frustratingly exciting that led to internalization and the establishment of the rejecting object and the exciting object as internal structures. This difference in the views of Fairbairn and Klein regarding the origin of the internal objects is one that has set the field for the major differing approaches to this issue in the psychoanalytic literature today (Robbins 1980; Mitchell 1981). I will further discuss this difference in relation to both theoretical and clinical issues in Part Two.

For Fairbairn this was a critical issue. It was closely related to his view of libido as object-seeking, rather than as seeking discharge. His emphasis was clearly on the individual's longing for good interpersonal relationships, with the internal world viewed as a defensive (and pathological) consequence of the frustration of this longing. It should be noted that this defensive nature of internal objects did not (primarily) refer to the kind of intrapsychic defence commonly discussed in traditional psychoanalytic theory. Fairbairn did not conceive of internalization as a defence against internal processes – for example, against drive impulses, as did Freud (1923b), who viewed the introjection of the parental images leading to the establishment of the superego as a defence against overpowering Oedipal impulses. Rather, he saw internalization as defensive mainly in the context of the interpersonal relationship with the (external) object. By internalizing bad aspects of the (external) object, the individual attempts to 'purge' the (external) object of its badness, so that the interpersonal relationship may continue undisturbed. The reason for this lies in the individual's complete dependence on the object (the paradigm for this being the infant's dependence on the mother). By 'taking in' the bad object, the individual attempts both to control it and to make it good (Fairbairn 1943: 67; 1944: 111, 114), and attempts, by taking on in himself the badness of the object, to allow the external relationship to go on undisturbed (1943: 65–6; 1955: 148).[27]

Of course, this defence does not really succeed, inasmuch as the internal structures thereby established reflect the bad (frustrating) nature of the (external) objects internalized, so that the individual's inner world too is populated by rejecting and exciting-but-frustrating objects. But, in Fairbairn's view, bad objects are better than no objects, as the ultimate psychic catastrophe with which the individual (especially the schizoid individual) is threatened is the 'loss of ego', consequent on the complete withdrawal from all object-relationships (Fairbairn 1941: 52; 1944: 113).[28] Thus the establishment of a world of internal objects, though not gratifying, does serve as a defence against an even more disastrous situation.

Here a note is relevant regarding the presentation of Fairbairn's view of internalization as involving specifically bad objects. Although this is definitely the gist of his view (for example, Fairbairn 1944: 99 – 'It is difficult to find any motive for the internalization of objects which are satisfying and good') – a qualification needs to be mentioned. Fairbairn did deliberate regarding the question whether internalization should be seen as related only to bad objects, or whether it could be conceived as related to the frustrating but pre-ambivalent object (that is, one that is not yet bad). Fairbairn's deliberations (as he described them in his paper of 1951: 117–19) were related to the chronological relationship between ambivalence and internalization, and he eventually decided that ambivalence could be considered to arise only after the original internalization of the (frustrating) object (ibid.). Thus the infant was considered to internalize the object because of the frustrating nature of the object, and only after this, and after the infant achieves the stage of ambivalence – following Abraham (1925), who designated the early oral stage as pre-ambivalent – came the process of the splitting of the (internal) object into its separate good (idealized) and bad (exciting and rejecting) aspects. This description also provided Fairbairn with an explanation for the existence of an idealized object structure, one for which his original theory of the internalization of bad objects did not account. Again, although this may seem to run counter to Fairbairn's declared view that only bad objects could be conceived as undergoing internalization, he actually did continue to maintain a slightly mitigated version of his original view, seeing internalization as an exclusively defensive process aimed at the frustrating object (Fairbairn 1963).

After discussing the issue of the origins of the internal objects in Fairbairn's theory, a word is in order in regard to their ongoing influence. As noted above, one of the basic clinical insights which Fairbairn was trying to account for in his theory of internalization was that of the withdrawal of interest in interpersonal relationships on the part of the schizoid individual in favour of a preoccupation with an inner reality. Thus, one of the basic functions of internal objects is to provide a substitute for interpersonal relationships, to which the schizoid individual withdraws, rather than risk the dangers of a 'real' relationship over which he has no control. (Fairbairn (1940, 1941), gave an exquisite description of the schizoid's fear of destroying his objects by his love for them.)

But Fairbairn also considered this inner world to influence the individual's interpersonal relationships in other ways, especially via neurotic (but also psychotic) mechanisms involving the externalization (or projection – Fairbairn did not seem to distinguish between these two terms)[29] of internal objects on to external reality. Thus, in spite of the fact that internal objects were considered to have been established as part of the individual's attempt to 'purge' external reality of its badness, they also tend to perpetuate this badness via various defensive techniques.[30] In addition, Fairbairn (1943) described a process which he called the 'release (or return) of repressed bad objects'. This refers to a psychotic process in which 'external situations acquire . . . the significance of repressed situations involving relationships with bad objects' (pp. 76–7). He considered this process to be related to, and capable of accounting for, the phenomena Freud described under the heading of the 'repetition compulsion'. Fairbairn viewed these phenomena as consisting of an experience of being 'haunted' by (previously repressed) bad internal objects which continually 'appear' in reality. He also considered this process as of potential therapeutic value, inasmuch as such a 'return of the repressed' allows (in therapy) a working through of the pathological tie to these internal objects. It was in the lessening of the pathological relationship with internal objects, leading to a lessening of the repression and split-offness of the internal structures, that Fairbairn saw the basic aim of therapy.

These formulations of Fairbairn regarding the influences of the internal objects on an individual's perception of, and attitude towards, other people (external objects), although limited to the area of pathology, paved the way for the eventual development of a more general theory of personality. Guntrip (for example, 1961) further generalized from Fairbairn's description of specific neurotic and psychotic processes, to a view that 'the inner and outer worlds have a two-way causal relationship and reciprocal influence' (p. 360). But Guntrip basically continued to regard the inner world of psychic structure as a pathological (though, to some extent, universal) phenomenon, its 'healthy' contrast being 'the pristine unitary wholeness of the psyche' (Guntrip 1971: 93–4). Thus, this view of the influence of internal structures on the perception of, and attitude towards, the external world, as a basically pathological phenomenon, remains a major difference between the theories of personality of Fairbairn and Guntrip, on the one hand, and North American views orientated towards ego psychology, on the other. This difference will be further discussed in the final chapter of this study.

Summary

In the history of psychoanalytic ideas, the concepts presented by Fairbairn have been cited as playing an important role in the shift from drive psychology, and its futher extension in Hartmann's version of ego psychology, to an object-relations orientation (Guntrip 1961, 1969, 1971; Greenberg and Mitchell 1983). Although the concept of internal objects was not Fairbairn's innovation, his theory of internal objects, and the centrality which this idea acquired in his theory of personality, constitute a very important contribution in the development of concepts of mental objects. I will here attempt to summarize the main points relevant to his concept of internal objects, those which have influenced the further development of this concept.

1 Fairbairn's basic position was that the internal organization of personality (internal structures) is a defensive reaction to emotionally frustrating experiences (primarily with the mother).
2 As a result of such experiences internal structures are established, internalizing frustrating aspects of the (external) object.
3 In addition, the individual will also experience themselves in accordance with the nature of their internal objects, viewing themselves as bad, and establishing internal structures of the ego (self) in accordance.
4 To the extent that a person experiences emotionally frustrating interactions (especially early in life), they will tend to withdraw from interpersonal interactions in favour of a preoccupation with their inner world. (Today we would tend to conceive of such preoccupation in terms of – conscious and unconscious – phantasying. For reasons discussed above, Fairbairn preferred the concept of internal structure instead of Melanie Klein's use of that of phantasy.)
5 To the extent that this process of internalization occurs, the phantasies with which the individual is preoccupied (their inner world) will

ultimately tend to reflect the emotionally frustrating nature of the original interpersonal interaction.

6 Aspects of this bad inner world may be externalized, thus influencing the individual's further experience of interpersonal relationships.

7 A person's emotional life may be understood in terms of the interactions of these internal structures, both ego structures and object structures, among themselves.

A number of issues raised in these views should be noted. First and foremost is the issue of the origins of the internal objects, and Fairbairn's clear-cut rejection of Melanie Klein's emphasis on their internal origin. Another important issue is the designation of internal objects as structures, in contrast with Klein's view of them as phantasies. This difference will be further discussed in the final chapter of this study in terms of concepts referring to the experiential and non-experiential realms. While Fairbairn's and Melanie Klein's own personal preferences in this regard may not necessarily be of major theoretical importance (although they themselves did consider them so – Grosskurth 1987: 320), the fact that each of them chose a different realm of concepts probably does reflect the ongoing difficulty in integrating (and also differentiating) concepts from these two realms.

Bion

The statement at the beginning of the section on Melanie Klein regarding the limited innovative additions of later Kleinian analysts to Melanie Klein's basic ideas regarding internal objects, certainly should not be applied to the work of Wilfred Bion. Bion's work definitely contributed much to Kleinian psychology in many areas, including the concepts under study here. Unfortunately, his work is of such scope and complexity as to be almost unapproachable by the uninitiated.[31] This short summary of some of Bion's ideas will necessarily ignore much of his later work, and focus on the ideas presented in his psychoanalytic papers on schizophrenia and thinking, from 1950 to 1962, which have been collected in *Second Thoughts* (Bion 1967) and in his first book, *Learning from Experience* (1962b). This restriction undoubtedly does not provide the extent of study which his ideas deserve, extracting them as it does from the ultimate flowering which his ideas attain in his later works. Due to the unusual nature and breadth of Bion's work, and the limitations of the present study,[32] we will have to limit this section to the period of time noted.

Bion's work may be seen to originate in a specific clinical problem, but one so basic to mental life as to lead him to extend psychoanalytic theory to an exploration of the substratum of mental life itself. The clinical issue was that of thought disturbance, and Bion followed the strands that led him from this issue to the origins and foundations of thought. It should be noted that the question of the basic structure and nature of thought was taken more or less for granted in psychoanalytic theory. Freud (1915c) had considered the drives to be represented in mental life by 'ideas',[33] and on that basis went on to explore the way drives influenced the content of those ideas and the complications to which this led. But the more basic constitution of those ideas, and their origin, were questions generally beyond his interest. One important exception to this was his distinction between 'word-presentation' and 'thing-presentation', a distinction made in the context of a discussion of the concrete nature of the schizophrenic's thinking (Freud 1915e). As we shall see, this distinction is very similar to a distinction Bion later made between two 'kinds' of thoughts (alpha and beta elements).[34] Bion's distinction, however, was embedded in a dynamic conception regarding the evolution of thought, as opposed to Freud's distinction which lacks a theory of the dynamics of these 'presentations'.

One of the important basic assumptions with which Bion set out in his exploration of thought disturbances in schizophrenia was the Kleinian view that the 'proper' concepts for an exploration of the mind are of a concrete nature.[35] As we mentioned above, in the chapter on Melanie Klein, the need for a distinction between the concepts used to describe subjective experience and the theoretical concepts used to account for such experience, as two distinct realms and levels of discourse, was not accepted by Kleinian analysts. This assumption must be borne in mind when we approach Bion's extension of the concept of part-object to include functions of the personality (Bion 1959).[36] As we have seen, the concept of 'partial object love' had been introduced by Abraham (1925) as a stage in the development of object-love. Melanie Klein similarly considered a relationship to part-objects to characterize the paranoid-schizoid position. This conception is based on the view that the capacity to conceive of, and relate to, another person is a capacity that develops via the capacity to relate to a 'part' of that person.[37] The incapacity to integrate the differing 'parts' is gradually overcome as the depressive position is worked through.

In Melanie Klein's theory, 'part-objects' refer to primitive phantasies based on the workings of the life and death instincts in the infant's mind, and on primitive body sensations (such as the nipple-in-the-mouth). Bion took this concept a step further in considering that all functions of the personality may be experienced and related to as part-objects. The individual may experience his own psychological capacities, such as verbal thought, judgement or specific perceptual senses (seeing, hearing and so on) as 'parts'[38] with which he has a relationship. The same dynamics which apply to other part-objects – especially projection and introjection – may apply to these functions. Accordingly, Bion conceived of the various defects of psychological functioning of his schizophrenic patients as the products of such internal dynamics, especially of internal attacks on those functions due to the unbearable anxiety the infant experienced in relation to those functions (Bion 1959).[39] Thus a patient experiencing his capacity for verbal communication as leading to unbearable anxiety may attempt to project that capacity into the analyst, leaving the patient without the capacity to speak coherently (Bion 1954).

Gradually, as Bion succeeded in working through these processes with his patients, he came to conceive of an underlying capacity which served as the basis for all the other specific functions of the personality. This function was considered to be that which transforms raw data received by the mind into meaningful information that could be processed by the mind. This information could thereupon partake in all those mental processes that constitute mental life. Bion (1962a) called this function 'alpha function', preferring to assign it a meaningless sign (alpha) rather than call it by a name which might prejudice future research as to its nature. The products of this function were designated 'alpha elements', and were distinguished from 'beta elements' in that they could be used by the mind for its processes. In contrast, beta elements could not be used by the mind for thought, and were appropriate only for evacuation (projective identification). The 'raw data' upon which the alpha function was considered to operate were either percepts, originating in the external world, or emotions. The latter were considered by Bion to be the counterparts of percepts, a kind of sense-data originating in the individual, which had to be processed by alpha function in order to be converted into alpha elements appropriate for use in the mental system. Bion likened the processing that these raw data had to undergo to digestion – with beta elements as the raw, undigested food, which could not be digested and had to be eliminated, and alpha elements as the digested particles which could serve as nourishment for the mind (Bion 1962b).

At this point I would like to pause a moment in order to reflect on the significance of these ideas for the concepts now under study. Clearly, Bion has greatly extended the area covered by the concept of the internal object (of which part-objects are a specific class) by applying it to functions of the personality.[40] If anything, this usage tends to widen the gap between Kleinian and ego psychology conceptualizations by including within the realm of experiential concepts an important concept that for ego psychology refers to the non-experiential realm – the concept of (ego-) functions. Bionian formulations, such as the projection into the analyst of the patient's capacity for verbal thought leading to a disturbance in that capacity, constitute a gross concretization from the point of view of ego psychology.

66

In spite of this, if we may bear these thoughts for a while, it is of interest to note that in the concept of alpha function Bion has presented an idea that has a clear counterpart in formulations orientated to ego psychology regarding psychotic thought disturbances. That idea is related to the (ego psychology) concept of representation. As we shall see in the conceptual analysis at the end of this study, the concept of representation came to be widely used to account for the disturbances of thought in schizophrenia (for example, London 1973), and it is to this account that Bion's concept of alpha function, and its disturbance, has a clear affinity. Bion's distinction between elements which may be used for thought processes (alpha elements), and those which cannot be so used (beta elements), opens up for investigation the idea that it is the capacity to represent that is disturbed in schizophrenia, the capacity to attach meaning to (raw) data. Whereas ego psychology theories tend to accept such disturbance as an accomplished fact (possibly accounted for by biochemical processes), Bion attempts to explore the psychological dynamics lying behind this situation. It remains, of course, to be seen which, if either, of these approaches will eventually be considered the more productive.

A second aspect of Bion's ideas that has direct bearing on the concepts of mental objects under discussion in the present study is related to Bion's extension of the concept of projective identification and his conception of the container–contained relationship. These ideas are especially important because of the widespread influence they have had in the psychoanalytic literature, both among Kleinian analysts and among others.

Whereas Melanie Klein's concept of projective identification referred to a phantasy regarding the projection of parts of the self into the object, Bion added an interpersonal dimension by asking what it was that the mother (analyst) contributes to the process.[41] His answer, following a patient who impressed Bion as being in need of the opportunity to be able to exercise projective identification but not being able actually to do so in the analytic situation (Bion 1958), was that the mother could stifle the infant's need for projective identification by not accepting the projection. According to this conception, projective identification is a link between patient and analyst, a form of communication (Bion 1959). By not accepting the projection, mother (analyst) blocks off this path of communication, leaving the infant (patient) unable to communicate.

By viewing projective identification as a form of communication between infant and mother, the first and most primitive form, Bion gave a whole new outlook to the process of projective identification. It became a need, a central need, crucial for the development of the emotional life of the infant. Melanie Klein had already defined the basic difficulty the infant must deal with, in terms of coping with the death instinct. According to this conception of early mental life, the primitive processes characteristic of the paranoid-schizoid position are designated to meet just that difficulty – the redirection (projection) of the death instinct outwards. Bion (1959) added to this view another element which had been completely missing from Melanie Klein's earlier descriptions (and his own) – the role of the mother in this process. Here his idea of the container–contained (Bion 1962b) served to add a new dimension to the process. Whereas earlier Kleinian views (including Bion's earlier papers from 1954 to 1958) greatly emphasized internal factors responsible for pathological processes, especially destructive impulses related to the death instinct and primal envy, Bion's extension of the concept of projective identification to the interpersonal realm made room for a view of pathogenic interpersonal processes within Kleinian theory. Bion expressly discussed the deprivation suffered by the infant as a result of the mother's unreceptiveness to his projections as 'the environmental factor in the production of the psychotic personality' (Bion 1959: 105; and further in 1962a). This discussion of Bion's in effect provided a conceptualization of early interpersonal processes that could be related to the intrapsychic dynamics described by Melanie Klein and her followers.[42] In addition, this conceptualization, especially in terms of the role of the analyst as container, linked these early processes with a theory of therapy. The latter had been clearly lacking in Kleinian theory previously.[43]

The concept of containment as a central process in both development and therapy led to further work by Bion (1962b) on his theory of the development of the capacity for thought (alpha function). According to these further formulations, the development of the capacity for thought is directly related (among other factors, mentioned below) to the existence of the mother's capacity for reverie (ibid.: 37). The mother's reverie provides the infant with the possibility of transforming intolerable emotions, sensations and so on, by way of projection into the mother (without the infant having to lose contact completely with those aspects of his personality). The mother's capacity to contain the projected 'parts', and eventually to return them to the infant, allowing him to re-introject them in more tolerable form, helps the infant develop a capacity for processing mental contents on his own (alpha function). Without such a benign container the infant is forced to seek continuously to rid himself of mental content, and the capacity for self-processing of thoughts cannot develop. Of course, these processes are not of an either-or nature, and alpha function may be considered to develop in every person to some extent, in accordance with Bion's earlier observations on the non-psychotic parts of the personalities of schizophrenic patients (1957).

In addition it also must be noted that the development of the infant's capacity for thought is not dependent only on the mother's capacity for reverie – Bion certainly did not adopt a simplistic interpersonal viewpoint.

Internal factors, related to the infant's own capacity to tolerate frustration, which in turn is related to such factors as primal envy, determine the extent to which the infant is in need of the mother's reverie in order to develop a capacity for thought. Thus an interaction is formed between the infant's tolerance of frustration and the mother's capacity for reverie, internal and external factors.

To summarize: Bion made two important contributions to the concepts of mental objects under study here. The first was in regard to that function he called 'alpha function', and the dynamics involved in its development and in its disturbances. This function may be seen to be similar to the capacity for representation discussed in ego psychology. The second point relates to the question of the origin of mental objects, and Bion's contribution of an interpersonal dimension (of external origin) to what had previously been a rather clear bias in Kleinian psychology in favour of internal factors. Bion's elaboration of the concept of projective identification, and that of containment as a crucial emotional relationship between mother and infant (and analyst and patient), provided conceptualization of interpersonal processes compatible with Kleinian theory. The application of these concepts both to processes of pathology and to a theory of therapy constituted an important contribution to concepts of mental objects in Kleinian theory.

Grotstein

A very recent contribution to the study of object-relations theory in general and of concepts related to internal objects in particular is the work of James Grotstein. In his book *Splitting and Projective Identification* (1981) and in a series of papers (1977, 1980, 1980/81, 1982, 1982/83, 1984) Grotstein has presented an elaborate metapsychology based primarily on a version of Melanie Klein's theory but also incorporating and critically discussing a vast portion of psychoanalytic literature.[44] In this short section I cannot do justice to Grotstein's extensive writings and have therefore presented only the specific points of innovation which are relevant to this study.

Grotstein's metapsychology is based on a Kleinian view of the ubiquity of 'internal object' dynamics in infantile psychology. Grotstein considers every experience to be experienced as an 'internal object': 'Every affect is an internal object . . . we function through the personification of experience. These personifications are internal objects . . . All affects, experiences and mental functioning can be seen as varying personifications and depersonifications of inchoately installed internal objects' (1982: 60–1). He adopts the Kleinian view of the 'phantasmal nature' of internal objects, and stoutly defends this view against its critics (1982/83). But he also accepts the criticism, based on Jacobson's, and Kohut's, ideas of degrees of fusion of self and object representations, of Klein's concept of 'internality': 'If one fuses with an object, one cannot internalize the object with which one is confused because the very boundaries which designate self have been obliterated in the confusion consequent upon impact between self and object' (Grotstein 1982: 67). His solution, which is a major tenet of his 'new metapsychology', is that development progresses on a 'dual-track' of both primary fusion and of primary separateness.[45] Thus, while on one track the object is experienced as merged (or confused) with the self, on the other track there will be an experience of separateness. The convergence of these two primitive experiences of the object gives rise to the experience of the self containing an object which is yet confused with the self – internal objects. In this way Grotstein retains both Melanie Klein's concept of internal objects together with Kohut's (early) view of the experience of the object as an extension of the self (selfobject); this is a good example of his attempts to synthesize various concepts from different theoretical frameworks into one whole theory.

Another example of Grotstein's integrative approach is his account of the development of internal objects and the relationship between internal objects (Kleinian theory) and object representations (ego psychology). Grotstein considers the differences between the Kleinian and ego psychology concepts (internal objects and object representations) to be related to different stages of development. The phantasmal, drive-related internal objects are considered to belong to the pre-separation-individuation phase of development, which in Kleinian terms is considered to correspond to the paranoid-schizoid position.[46] These primitive structures[47] are closely related to the infant's body-sensations; that is, the (internal) object is 'felt' by the infant at a body-level. As development progresses the infant becomes able to 'imagine' the object without experiencing it physically; that is, he attains the capacity to 're-present the object in its absence.[48] Grotstein considers this to be related to Mahler's phase of separation-individuation and to Melanie Klein's depressive position. But this developmental process does not eliminate the existence of internal objects at the later developmental stage. In Grotstein's view (and here we see another example of the Kleinian emphasis in Grotstein's approach), even after the development of object representations, internal objects 'continue to evolve as imagined and imaginary phantoms comprise psychic structure in an internal world which becomes progressively more eclipsed by a representational world responsive to issues pertaining to external reality' (Grotstein 1982: 68). This view makes room both for Kleinian and ego psychology concepts, trying to integrate both into a single theoretical framework.

At a very general level, Grotstein's theory of personality and psychopathology seems to be based on the basic view of the individual striving for, and shying away from, an integration of 'separate subselves or separate personalities which have never been totally unified into a single oneness' (Grotstein 1981: 18). These 'separate subselves' are conceptualized by Grotstein as 'selfobjects' (or internal objects), and he presents a 'cast' of six of these. They may be of a 'helpful' nature or may be 'pathologically transformed' by virtue of destructive impulses.[49] The specific nature of the pathology is determined by the 'sociology and politics' of this internal cast. Grotstein considers the dynamics of the subject's relationship with different aspects of himself embodied in these internal objects to constitute his inner world. Therapy consists (to a large extent) of the therapy of 'splitting' – 'At-one-ment is not only the goal of analysis; it also is the goal of life' (Grotstein 1981: 18).

To summarize: Grotstein's theory of personality is based on a Kleinian model according to which personality is seen as consisting of a 'cast' of internal objects. His unique contribution is his attempt to integrate various non-Kleinian concepts into the Kleinian framework. Especially prominent are his integration of Klein's concept of internal objects together with Kohut's concept of selfobject and the ego psychology concept of object representation. In addition, Grotstein is in the process of developing a description of the dynamics of personality based on the dynamics of a set 'cast' of internal objects (or selfobjects). Two interesting ideas very relevant to the subject of this study are the similarity between Kohut's 'selfobjects' and Melanie Klein's internal objects, and the possibility of a developmental relationship between internal objects and 'object representations'.

In closing I would like to emphasize the basic difference between Grotstein's overall 'methodology' and that employed in this study. While Grotstein is endeavouring to expand Kleinian theory by encompassing concepts from differing theoretical frameworks, it is my objective in this study to examine the different relevant concepts within the theoretical framework to which they belong. Thus, rather than synthesizing, this study emphasizes the conceptual divergencies of the different theories.

3

Orientations in ego psychology

Bychowski

The work of Gustav Bychowski is an interesting example of the difficulties facing a theoretical exposition of processes relating to introjects in the absence of a theory of mental structures. While Bychowski was deeply interested in the dynamics of introjects and wrote extensively on this subject, his work remained at a descriptive level and did not develop into a fully fledged theory.

Bychowski belonged to the generation of analysts that had been in contact with Freud in Vienna (in the 1920s), and eventually, in 1939, emigrated to the United States. Although writing in the United States, his writing reflects the ideas of European analysts, and was not much influenced by the development of North American ego psychology. (Bychowski's use of the term 'ego' is closer to the phenomenological 'I-ness' of Federn than to the ego as a structure in the structural model.) His interest in processes related to introjects was heavily determined by his extensive work with psychotic patients. The core of his views regarding introjects is contained in a series of papers on that subject (Bychowski 1956a, 1956b, 1956c, 1958), although references appear also in other papers and especially in his book on *Psychotherapy of Psychosis* (1952).

Bychowski considered the ego's difficulty in dealing with 'ambivalently introjected images of the early objects' to be the core problem with which many of his patients were struggling. He found his patients' pathologies to be related to their ongoing attempts to find some solution to the un-bearable condition of both loving and hating objects that were experienced as both satisfying and threatening. The two processes which he specified in relation to these attempts were 'splitting of the ego' and 'externalization (or release) of the introjects'. His discussions of these two processes abound in clinical examples, but lack any attempt to relate them to a more general theoretical framework. Rather, he described, in case after case, how the patients' pathology may be conceived as exemplifying these two processes.

72

In terms of the present study, Bychowski was pointing to two sets of processes between which we may distinguish:

1 processes in which aspects of the self come to be felt as not being aspects of the self but rather as belonging to some other entity;
2 processes of the distortion of perception of and relations with external objects in accordance with the emotionally charged images originating in early childhood.

It is to the combination of these two groups of processes that Bychowski referred when he wrote, in the last of his series of papers on introjects, that:

> An important concept that emerged in the course of these investigations was the externalization of various aspects of the self. In this process they, too, having become fused with various aspects of the original objects, become externalized together with them, so that, for instance, in male homosexuality, the homosexual partners proved to be substitutes, not only for the parental objects, but for the self as well.
>
> (Bychowski 1958: 182).

Bychowski considered the process of the externalization of introjects to be especially significant both in psychotic production and in relation to the reorganization of psychic structure in the process of psychoanalysis (1956c). He preferred the term 'release' to 'externalization', it would seem, to emphasize the fact that the process is not necessarily (or even primarily) under the control of the ego, or actively used for defensive purposes. Constantly aware of the manner in which such 'release of introjects' interferes with the ego's attempts at dealing with reality in his psychotic patients, Bychowski did not develop a theory of motivation concerning externalization, but rather saw it as involving a weakening of the ego's ability to cope:

> It seems then that, at critical times, the ego feels the need to re-experience the object as lying outside the ego boundaries, that is, as being external. Or we may also say that at certain times the ego is no longer able to maintain the internalized objects within its boundaries, and consequently is bound to release them.
>
> (ibid.: 335)

Thus Bychowski was referring to a number of processes:

1 objects felt to be inside the subject come to be experienced as being outside;
2 the distortion of the present perception of objects in accordance with distorted early childhood object representations;

73

3 dormant or unconscious phantasies gaining access to consciousness.

Although these three processes may be interrelated, and in specific cases may appear together, the fact that Bychowski did not have the theoretical concepts necessary to distinguish between them limited his ability to do more than describe these processes. But in spite of the fact that Bychowski's writings on introjects seem to have had little influence on the development of psychoanalytic theory on this subject, he does seem to have provided American psychoanalysis with a reminder of the importance of the study of the dynamics of mental objects (or introjects) for an understanding of psychotic and latent-psychotic processes (Barchilon 1973; Ehrenwald 1973).

Spitz

In the process of intensive and extensive research on infancy (from the 1940s until his death in 1974), and using a combination of experimental methodology and psychoanalytic theory, Rene Spitz developed two concepts of great importance in the development of ego psychology concepts relating to objects: the concept of the preobject and the concept of the libidinal object. Although the latter had often been discussed, Spitz's whole theory of early infantile development gave it a very specific and well-defined meaning, which, together with the concepts of Hartmann and Jacobson, influenced the later theories and concepts of ego psychology.

Spitz sought to document, describe and form a theory of very early infantile development, especially during the first year of life. Basing his theory on observable phenomena (rather than on reconstruction from the analysis of adult patients) he described three central 'organizers' in the early development of infants. The concept of 'organizers' was borrowed from embryology, where it refers to the convergence of several lines of biological development at a specific location – the embryonic organism. Spitz considered that in psychic development too, integration of several lines of development bring about a restructuring in the psychic system at a higher level of complexity. Thus a new function or capacity is attained – not singly as a gradual progression on one line of development but rather as a result of the integration of different aspects of functioning. The organizers become known to outside observers by means of certain visible signs of behaviour which indicate that the organizer has emerged. The three well-known indicators noted by Spitz in his empirical research were:

1 the smiling response to the *Gestalt* of the human face in the third month;
2 stranger-anxiety in the eighth month;
3 the 'no' gesture at approximately 15 months.

It is the first two of these that are relevant here in connection with the development of concepts of mental objects.

Spitz referred to the first two months of the infant's life as the 'objectless stage' (1965), which he considered to coincide with what was generally termed 'primary narcissism', and what Hartmann (1939) referred to as the 'undifferentiated phase'. He emphasized that at this stage the infant cannot distinguish between the surroundings and his own body. He considered that the neurophysiological system of perception was basically different at this stage from later, and he termed it the 'coenesthetic organization' to emphasize this difference. In contrast to later sensory perception of external reality, the infant at this stage is receptive (rather than perceptive), sensing interoceptive stimuli rather than organizing stimuli to achieve meaning. Thus the neurophysiological system of perception itself is not geared to make perception of an object possible.

As gradually the neurophysiological perceptive system matures and perception develops from contact perception to distance perception, the infant becomes capable of recognizing external stimuli. This capacity is dependent on a number of component capacities: for example, the capacity to suspend the absolute functioning of the pleasure–unpleasure principle, which interferes with his devoting attention to outside, as opposed to inside, stimuli; the capacity to shift back and forth between the perceptual presentation (for instance, of the human face) and the memory of that percept, and so on. This maturation makes it possible to initiate recognition of the external object.

Spitz (1946, 1965) emphasized the smiling response to the human face as the indicator of the capacity to recognize and actively respond to the external object. But, and this distinction is a central one, the smiling response is an indicator of 'preobjectal' capacities, and not of those related to the libidinal object. By this Spitz meant that the 3-month old infant recognizes a sign *Gestalt* of the human face (forehead, eyes and nose) and is as yet incapable of recognizing the specific love-object (namely, the mother). The infant is capable of recognizing a sign *Gestalt* related to his earlier and ongoing experiences of need-gratification (especially in the nursing situation) and of responding to that positively toned affective experience with a smile. But for the infant the sign *Gestalt* signals a 'thing' rather than a libidinally cathected object. This is so because it is the interoceptive experiences which are primary. Therefore the gratifying and frustrating images of the mother are yet separate images, which the infant is still incapable of unifying into one image. In spite of the infant's smiling response to a face, it is primarily the positive affective experience to which he is responding.

Only as the infant becomes capable of recognizing the 'bad' and 'good' (frustrating and gratifying) images of the mother as identical, in spite of the different affective tones to which they are related, can a unified image emerge. Then the infant becomes capable of recognizing the mother as an object of love, independent of the specific affective experience of the present situation; that is, even when she is frustrating. This capacity constitutes the third stage in the development of the object-related capacities of the infant – that of the 'libidinal object'. (Spitz referred to the '*libidinal* object' in spite of the fact that his emphasis was on the ability to fuse the libidinal and aggressive drives in relation to a single object image. He explained that this was 'because the child's libidinal drive outweighs the aggressive one . . . . Consequently the good object appears to predominate in this fusion' (Spitz 1965: 170).)

Spitz's emphasis was developmental, and even the pathology he investigated – such as anaclitic depression (1946), hospitalism (1945, 1946) and psychotoxic disturbances (1965) – consisted of emotional disturbances in infancy. He did not reconstruct early childhood or infantile development on the basis of the analysis of adult psychopathology (as did Edith Jacobson). This is no doubt one of the reasons that Spitz's work had an influence primarily on specific developmental concepts rather than on the main body of psychoanalytic literature.

In summary, it should be noted that his concept of the 'libidinal object' as an ego capacity, and his detailed theory of the developments (especially in the perceptual organization) leading to its emergence, provided, together with the ideas of Hartmann and Jacobson, an impetus to the development of ego psychology concepts related to objects.

Edith Jacobson

Outstanding among the ego psychologists for her development of object-relational concepts within the general framework of ego psychology was Edith Jacobson. She was the first to build a theory using the concepts of self and object representations (after these concepts had been introduced by Hartmann in 1950), and she did so in a unique manner. Her major theories and concepts grew out of her work with psychotic, and especially depressive psychotic, patients. Although her major work, *The Self and the Object World* (Jacobson 1964) deals primarily with development, her theory of development is closely grounded in her theories of pathology. We shall see how her specific interest in the pathology of psychosis affected her use of the concepts of self and object representations.

Edith Jacobson's writing is very intricate, and the task of extracting a specific theory from her complex web of concepts is a difficult one. In spite of this difficulty, I will attempt to isolate those concepts dealing with mental objects and their place in her general conceptual framework. Of special interest is, of course, her use of the concept of object representation[1] and her theory of the superego.

In additon to bearing the stamp of her work with a specific group of patients (depressive psychotics), Jacobson's work exhibits the influence of two outstanding, though radically differing, theoreticians – Hartmann and Melanie Klein. Hartmann and his collaborators formulated the basic framework of ego psychology, and Jacobson's work is undoubtedly within that framework. Especially prominent in this regard are her views on the development of the superego as an abstract depersonified structure and the various functions which she attributes to this structure. Also, her intensive application of energy concepts and her emphasis on the importance of neutralization in the process of development (and deneutralization – in the process of regression) demonstrate her ego psychology bearings.

In radical contradistinction to her ego psychology approach is Edith Jacobson's appraisal of the work and ideas of Melanie Klein. This affinity seems to be due not only to the fact that both belonged to the Berlin Psycho-Analytic Society (Jacobson, some ten years after Melanie Klein) and that Jacobson's patients were psychotic depressives producing delusions remarkably similar to the phantasies described by Melanie Klein. Jacobson's deep interest in the imprint left by the mothering 'object' on the infant, not only as a gratifier or frustrator of instinctual wishes but rather as a person for whom the infant has an intensely dependent need in order to exist, is very close to Klein's emphasis on the role of the object (though not necessarily the 'real' object) in the infant's psychic make-up. The differences between Klein's and Jacobson's concepts are no doubt very great, but it appears at times as if Edith Jacobson were trying to formulate some of Melanie Klein's insights within an ego psychology framework. In fact we shall see that one of Jacobson's most important innovations – the concept of the fusion of self and object representations – may be considered precisely that: an ego psychology formulation of the Kleinian concept of the internal object.[2]

Edith Jacobson's interest in the development of the superego dates back to some of her earliest work and was closely connected throughout with her writings on depression (Jacobson 1946, 1953, 1954a, 1954b). More specifically, she examined the effect of disappointment (or 'disillusion') on the development of self and object images and of the superego. She traced the depressive development back to 'coinciding severe disappointments in both parents at the beginning of the oedipal period' (Jacobson 1946: 122) and the consequent narcissistic injury.

She followed her patients' fluctuating and alternating devaluations and aggrandizements of self and object, and she found these to be expressions of aggression born of recurring disappointment. An overpowerful superego is formed, which, instead of providing the ego (self) with narcissistic support, attacks and degrades it. But, in contrast to Freud and other writers, she did not consider the attacking superego (in the form of self-accusations, guilt and feelings of unworthiness) to be the ultimate source of the depressive phenomenon. Rather, she emphasized that the superego activity is part of a secondary attempt at restitution, underlying which may be found a primary depressive experience. The primary depressive experience consists of the 'deflation of the ego' (self) due to the 'aggressive deflation of the disappointing parental images'. It is that 'deflation of the ego' that Jacobson considered to give rise to the fatigue and exhaustion, emotional emptiness and lack of initiative that constitute primary depression.

Her conclusions in 1946 regarding the development of the depressive's superego serve as an example of her ego psychology approach. She emphasized the developmental defect that interfered in the development of 'firmly integrated depersonified reaction-formations with self-critical functions' that constitute the mature superego. Thus Jacobson conceived of depression in terms of the faulty structure of the superego, due to developmental deficiencies, rather than in terms of an upsurge of aggression – as had Freud (1917e) and Melanie Klein (1935) – or an oral fixation – as had Abraham (1924) and Fenichel (1945).

In 1953 Jacobson devoted a paper to the metapsychology of depression. Drawing on Hartmann's (1950) distinction between ego and self representation, she explored the vicissitudes of narcissism in the depressive and in normal development in terms of fluctuations in the cathexis of the self representation. Following Freud (1914c) and Hartmann (1950), she traced the changing distribution of cathexis between self and object representation. One of her major innovations in that paper was her discussion of the vicissitudes of the aggressive cathexis of self and object representation in her account of depression. Her use of representational terminology in her explanation of the dynamics of development and pathology was the first such exposition. It laid the basis for much of the later use of these concepts and exemplifies some of the conceptual problematics involved in this usage.

The concept of self and object representations (or images) implied, for Jacobson, more than just the conglomerate of memories, perceptions and phantasies regarding the self and object. In Jacobson's theory they become the basic building-blocks of the mature ego (and superego). Whereas the neurotic (that is, mature) ego copes with psychosexual conflicts with the use of neurotic defences, the psychotic (or prepsychotic) ego cannot cope in such a manner due to its defective structure (Jacobson 1953: 63). The defect in the psychotic ego is considered by Jacobson to rest in the self and object representations. More specifically, the unstable boundaries between the self and object representations, and their tendency to fuse, constitute a structural defect.

The superego, the object-and-self-representation, will be prone to a regressive fragmentation, to a splitting up again into primitive early images and, on the other hand, to fusions with one another. There will be a tendency to react to conflicts with the object world not by ego defenses against unacceptable strivings but by withdrawals and shifts of libidinous and aggressive cathexis, not only from one object to the other . . . but from object-to-self-representation and the reverse . . . . This goes along with a severe regressive distortion of the object-and-self-representations, leading to their breakdown and their eventual dissolution into primitive images, in the system ego . . . . These processes may reach the point of a collapse of the psychic system . . . . Naturally, severe disturbances of the sense of reality, i.e. of the perception of and the judgment regarding the object world and their own self will develop. The ego functions and emotional relationships with the real objects will deteriorate.

(Jacobson 1953: 62–4)

Thus, for Jacobson self and object representations are not simply conglomerate images, the schemata of experience. Rather, they are basic structures of the mental apparatus. Jacobson's use of these terms may be compared with an electrical metaphor of the mind: object and self representations appear similar to the positive and negative poles of a source of energy, which when sufficiently well isolated from one another can produce an effective electric current, but when not sufficiently isolated will cause a short circuit. Such a short may damage the electrical appliance (in this metaphor – the ego) to which the energy source is connected. This metaphor is also consistent with Jacobson's emphasis on the fluctuations of cathexes of the self and object representations. But it is not just this electrical metaphor, with its structural connotations, which should be noted. Jacobson's use of concepts of representation, with the implication of concrete structures, seems to have been related to her use of these concepts specifically in regard to psychosis. She considered shifts of cathexis between representations to be a psychotic phenomenon, as, of course, are fusions between them. Projection and introjection, involving shifts between self and object representation, are not used by Jacobson to refer to neurotic defences because they imply unstable representational boundaries (Jacobson 1954a).[3] Mature identification is considered to refer to stable changes in the ego, rather than to changes in the self representation (Jacobson 1964). Thus, Jacobson uses concepts of representation not as defined in the introduction to the present study – that is, as amalgams of memories serving as anticipatory sets; rather, they seem to constitute a new structural theory, especially for the area of psychosis (and what Jacobson calls 'prepsychosis'). We will see how Kernberg developed this aspect of Jacobson's concept in his theory of the borderline level of organization of personality.

Jacobson's theory of psychosis, in which the representations of self and object played such a central role, was intimately related to a theory of the development of these structures. The structural defect of fusion (or the tendency to it) was considered by Jacobson to be related to a developmental injury at those stages of development at which the child had not yet attained full differentiation of the object and self representations. From a developmental perspective Jacobson considered differentiation to be a long-term process. Although she did not strictly define a timetable, she mentioned 3 months as the earliest beginning of this process (Jacobson 1964: 39), and that the tendency towards fusion continues 'far beyond the preoedipal period' (ibid.: 41).

Thus she stated, regarding the prepsychotic personality:

> Because of their inherited constitution and their infantile history of emotional deprivations and instinctual overstimulation and/or frustration, these patients are evidently predisposed to a total regressive process by an arrested, defective ego and superego development . . . .
> In the prepsychotic personality the self-and-object-representations and the ego ideal will not be sharply separated; they will retain attributes of early infantile object-and-self images. . . . The superego, the object-and-self-representations will be prone to a regressive fragmentation, to a splitting up again into primitive early images and, on the other hand, to fusions with one another.
>
> (Jacobson 1953: 62)

In her paper (and later, book) on the development of the 'self and the object world' (1954c, 1964), Jacobson devoted extensive discussion to the gradual maturation of the primitive, fused self and object representations. She emphasized both the role of perception and the role of (optimal) frustration in the differentiation of fused representations of self and object. Of special interest is her emphasis on the close connection between the development of the superego and that of the self and object representations. Like the concept of fusion, this view of Jacobson's originated in her theories of depression. There she noted the close connection between the regressive quality of the depressive's superego, its disintegration into primitive self and object images of a sadomasochistic nature on the one hand, and the regressive fusion of self and object representations on the other. I will elaborate on this subject in the section on Jacobson's theory of the superego.

Fusion of self and object representations

Probably the most influential of Jacobson's concepts was that of the fusion of self and object representations. In this concept she crystallized processes occurring both in normal development and in pathological regression. As we have seen, this concept was used by Jacobson to refer to a structural defect which had severe pathological consequences. It also was used to account for various aspects of the relationship with the object, aspects that later writers further distinguished from each other. Jacobson did not consider fusion to be an all-or-nothing phenomenon, but rather considered there to be different levels of fusion/differentiation. She illustrated these in the words of a schizophrenic patient:

> Do you know the difference between closeness, likeness, sameness, and oneness? Close is close, as with you; when you are like somebody, you are only *like* the other; sameness – you are the same as the other, but he is still he and you are you; but oneness is not two – it is one, that's horrible – horrible.
>
> (Jacobson 1954c)

These descriptions are considered by Jacobson to represent the range from object relations, to identification, to magic total identification, to complete fusion of self and object images. This is a good example of the way Jacobson integrated the experiential and non-experiential aspects of her concept of fusion.

Jacobson also considered the fusion of self and object representations to be related to a wish – a wish to be at one with the mothering object, which in turn was related to the wishful phantasy of oral incorporation of the mother's breast. While she did not define the relation between the drive aspect (the oral wish) and the object-related aspect (wish for merger) systematically, her emphasis (1954c, 1964) was generally on the latter.

> Induced by repeated unpleasurable experiences of frustation, of deprivation and separation from the love object, phantasies of (total) incorporation of the gratifying object begin to arise, expressive of wishes to re-establish the lost unit (mother–child). This desire probably never ceases to play a part in our emotional life . . . the wishful phantasies of merging and being one with the mother (breast) are the foundation on which all future types of identification are built . . . the hungry infant's longing for oral gratification is the origin of the first, primitive type of identification, an identification achieved by refusion of self- and object-images and founded on wishful phantasies of oral incorporation of the love object. This refusion of self- and object-images will be accompanied by a temporary weakening of the perceptive functions and hence by a return from the level of beginning ego formation to an earlier, less differentiated state.
>
> (Jacobson 1954c: 98–9)

This emphasis on object-related motivation (in the form of a wish for merger with the mothering figure, a wish to be at one with her) and its corresponding representational (that is, structural) aspect (in the form of fusion of self and object representations, leading to a weakening of the ego functions of reality perception) is characteristic of Edith Jacobson's integrative approach.[4]

Another aspect of Jacobson's fusion concept refers to the attitude towards the object. The tendency towards fusion of object and self representations that characterizes the child is considered to be related to the child's ability to *care* for the object as an autonomous person. As long as the boundaries between self and object representations are not stable and there is a tendency towards fusion, the child relates to the object as 'an extension of himself . . . [he is] as yet unable to love in the sense of caring for others . . . he cannot understand and respect the parental needs unless they serve his own or are in accordance with them' (1964: 41–2).[5] Here Jacobson may be seen to be following Abraham's (1924) conception of a stage of partial love for the object (or, as it is often referred to – part-object), at which stage the child is as yet incapable of taking into consideration the autonomous needs of the object. Again, she was integrating the various object-related phenomena of childhood development – in this case the narcissistic attitude towards the object – with her own theory of self and object representations. This attitude towards the object refers, of course, to a very different aspect of fusion than the psychotic perceptual confusion between self and object that originally led Jacobson to formulate the concept of fusion. In fact, Jacobson did not frequently use the concept of fusion for such non-psychotic phenomena. While she did distinguish between different 'depths of narcissistic regression and dedifferentiation of psychic structures' in regard to the degree of fusion (for example, Jacobson 1967: 55), she did so almost exclusively within the field of psychosis (or prepsychosis).[6]

In her 1964 book, *The Self and the Object World*, which was an expansion of her 1954 paper of the same name, Jacobson added an extensive discussion on the subject of identity. This is a good example of yet another aspect of experience that she felt could be related to the concept of fusion/ differentiation of self and object representations. In her discussion of identity formation she emphasized the roles of both libidinal and aggressive strivings in the differentiation of self and object representations. She also discussed the processes whereby 'total' concepts of good-and-bad self are formed out of the earlier separate good and bad images. These are the processes which she considered to participate in identity formation, and the sense of self which constitutes identity is an expression of mature differentiation.

In this context it is of interest to note her disagreement with Lichtenstein

(1961) as to the ubiquity of disturbances of identity. Whereas Lichtenstein saw man as 'forever threatened with loss or breakdown of his identity', Jacobson emphatically stated that her clinical experience was that neurotics do not suffer from identity problems. These are limited to 'neurotics with specific narcissistic conflicts and to borderline and psychotic patients' (Jacobson 1964: 29).[7] This view is in keeping with Jacobson's restriction of representational defects to the non-neurotic areas of psychopathology, as I mentioned above.

We have seen the variety of meanings that Jacobson attributed to her concept of the fusion of self and object representations. Undoubtedly it was this concept that was the most 'powerful' one (that is, loaded with meaning and explanatory functions) in her conceptual framework. This is not to say that Jacobson wrote exclusively about the concept of fusion, but it did play a central explanatory role in her account of those aspects of the psychotic phenomena which we have seen above. What is of special interest is to note that Jacobson's use of representational terms implied a specifically structural aspect. She regarded self and object representations as the basic building blocks of the ego, such that a defect in them (namely, their tendency to fuse) constituted a defective ego with a tendency towards psychosis.

The superego

After discussing Jacobson's use of the concept of self and object representation we will turn to the concept of the superego (and ego ideal). Jacobson's writings on the superego have been referred to as 'the most comprehensive analysis of the superego in the psychoanalytic literature' (Kernberg 1981). In relation to the subject of this study three aspects of Jacobson's view of the superego are of special relevance. These are:

1 superego precursors;
2 the nature of the mature superego as an abstract depersonified system;
3 the 'survival' of a 'relationship' aspect in the mature superego.

Regarding the precursors of the superego, Jacobson specified three aspects of the primitive self and object images that will eventually constitute the superego. These primitive images were considered to derive from instinctual, reality-related and narcissistic impressions, respectively (Jacobson 1964: 124).[8] Although these primitive images eventually contribute to the formation of the superego, they do not constitute, in themselves, the superego. This is a point on which Jacobson (as an ego psychologist) was in sharp disagreement with Melanie Klein (ibid.: 94–5), who considered the primitive object images to be equivalent to the superego. Jacobson emphasized that these superego precursors are 'disconnected components originating in self and object imagery of different instinctual and ego stages and levels' (ibid.: 125). Although they 'here and there . . . begin to merge and to assume the character of compelling inner standards' – however, they 'lack maturity, uniformity, coherence . . . [and] are not yet a masterful organized functional unit, a system in its own right' (ibid.). Jacobson considered the superego itself to be a coherent depersonified, abstract system with various functions, such as self-evaluation (both critical and rewarding) in terms of moral codes and value systems, direction-giving (to the ego) and enforcing functions. This emphasis is central to Jacobson's view of the mature and healthy superego as opposed to the defective or regressed, pathological superego. In the latter, the primitive imagery of the superego precursors is revived, as Jacobson frequently illustrated in cases of depression.

Regarding the mature nature of the superego, Jacobson devoted specific discussion to the question of how this depersonified system is formed out of the varying object images which are its precursors (ibid.: 119–26). She did not consider Freud's formulation regarding the role of castration fears in the renunciation of Oedipal strivings as sufficient. Rather, she emphasized the role of the maturation of ego functions – for example, perception and reality testing, conceptual (as opposed to concrete) thought, and the sense of time (future) – as central for the capacity of the psychic organization to construct a superego system. 'Only at this stage [of the maturation of ego faculties] can selected ideal, directive, prohibitive, disapproving and approving parental traits and attitudes and parental teachings become constructively correlated and gradually blended into a consistent, organized set of notions' (ibid.:126).

Jacobson's emphasis on the abstract nature of the superego is compatible with her ego psychology orientated approach. It is therefore fascinating to see her attempt to preserve the object-related (that is, personified, non-abstract) nature of the superego concept in spite of its supposedly abstract nature. Although the two approaches appear to be diametrically opposed, Jacobson, in full awareness of the contradiction involved, adopted both. 'Whereas I have thus far done my best to stress the depersonified, abstract nature of the superego, my emphasis here is back again on the sort of *personal relationship* that we usually maintain, to some extent, with our conscience' (ibid.: 128 – emphasis mine). In Jacobson's view, in spite of the abstract nature of the superego, there does survive in its relationship with the ego something of the child's relationship with its parents. This accounts for the fact that the conscience is not only prohibitive (that is, active in conflict) but also actively approving, as illustrated by the feeling of elation when one feels 'moral self-satisfaction'. Jacobson referred to the ego ideal as that aspect of the superego system that, in spite of its maturation, retains idealized self and object images. While she emphasized that the mature ego ideal, like the superego, is of an abstract nature, she pointed out that even the 'abstract conceptions' of the ego ideal consist of the persistence of 'magical' non-realistic phantasies (ibid.: 110–11).

This two-sided view of the superego is a good illustration of Jacobson's attempt to integrate an object-relations approach into an ego psychology framework. The difficulty in determining whether the superego is a strictly depersonified structure, or whether it remains in some way personified, giving a feeling of a relationship with another, is a basic difficulty of the superego concept. Jacobson's suggestion that both aspects be retained does not resolve the conceptual difficulties involved, but does show that the two aspects of the problem must in some way be acknowledged.

Summary

We have viewed Edith Jacobson's use of the concepts of self and object representations, and some aspects of her theory of the superego, as outstanding examples of an attempt to integrate object-relational considerations within an ego psychology framework. Jacobson contributed significantly in this direction, formulating concepts of mental objects and applying these concepts especially to the areas of psychosis and development. The restriction of the use of representational concepts to the area of psychosis and defective (or primitive) ego structure is a unique contribution of Jacobson's. This, together with her emphasis on energic concepts of cathexis, combines to give some of her discussions of self and object representations a very abstract, mechanistic flavour rather than the more 'experience-near' quality of the work of others using representational terms.[9] This difference is so blatant as to suggest that Jacobson's use of representational terms constitutes a unique meaning-space, in which the emphasis is on the structure of the representations rather than their content. This emphasis carries important implications in regard to conceptions of developmental deficit, as will be further explored in the final chapters of this study.

The representational theorists

The 1960s introduced a period during which the concept of mental representation gained a secure place in the psychoanalytic literature, and served, among other roles, to provide ego psychology (in the United States) and 'Freudian' psychoanalysis (in London) with a concept that would allow a growing emphasis on object-related aspects within a more classical framework. The greatest impetus to the development of this concept was probably provided by the work of Sandler and his co-workers at the Hampstead Clinic. But others too devoted serious interest to this concept.

Novey

Samuel Novey was one of the first, and his work demonstrates some of the issues with which psychoanalytic theory was dealing via the concept of mental representations of objects. Two of his papers dealt extensively with this concept. The first (1958) was devoted specifically to the concept of object representation, and in the second (1961) he integrated his work on object representations with his formulations of a psychoanalytic theory of affect (1959) in a manner which was very fruitful to both areas.

However, Novey did not succeed in constructing a systematic distinction between the processes and phenomena related to the self, and those related to object representations. In fact, an interesting aspect of his 1961 paper was the role he ascribed to the object representations in maintaining the 'inner sense of self'. He conceptualized what he called 'curative changes in the superego' in terms of shifts of cathexis from archaic to mature mental representations of objects, which promotes reality orientation (or testing).

Novey emphasized three aspects of the concept 'mental representation of the object':

1 The mental representation of the object is not the product of simple sensory experience alone.
2 The mental representation of the object is in some (or various) way(s) related to, but not identical with, the self.
3 The mental representation of the object is an amalgamation of both affective and ideational (perceptual) aspects, of which Novey considered the affective to be (by and large) of primary importance.

All three of these aspects have therapeutic implications which Novey discussed, giving us a more concrete idea of what some of the implications of his ideas were.

Regarding the first point – that the representation was not simply a perceptual image – Novey seems to have been trying to correct a bias of Fairbairn's theory (to which he referred in Novey 1959) which favoured the *realistic* aspects of experience in determining the nature of the individual's objects. Novey emphasized that we do not simply perceive reality, but that apperception (rather than direct perception) encompasses the reactions of the unconscious to the sensory data before the latter achieves consciousness.[10]

Regarding therapy, Novey used this point to emphasize that the patient's *memories* of their significant objects reflect not so much realistic aspects of those objects, but rather the products of the patient's own personality. Novey emphasized that mental representations are products of the mind and personality of the individual and not external agents, and that therefore they are open to processes of change as the patient's personality changes in analysis.

The first point is directly related to the second: Novey considered object representations to play an important role in maintaining a stable sense of self. He referred to Jacobson's concept of the fusion of self and object representations as the pathological process that ensues when the object representations are disturbed. In the case of borderline or psychotic patients, object representations are 'inadequate' due to these patients' very disturbed early interpersonal experiences. Novey referred to their object represent-ations as constituting 'empty spaces' in the patient's experience, as a result of which they are incapable of fulfilling the self-supportive roles that object representations do in neurotics.[11] Also he considered the therapeutic task to include the construction of more adequate mental representations, on the basis of identification with the therapist. Unfortunately, he did not elaborate on this idea, but it would seem that he was referring to the therapist's role as a 'good object' for the patient to experience, allowing him to construct on the basis of this good experience a correspondingly 'good' mental representation. He did not discuss how this was to take place.

The third point, regarding the primarily affective nature of the object representation, did not appear in Novey's first paper (1958), but was added in his later one on affects (1961). This point represents a very interesting departure from the more popular aspects of the concept of mental repre-sentations in ego psychology. In a radical expansion of his earlier view that object representations are not simply the products of perceptual experi-ence, he asserted, in 1961, that it is primarily the *affective constellation* that constitutes object representations, with ideational and perceptual aspects of secondary importance. Thus it is a person's affective experience of their relationship with other people, rather than the perceptual or ideational aspects of the experience of other people, that are predominant in the object representation. As an example of this view, Novey referred to the concept of the superego. Rather than conceive of it in 'ideational' terms relating to internalized parental images, Novey suggested that the superego is experienced primarily as an affective state – for example, of guilt. It is this affective experience that is definitive of the superego, with perceptual/ideational aspects of the parental figures of decidedly secondary importance. 'In our limited verbal attempts to define internal representations, we reach a point at which we no longer experience them as organized and clearly delineated things, but rather as if they resembled or were emotions' (Novey 1961: 26).

This latter view of Novey's is difficult to conceptualize, and it raises a wealth of questions demanding explanations – questions to which Novey did not address himself.[12] Part of the difficulty resides in the present condition of the psychoanalytic theory of affect, immersed as it is (or was, until very recently) in questions of energy and discharge incompatible with the representational concepts that Novey was striving to formulate. But, beyond the difficulties, it is important to note that Novey's idea emphasizes an important aspect of the psychoanalytic concept of mental represent-ations, one that is sometimes forgotten under the influence of the use of the term 'representation', with its heavily Piagetian – cognitive – con-notations. That aspect is, of course, that the primary area of psychoanalytic interest, especially in regard to object relations, is that of affective ex-perience. In this regard Novey's view surprisingly brings to mind that aspect of Melanie Klein's concept of internal objects which emphasized them as representatives of the (life and death) instincts. As such, they primarily were seen as consisting of the basic emotions of love and hate and their various derivatives. This confluence of views in the very differing theoretical frameworks suggests that the question of the affective aspect of object representations is one that requires further thought and discussion.

In summary: following Edith Jacobson's development of the concepts of self and object representation to refer to basic structures of the personality, with implications regarding development and pathology, Novey was the first of a group of analysts who developed the concepts of representation in a different, more general direction.

In the present study, representation has been defined as an amalgam of experience (including phantasies) which serve as an anticipatory set for future interactions (again, including phantasied interactions). Novey's use of representation was very close to this definition, although a number of differences must be noted. The first is Novey's emphasis on the experi-ential aspect of representations (for example, the 'empty space' experience of individuals with defective representations). Closely connected with this emphasis on experience is Novey's view of representations as affective phenomena. While the definition presented in the present study does include the affective aspects of representation, Novey's emphasis on this aspect is much greater.

In addition, Novey emphasized the functions of the object represent-ations *vis-à-vis* the sense of selfness, adding a motivational aspect to the concept of object representation not commonly stressed. Although his ideas did not achieve the popularity of the other representational theorists presented here, they did point the way for much of the ongoing discussions of the different theoretical issues related to this concept.

Beres

Another North American psychoanalyst who devoted considerable thought and study to the concept of mental representation is David Beres. In two papers on the subject of imagination (1960a, 1960b) and in a later paper devoted specifically to mental representation (Beres and Joseph 1970), Beres discussed various aspects of this concept. It is of interest to note that Beres' earlier discussion of mental representation (1960a, 1960b) was part of, and played a central role in, his development of a psychoanalytic theory of imagination. Beres viewed phantasy as a ubiquitous psychic manifestation essential to almost all mental processes, rejecting the primacy attributed by the Kleinians to phantasy at the expense of nearly ignoring processes of realistic perception. Beres, in the framework of ego psychology and integrating research of academic psychology on perception, attributed a more central role to perception in the mental processes, and on the basis of that view proceeded to delineate the concept of mental representation *vis-à-vis* perception on the one hand and 'mentation' on the other.

Beres included all the mental processes leading to the formation of mental representations under the general term 'imagination'. He emphasized that both primary and secondary processes participate in an adaptational process – one that shapes the individual's conception of reality. Representation is considered to be a third level of perception, after the neurophysiological sensation and the organization of the sensory data into percepts. The lower two levels exist both in humans and in the animal world. In contrast, the representational level is unique to humans. It consists of the capacity to represent and evoke the image of an absent object. It gives a person the capacity to be independent of immediate physical stimuli, to entertain wishes in the absence of the physical presence of their objects. Mental representations in human beings also take the place of the mental registrations or signs whereby animals recognize reality. Thus people do not respond directly to the second level of perception of stimuli, but, rather, further process percepts via mental representations before responding. Mental representations thus also serve as the schemata whereby the individual's perception of reality is organized. As such it refers especially to an unconscious level of organization, of which conscious images, wishes, phantasies and so on may be considered derivatives.

This emphasis on the unconscious nature of mental representations is one of the central features of the paper devoted to the concept of mental representation (Beres and Joseph 1970), as it provides a uniquely psychoanalytic perspective on representation, in contrast to Piaget's theory. The idea that mental representations constitute a higher level of mental organization (higher than lower-level percepts) is closely related to the view that dynamic factors (drives, wishes, anxiety and so forth) play an important role in shaping these representations. It is this view that is expressed when Beres (1960a, 1960b) equates mental representation with imagination. Placing representation at the upper level of perception on the one hand, and defining it as synonymous with imagination on the other, Beres has formulated his approach to the drive/reality issue of representation. Psychic reality is thus considered to be both closely related to external (perceived) reality, but also open to the ongoing distortion of drives, wishes and so on. This issue will be further discussed in the framework of the question of the internal or external origin of mental objects (Chapter 5).

Another noteworthy aspect of Beres and Joseph's (1970) conception of mental representation is their adoption of the Piagetian conception of representation as specifically related to the capacity to 're-present' an object that is not present. This emphasis is not part of the definition represent- ation that has been adopted in the present study, because of the attempt that is being made here is to distinguish between representation as an anticipatory set and the issue of developmental capacities and defects. Beres and Joseph's definition of representation in terms of the capacity to represent does not lead them to explore developmental issues such as the line of development leading up to this capacity, or the possible conse- quences of the disturbance of this capacity. Rather, it serves to distinguish between processes of perception in humans, as opposed to such processes in the animal kingdom. Therefore the issue of whether representation in psychoanalytic theory is best defined as implying the capacity to 're- present', does not find supportive arguments in Beres and Joseph's discussion of this point. This question is further explored in Chapter 11 in regard to the comparison of Piaget's concept of representation with that of psychoanalysis.

Sandler

The most influential work on the concept of mental representation is probably that of Joseph Sandler and his co-workers at the Hampstead Clinic. In three papers (Sandler 1960, 1962; and Sandler and Rosenblatt 1962) Sandler put forward an approach regarding concepts of mental objects that served as the conceptual framework for the extensive work of Sandler and of many of the Hampstead analysts.[13]

Again, as in the cases of Novey and Beres, it is useful to note the context in which the concept of mental representation was studied. Sandler's first discussion of this concept appeared in his paper on the superego (1960). There he noted what he called the 'conceptual dissolution' of the superego concept, and the various theoretical problems which led to the situation in

which Hampstead analysts were avoiding use of the concept of the superego in their Index project.

As part of an attempt to establish an accepted conceptual framework,
Sandler distinguished between various processes often confused in the
psychoanalytic literature. The most important distinctions were between
processes of internalization (which he referred to as 'organizing activity'),[14]
identification and introjection. The products of each of these processes
were considered to be different. Internalization (or 'organizing activity')
was considered to be that process whereby mental models or schemata
(later to be termed 'mental representations' in Sandler and Rosenblatt 1962)
of the external world (and of the self) are gradually built up in the mind of
the infant. This organizing activity eventually creates a 'representational
world' which provides a perceptual mapping of the external world (and of
the person themselves – self-representation). This process was considered
to serve as a basis for all later processes which made use of the mental
representations of objects and self. Identification and introjection were
considered to be processes dependent on the existence of such mental
representations.

Identification was defined as the alteration of the ego (or self-
representation) so as to attain a similarity with (some aspect of) the object
representation. This was considered to be the process whereby the ego's
traits and functions were established.

The term 'introjection' was reserved for the special process whereby the
superego was formed. Sandler emphasized that in this process there occurs
a transfer of authority from the external objects (the parents) to that mental
structure called the superego. Whereas before this transfer the child was
dependent on his parents as his major source of self-esteem (narcissistic
gratification), subsequently the child acquires the capacity to maintain a
certain narcissistic balance via his relationship with his own superego.
While mental representations of his parents certainly existed before the
introjection of the parental images, they did not possess the capacity to
'substitute . . . for the real object as a source of narcissistic gratification'
(Sandler 1960: 153). This capacity is considered to be the unique contribution of the process of introjection.

Thus we see that in Sandler's proposition the level of mental representation serves as a substratum for later mental processes. Sandler especially
emphasized the perceptual basis of the representational world. Distortions
due to emotional factors, such as projection or identification, were considered to consist of a defensive distortion of the representations. 'The child
who feels angry at one moment and the subject of attack at another, shows
a change in the shape of his self-representation' (Sandler and Rosenblatt
1962). Id impulses too were considered to consist of the wished-for
interaction of self and object; that is, an unconscious 'perception' of self

and object representations in a wished-for interaction.[15] Representations themselves are not considered to be active agents, but rather the 'material' which serves the ego in perception, phantasy, thought and so on.[16]

In terms of his later distinction between concepts referring to the 'experiential' and 'non-experiential' realms of the mind (Sandler and Joffe 1969), Sandler would seem to consider mental representations to refer to the experiential realm. In fact, it would seem that his concept of 'the representational world' is largely synonymous with the experiential realm, which 'is not an active agent [but rather] is a *guide* to the mental apparatus' (Sandler and Joffe 1969).[17]

In these papers, representations function to 'inform' the mental apparatus as to the state of the organism. Discrepancies between wished-for and perceived states (representations) lead to pain, and congruence between them lead to feelings of pleasure and of safety and well-being. Instinctual wishes, reality considerations and superego demands are all considered to operate via the representational world. As such, the representational world is not an autonomous agent but rather the 'substance' upon which different forces operate and the condition of which fosters the further operation of those forces.

In 1978 Sandler (together with A.-M. Sandler) presented a paper in which he brought together different trends of thought that he had developed in earlier papers, and which constituted an interesting shift in his conception of the representational world. The other trends of thought, embodied in the title of the paper, concerned object relationships and affects. Sandler's growing emphasis on feeling states as the basic regulatory principle of psychic life (Sandler and Joffe 1969; Sandler 1972) had previously been explored in terms of his already existing concepts of the representational world. He had viewed psychic adaptation in terms of an 'economics of feeling states' in which the feeling of safety or of well-being played a central role. He viewed object relationships, in the framework of the economy of feeling states, as an attempt to actualize that interaction with the object which would maximize the feeling of well-being.

In the 1978 paper he brought these ideas regarding feeling states to bear on the construction of the representational mental world itself. He suggested that feeling states themselves could be considered to be the first and primary 'objects' of the child, before he is capable of recognizing the external world as such. These feeling states are divided into two classes – the pleasurable, comfortable experiences associated with safety on the one hand, and unpleasant and painful experiences on the other. These two classes of experience may be conceived of as constituting good and bad objects for the infant, before the infant is capable of distinguishing between self and objects. As representations of objects (that is, people) are built up,[18] they come to be associated with the various feeling states which these objects engender in the infant, and take their emotional significance from that association. The child's later wishes for various interactions with, for example, his mother, are related to his striving to perpetuate the good feeling state associated with his mother. It is these interactions which continue to be represented throughout life as the wished-for interactions with objects. Actualization of these wishes evokes an experience of the presence of the longed-for object, and it is this experience of presence which gives the feeling of well-being. This experience of presence was later described by Sandler (1981) as a subliminal or preconscious illusion.

In this elaboration of his theory, Sandler succeeded in integrating the two aspects of motivation which he had so emphasized in his previous papers – feeling states, and wished-for relationships with the object. In regard to his concept of mental representation too, the revision supplements an important aspect not dealt with in his previous work – the connection between the representational world and affective experience. Here Sandler formulated the affective experience as the substrata of the representational world, via the concept of 'object'. He thereby concurred with Novey (1961), who also strove to formulate a model whereby affective experience would play a central role *vis-à-vis* mental representations. Sandler has further extended this connection by developing a specific theory of the way in which object-relationships come to be associated with the internal economy of feeling states. The representation of the (wished-for) interaction between self and object functions as a 'guide' to the person's interpersonal activities, so as to attain the illusion of the presence of the gratifying object (that is, one providing safety). This theory also provides a rationale for the 'striving for the object' which Fairbairn viewed as the basic motivational principle, in place of Freud's pleasure principle.[19]

Recently, Sandler (1990a, 1990b, 1991, 1993) has returned to his earlier formulations regarding representations, updating some of his earlier views and adding to them. From these papers, two points stand out. Regarding mental representations, Sandler (1990b) clarified the previous ambiguity regarding their status as belonging to the experiential/non-experiential realms. He explicitly distinguishes between these two usages of the term, concluding that there is need of both. But, using this distinction, he defines the Kleinian term 'internal objects' as belonging to the non-experiential realm, referring to structures and not to experiences (whereas Melanie Klein emphasized that internal objects were experienced as such). Sandler defines 'internal objects' as structures that give rise to an experience of the presence of the object through current phantasies, thereby contributing to the individual's feeling of safety (due to the nearness, or presence, of these objects). It would seem that this definition is similar to Sandler's earlier definition of introjection (1960). It is important to emphasize that Sandler reiterates his previous position that these concepts (mental representations, internal objects) are not to be thought of as sources of motivation or as active agents.

Another point of interest in Sandler's recent formulations (1991) relates to his views regarding the tension between the viewpoints of one-person and two-person psychology. Loyal to the view he had expressed a number of years previously (1983), that psychoanalytic theory is still in need of sufficient flexibility to allow seemingly incompatible theoretical models between which analysts can move according to their clinical needs, he does not attempt to determine between these two models (Sandler 1991). However, his preference is clear, and it is clear that he considers the concepts he developed in relation to mental representations to be sufficient to define interpersonal interactions in one-person psychology terms. As an important example of this, Sandler (1993) discusses processes subsumed by Kleinian analysts under the heading 'projective identification', using a representational framework to distinguish among these various processes. He prefers to use the term 'projective identification' only for those instances in which it is the patient's (unconscious) intention to make the analyst experience that which is projected.

Sandler argues that not everything that the analyst experiences in his countertransference reaction to the patient is necessarily unconsciously meant by the patient to be so experienced. He defines the details of processes of unconscious communication in terms of what he calls 'recurrent primary identification' by the analyst, which do not necessitate intention on the part of the patient. This process entails an extremely short and unnoticed suspension of the boundaries between self and object representations (in the analyst), due to which the analyst may experience the verbal expressions of the patient as his own. As a result of this, these contents will (unconsciously) affect the analyst's own latent thoughts, phantasies and so on. This happens, therefore, not as a result of a projective identification on the part of the patient, but rather as part of normal processes of unconscious communication. In this way, Sandler succeeds in defining thse processes in one-person psychology terms, rather than the two-person psychology model used by Bion in his understanding of the use of projective identification in unconscious communication. Projective identification, in Sandler's terms, depends on the intention of the patient (the projector), which returns us to one-person psychology terms. The fact that the analyst subsequently, via his own recurrent primary identification, experiences these contents as his own, is part of an interaction of two separate psychological systems, and not the result of 'projection into' the object.

The psychoanalytic concept of the mental representations of objects as developed by the three writers reviewed here constitutes an attempt on the part of those theorists orientated towards ego psychology to develop a framework capable of integrating concepts related to objects. This was especially necessary in the context of complex theories developed by Melanie Klein and other analysts from the British Society (especially Fairbairn), theories which presented difficulties for the conceptual framework of the early 1960s regarding ego psychology. As noted above, Freud's conceptual framework of 'objects' as an aspect of the drives, an aspect to be invested ('cathected') with mental energies, was not adequate to encompass a shift of views from a strictly drive-defence model to a growing emphasis on the role of interpersonal relationships in the development of personality. The concept of object representation, as used by the theorists presented here, combines a number of characteristics that allow it to play a 'bridging' role between the different approaches.

First, the mental representation is considered to be a product of the mind, a construct which the mind develops and uses to comprehend reality. As such it is considered to span the (unbridgeable) gap between the drives, on the one hand, and reality, on the other. Here the issue of the origin of the object representation – internal or external – is very relevant. Different analysts will emphasize to different extents the aspects of realism or phantasy of the object representation, but it is clear that the concept is used to provide for both.

Second, closely connected with the above point is the emphasis of both Novey and Sandler on the affective aspect of the representations. Both came to regard the affective aspect as primary, both finding their way to formulations of affects as (some form of) object representation. While neither expressed this in the concrete terms of the Kleinians, it is interesting that both seem to have been drawn (*post facto*) to a view integrating the Kleinian perspective. This notion, that affects (or feeling states) stand in some relation to the self, a relation similar to that of objects, and that objects take their meaning from their association with those affects, emphasizes the distance of the psychoanalytic idea of representation from the Piagetian concept.[20] Again, the question regarding the extent to which object representations reflect reality versus the extent to which they reflect emotional states of the subject is a central issue.

It is of special importance to note the very different realms of meaning encompassed by the conception of mental representations of objects as presented by Novey, Beres and Sandler, and those encompassed by the same terms as used by Edith Jacobson. Although Jacobson was herself also struggling with the integration of object concepts into an ego psychology framework, her concepts bear the stamp of a very specific insight that she was trying to express. Her concept of the fusion of self and object representations as an explanatory concept related to psychotic states, restricted her development of the concepts of mental representations to that area of psychopathology. Representations in her usage took on a structural meaning, such that her theory constituted a distinct theory of mental structures. In contrast, Novey, Beres and Sandler all take a wider view of the concept of representations, a view most fully expressed in Sandler's concept of the representational world. Representations here come to refer to significant constellations of experience, and among these the experiences of objects occupy a central position. It is of special interest to note Sandler's (1993) view of the temporary suspension of the boundary between self and object representations as part of the normal process of communication, in contrast to Jacobson's view of such suspension of boundaries as a deeply regressive phenomenon.

In conclusion, the mental representation of objects as developed (separately but similarly) by Novey, Beres and Sandler has become a basic concept in the framework of thinking related to ego psychology. It is today widely used (as may be verified by a perusal of the subject index of recent volumes of psychoanalytic journals), and appears to have been accepted as a useful concept. Its basic contribution has been to provide ego psychology with a concept that will: (1) bridge the gap between the influences of reality and of the drives (and other internal factors) on the individual's perception of, and attitude towards, his environment, providing for both types of influence; (2) account for the influences of the interactions with, and personalities of, emotionally significant people on the formation of personality in a wider range of experience than that specified by the drive-defence model.

Although the concept of mental representations has been widely accepted there has been some criticism of its use. We will now turn to examine this criticism.

Two important papers, both dedicated specifically to a critique of the concept of mental representation from the perspective of ego psychology, appeared in the early 1980s – Friedman (1980a) and Boesky (1983). Both may be seen in the context of an attempt by analysts orientated towards ego psychology to defend ego psychology against the inroads made by concepts close to an object-relations approach. Indeed, both these analysts openly declare in their critiques that one of the reasons they are critical of the concept of representation is that it is the tendency of those who use it to do so in the context of ideas embedded in object-relations theory.[21] But beyond this specific critique (to which I shall return), there are a number of points raised in these papers worth discussing.

The brunt of criticism in both papers relates to the implication, and in some cases the outright declaration, of those using the concept of mental representation that it is not to be considered as a source of motivation. As we have seen, both Sandler (Sandler and Joffe 1969) and Schafer (1968) specified that representations are to be considered 'material' or 'information' and not sources of motivation. This was especially prominent in Schafer's work, which repeatedly emphasized that representations were not to be confused with motives, even when the subjective experience is of the influence of an introject or psychic presence on an individual's feelings and behaviour. In spite of these disclaimers, both Friedman (1980a) and Boesky (1983) contend that motivational implications become tied in with the concept of representation when representations are considered to guide the individual (or the mental apparatus) in regard to those wished-for states (as they are, by both Sandler and Schafer). Thus, although representational theorists may intend to adhere to a drive-defence model of motivation that is strictly orientated towards ego psychology, in effect they do not.

A second point of criticism, emphasized especially by Friedman (1980a) has to do with the more basic question of how to use concepts of representations without using them concretely, as to refer to (visual) images, on the one hand, or to use them so abstractly as to refer to 'meaning', on the other. Friedman contends that the whole question of how experience is organized, and whether the distinctions between (for instance) self and object representations are basic to the organization of experience, as the representational theorists seem to suppose, must be opened to discussion. In fact, he says, the organization of experience is just what the psychoanalytic theory of motivation is all about – it is a theory of how experience is organized. This, of course, returns us to the issue of ego psychology. One meaning of the concept of representation which Friedman is willing to accept is that of 'capacity' (Friedman 1980a: 222–3). This, in conjunction with his example of Mahler's work as exemplifying the proper study of changing representations without ignoring the motivational underpinnings of those changes, points to the definition of mental objects as developmental capacities, which will be discussed in Part Three as the aspect of the concept of representation that Friedman finds to be compatible with his version of psychoanalytic theory.

To return to the criticism that pervades both papers – that the concept of representations leads to object-relations theory – I find this point to be well taken. As I will describe in the chapter on 'representation' in the last part of this study, I consider the various concepts of representation to be part of the response of ego psychology to the challenges of a developmental point of view. The latter views the formation of personality not only in the context of the vicissitudes of drives and defences, but also in response to the emotional interactions with others during the different stages of development. Thus, from the perspective of a strictly drive-defence model, the concept of representation tends to blur the well-defined contours of the drive-defence organization of experience. Whether such a tendency is considered progress or regression depends on one's preferences in psychoanalytic theory. The perspective of this historical survey is to describe the development of the various trends in psychoanalytic theory, and from that point of view I tend to concur with Friedman's (1980a) and Boesky's (1983) analysis of the place of the concept of representation in the development of psychoanalytic theory.

Schafer

One of the most learned and detailed studies of a theoretical nature in the psychoanalytic literature is that of Roy Schafer, *Aspects of Internalization* (1968), which has direct bearing on the concepts under study in the present work. Schafer's study seems to have come about in order to fill a gap in the development of ego psychology as it developed in North America. For, while many psychoanalytic concepts were studied, redefined and clarified in the works of Rapaport and his associates (of whom Schafer was one), concepts related to processes of internalization seem to have received relatively less intensive study than others.[22] Schafer's study undoubtedly helped to fill that gap.

It is noteworthy that his study came at the end of the period of the unchallenged predominance of interest in ego psychology-orientated metapsychology in North America. The 1970s witnessed a revolt against metapsychology, in which George Klein (1969, 1976) and others of Rapaport's earlier associates (Gill, Holt and Schafer) played a major role. Schafer's participation in this new wave of interest took a unique form in his work on 'action language' as a wholesale alternative to accepted metapsychology (Schafer 1972, 1976). In fact, one of his first papers to be published after *Aspects of Internalization* was a critique of the very concept to which he had devoted such careful study – internalization (Schafer 1972). Thus it came about that Schafer himself did not continue to develop those lines of thought which he had presented in his book, and basically rejected the legitimacy of the direction of study to which he had previously contributed so much. In spite of this quirk of personal interest on Schafer's part, his study on internalization was very highly regarded and continued to influence psychoanalytic thought on this subject. Of special interest in the present work is his continuation of that line of thought developed by the representational theoreticians discussed above, in regard to the concept of representation.

Three major influences loom large in the theoretical background of Schafer's book, theoreticians with whom Schafer may be considered as being in dialogue – Hartmann, Jacobson and Melanie Klein. Hartmann set the foundations of the ego psychology framework within which Schafer was working, but Schafer preferred an emphasis on dynamics, on motivation, to Hartmann's emphasis on the adaptive point of view (Schafer 1968: 11–12). Schafer was less interested in the processes whereby ego functions develop, and more in the processes whereby the motives of the individual develop and change (Schafer's concept of identification). The former belongs to the domain of general psychology, which Hartmann worked to bring under the scope of psychoanalytic theory (Hartmann 1964), while the latter is closer to the clinical interests of psychoanalysis.

Edith Jacobson, as we have seen, was the first theoretician to make major use of the concepts of self and object representations in her theoretical writings. But Jacobson developed a unique approach to these concepts, which became the basic building blocks of personality. Although Schafer draws heavily on Jacobson's work, he is critical of the tendency, present in her work, to formulate motivation in terms of shifts in the cathexes of representations.[23] One of the major principles of his study is that the concept of representation should not be used to refer to motivation, but rather should be restricted to the content of experience. This is a crucial point in Schafer's discussion on introjects.

Last, in regard to Melanie Klein, Schafer uses her work as a contrast to his own effort, almost as the disorder for which he wishes to provide a remedy. Impressed by the clinical observations in the work of the Kleinians, especially in regard to introjects, he considers their theoretical framework to be quite lacking. One of the major thrusts of his study is to provide theoretical conceptualization in accord with ego psychology for these phenomena.

Schafer distinguishes between the two major processes under the general heading of internalization – introjection and identification – and it is these two processes to which the bulk of the book is devoted.[24] Introjection is defined wholly in terms of the phenomenon of introjects. These are defined as 'an inner presence with which one feels in a continuous or intermittent relationship' (1968: 72).[25] The crucial point defining introjects is that they are not experienced 'as an aspect or expression of [the individual's] subjective self' (ibid.), but rather as another person (or thing). Because they retain the quality of 'otherness', Schafer considers introjects to be a certain kind of object representation – not a realistic, secondary-process object representation, but rather a primary-process one. Introjection was thus defined as the process whereby introjects, and other primary-process object representations, are formed, presumably on the basis of already existing secondary-process object representations. In contrast with introjects, which are experienced as 'other', identification is defined (1968: 140) as leading to changes in the individual that are reflected in the self representation – that is, are experienced as 'self'. Although these changes are also considered to be based on already existing object representations, the outcome is a change in 'self'. I will return to this distinction later.

In the process of the study of these two concepts many others come up for definition and description; of these, those of representation are of special interest here. For Schafer the concepts of representation are basic concepts which, while in need of definition among other 'auxiliary terms', do not seem to need intensive discussion and study on their own. In spite of this, much may be learned from Schafer's discussions of the 'principal terms' about the concept of representation.[26]

The most important aspect regarding representations, which Schafer emphasizes again and again, is that they are not to be used as referring to motivation. Representations provide the material, the content of experience, but do not themselves direct or influence behaviour.[27] This point is especially important to Schafer in relation to the concept of the introjects. The latter are defined as 'primary process object representations' – that is, a specific kind of representation. But, as representations, introjects do not actually influence the behaviour of the individual, in spite of the fact that they are experienced as doing just that. Here Schafer is correcting one of the 'mistakes' of Kleinian psychology which describes the introjects as guiding and directing behaviour.

This view, in Schafer's opinion, leads to a 'demonology' in which the mind is seen as populated by numerous objects doing battle with each other. Schafer considered the subjective experience of introjects to be an important phenomenon, but one that should not be directly translated into theoretical terms. Thus, the experience of being influenced by another person who is neither present nor necessarily experienced realistically, points to the primary-process nature of the experience. In the regression to primary-process ideation, the distinction between phantasy and reality may be (temporarily) suspended, leading to the phantasy being felt as actually influencing behaviour (without, of course, this being so). Introjection, thus defined, constitutes 'a regressive change in ego organization which obscures the distinction between the idea of the object and its external and temporal referents' (1968: 78).

Another point on which Schafer strongly differs from Kleinian views regarding introjects is in relation to what he calls their 'localization'. As we saw in the section on Melanie Klein, she laid great emphasis on the 'internality' of internal objects, on their being experienced (primarily) as existing physically within the individual's own body. This view was closely related to Melanie Klein's emphasis on introjection and projection as the two basic processes of mental life. Schafer, of course, considers introjection as only one of very many mental processes, functioning, as do all the other processes, in the service of the various motivations which direct mental life. The experiences of the internality of the introject, while definitely an important clinical fact to be explored for its meaning for the patient, is of little import at the theoretical level. Primary-process object representations

– or, as Schafer prefers to call them, 'primary-process presences' – may be indeterminate as to localization. The case of introjects, which are specifically experienced as 'inside', are but one kind of such 'presences'.

Regarding the difference between identification and introjection in Schafer's framework, two aspects need to be noted. First, there is the simple distinction based on whether it is the self representation or the object representation that is undergoing change. In introjection it is the object representation, while in identification the self representation undergoes a change. The introject is experienced (not necessarily at a conscious level) as 'not-self', while identification leads to changes in the content of the experience of self. But beyond that level, an important distinction between the two may be seen to involve the 'realness' of the change effected by the two processes. (Schafer himself did conceptualize the difference he described in these terms, but I think that such a distinction is a straightforward outcome of his discussion.) While introjection leads to changes in the *content* of experience (that is, in the object representation), identification leads to changes in the *motives* of the individual – 'in this process [identification] the subject modifies his motives and behaviour patterns, and the self representations corresponding to them' (1968: 140). And while Schafer emphasizes that identification does not create new capacities but only 'selectively reorganizes' previously existing factors (pp. 147–8), by giving certain motives primacy over others, identification can lead to 'fundamental systemic change' (p. 148). This difference, between a process that just *seems* to lead to change (introjection) and one that *really does* (identification), carries, of course, interesting judgemental connotations; unfortunately, Schafer does not follow up on these.

Another seemingly judgemental distinction that Schafer makes, in the final chapter of the book ('The fates of the immortal object' – a title in interesting contrast to the clear-cut titles of the other chapters), is that between three possible 'fates' of the (mental) object. The three fates correspond to the three basic concepts that came into play in Schafer's study: (1) the object as introject (or primary-process presence); (2) transformed into an identification; and (3) 'the objects' being preserved as such, that is, with their index of being external to the subjective self' (1968: 234), namely as an object representation. It is interesting to note Schafer's laudatory comments on the third possibility (pp. 235–6), and despite his own disclaimer (p. 236) it would seem that there is something in that possibility that appeals to Schafer more than the first two. Whereas introjection and identification are both processes serving defensive and security-seeking functions, in the third possibility 'the subject takes his chances with the external world [and] leaves himself vulnerable to the independent activity of the external object' (p. 235).

Here we catch a glance at an interesting point of view on Schafer's part, one which does not come up for direct examination throughout the study, related to the concept of representation. For, while Schafer discusses in detail the many aspects of the changes of the object representation that constitute introjection and identification, he does not discuss the origins of the representations themselves. From the above-quoted statement regarding the third 'fate' of the object, and from various other hints throughout the book (for example, pp. 35, 130, 136–7) it would seem that representations are considered, first and foremost, the representation of external reality, and that the origin of the object representations is in the (external) object. This point, so seemingly simple, is of course not to be taken for granted in psychoanalytic theory, where precisely the question of the relative roles of internal versus external factors, or drives versus reality, is such a critical one. Schafer's usage of the concept of representation as primarily a representation of external reality, without detailed discussion of the dynamic factors involved in its emergence, further emphasizes the trend developed by the representational theoreticians discussed above regarding the use of this concept.[28]

As mentioned above, Schafer was to abandon the line of study he developed in *Aspects of Internalization* shortly after its publication. In a paper entitled 'The psychoanalytic vision of reality' (1970), he began the journey that would lead him to the hermeneutic version of psychoanalysis which characterizes his more recent works (1983). It is interesting to note that the hermeneutic version leaves (almost) untouched the very question that Schafer abstained from broaching in *Aspects of Internalization*. That question may be formulated in different ways – in terms of the origins of the self and object representations, in terms of the relation between psychic and material realities, or in terms of the relation of the 'second reality' (1983: 255–7) and the first. As we shall see in Part 2, this is a central question in psychoanalytic theory today. Schafer's (1968) discussion and clarification of concepts of introjection and identification, and especially his widespread use of concepts of representation, give him an important place as a continuer of the line of thought developed by the representational theoreticians orientated towards ego psychology discussed earlier. While not directly involved in the study and development of the concept of representation itself, the concept gains an important place and context as it is consistently used in the study of the theories of internalization. Most notably, Schafer's definition of representation as content, in contrast to motivation, contributed to the more consistent use of this theory in the psychoanalytic literature.

Kernberg

Otto Kernberg has probably done more than almost any other psychoanalyst to introduce object-relations theory to the North American psychoanalytic scene, striving for an integration of that theory with that of ego psychology. He considers himself to be continuing the theoretical approach of Edith Jacobson (Kernberg 1981), and in fact there are very evident similarities between their approaches. Beyond the specific theoretical similarities there is also a more general – one might call it methodological – similarity between them: both have based their theoretical innovations on the understanding of a specific area of psychopathology. Jacobson, as we have seen, focused on the study of psychotic phenomena, especially psychotic depression. From this she developed her (structural) conception of mental representations, and especially of the fusion of self and object representation.

Kernberg, as is well known, has focused on the area of borderline phenomena (which he expanded in his concept of the borderline personality organization) and in that context developed his concept of the *splitting* of self and object-representations.[29] It is this concept that constitutes Kernberg's most basic and consistent insight, and his conception of it is the core around which much of his theoretical framework revolves. Although he has introduced radical changes in some of his views on theory, his concept of splitting has remained constant. We will begin by examining this concept and its implications.

Kernberg's (1966) work with borderline patients led him to a realization that in spite of these patients' difficulties in the control of their impulses, it would be incorrect to characterize them as lacking impulse control. His observations led him to conclude that there was a certain selectiveness in his patients' impulse control, such that a specific impulse (lying, sexual promiscuity and so on) could sometimes be freely (that is, ego-syntonically) expressed and at other times be strictly controlled. He noticed that at times when an impulse was under strict control there was also the feeling that that impulse had no place in the patient's personality – that is, that the patient was no longer emotionally in touch with the impulse. Impressed by this compartmentalization of his patients' experiences, he conceived of this phenomenon as alternating ego states, thereby emphasizing the ego's alternating attitudes to the impulse as the central determining factor.

It was Fairbairn's conception of the ego as a structure subject to splitting that provided Kernberg with the appropriate theoretical conceptualization.[30] Fairbairn, in his rejection of Freudian drive-psychology, had emphasized impulses as aspects of the ego, leading him to a conceptualization of an ego split into libidinal and anti-libidinal parts. He considered this splitting of the ego to come about due to frustrating experiences with the longed-for object. Splitting occurs, to begin with, in the (subject's mental representation of the) object. But the ego (self), being in close relationship with the (mental representation of the) object, must split accordingly. Kernberg (1966) quoted Sutherland's (1963) summary of Fairbairn's view: 'Such a split involves a division of the pristine ego into structures each of which contains (a) a part of the ego, (b) the object that characterizes the related relationships and (c) the affects of the latter' (p. 239). Using representational terms, Kernberg formulated his 'basic unit' (of the ego) as composed of: (a) object images or representations, (b) self images or representations, and (c) drive derivatives or dispositions to specific affective states (1966).[31] His concept of splitting (like that of Fairbairn) emphasized the affective quality of the interaction between the individual and his objects as the organizing principle according to which the self-object-affect units were organized, leading to separate positive and negative self-object-affect units.

Kernberg used this basic conception in his construction of a theory of ego development, elaborating on that of Jacobson. Fairbairn's model did not provide for any notion of the development of the ego as an organization of functions. Fairbairn's use of the term 'ego' was closer to Hartmann's definition of self (or self-representation) and he made no attempt to integrate his model with that of (Hartmannian) ego psychology.[32] Kernberg did just that. Noticing the close connection between his borderline patients' alternating ego states (which he conceptualized in terms of split self-object-affect constellations) and their more pervasive ego weakness, he strove to construct a theory that would relate the splitting of representation with the development of ego functions. (Note that for Kernberg this meant ego in the Hartmannian sense; that is, that structure responsible for anxiety tolerance, impulse control, sublimation, thought processes – primary versus secondary – and defensive organization.)[33]

Kernberg's (1966) developmental scheme employed Erikson's (1956) conception of the development of ego identity via primitive introjection and childhood identifications. He considered introjection to refer to the earliest construction of self-representation–object-representation–affect units. This is accomplished by primary autonomous apparatuses of the ego – such as perception, memory and so on. Kernberg does not consider introjection to be an instinctual process, related to oral incorporation. His view in this is similar to Sandler's opinion (Sandler and Rosenblatt 1962) regarding the 'organizing activity' of the ego as responsible for the construction of the representational world, rather than to Melanie Klein's and Fairbairn's more dynamic – that is, motivated – conceptions.[34]

He considers the early introjections to be organized on the basis of their valences (their affective quality) such that positive and negative introjections will be separately organized. No special mechanism is needed to effect this separation; rather, it is considered to be the natural mode of organization. Only as the ego functions of perception and memory mature, and as self-representations and object representations become differentiated, is the ego capable of integrating positive and negative introjections in spite of their contrasting valences. Concurrently with the capacity to combine the introjections there is also a development of the ego's active use of the separation of contrasting introjections for defensive purposes – splitting. This defensive use of splitting protects the developing ego by 'preventing the generalization of anxiety throughout the ego from the foci of negative introjections, and protects the integration of positive introjections into a primitive ego core' (Kernberg 1966: 244).

It is precisely at this juncture that Kernberg considers the borderline patient to be stuck. Due to factors either constitutional (such as lack of anxiety tolerance, over-intensity of aggressive drives) or environmental (severe early frustrations), synthesis of introjections of opposite valences has not taken place and active (defensive) splitting persists. The ego alternates between identification with the different introjects, leading to what seems to be a lack of impulse control, but is actually an identification with 'non-metabolized' (that is, unintegrated) primitive introjects. Due to their primitive nature, the early introjections are of an intensely affective nature, unmitigated by reality considerations. As a result of the persistence of active splitting, ego development is retarded. The integrative powers of the ego are affected by the splitting, and higher development of ego functions and of the defensive organization is disrupted. The result is not only that the specific mechanism of splitting persists, but also that general ego development is impaired, leading to the general ego weakness of borderline patients (Kernberg 1967).

If we pause here to examine the concept of representation implied in Kernberg's theory of splitting, we will see that a central aspect of the splitting of representations is that this process entails the disruption of (general) aspects of ego-functioning. In fact, that is one of the main aims of Kernberg's theory – to specify the connection of splitting of self and object representations to ego pathology. As with Edith Jacobson, so also with Kernberg, self and object representations are seen as basic building blocks of the personality, more than 'patterns of experience'. Kernberg discusses this aspect of his theory in his discussion of the close connection between self (representations) and ego.[35] Thus, in the terms employed in the present study, he attributes both experiential and structural meanings to the term 'representation'. This is an important point for the understanding of Kernberg's theory. It is based on his view that the structural ego grows out of the developing organization of representations, a process to which he devoted an elaborate description (Kernberg 1966: 252).

In a later paper (1982), Kernberg further reiterated his opinion on the close connection between self and ego, rejecting Hartmann's clear-cut distinction between them: 'In my view, historically speaking, Hartmann's fateful separation of ego from self and of self from self-representation created a problem in the development of psychoanalytic theory, namely, the artificial separation of structural, experiential and descriptive aspects of ego functions' (p. 898).

But Kernberg here is not simply adopting the Kleinian view, emphasizing the centrality of experiential aspects of the mind and rejecting structural concepts.[36] Rather, he is following Edith Jacobson in expounding that the self and object representations constitute the basic or primitive structures upon which later structures (namely, ego and superego) are constructed. It is this aspect of his theory that has been criticized for confusing these two levels (Boesky 1983).

We have seen that Kernberg's concept of the splitting of self and object representations occupies a central place in his theory of the borderline personality organization. Kernberg's use of this concept stresses his view that structural and experiential aspects are inseparable, and it is in accordance with this view that Kernberg considers the self and object representations to be the basic building blocks (structures) of the personality. We shall now turn to an examination of the specific place of object representation in Kernberg's theory and the relationship of Kernberg's views with those of Melanie Klein and Fairbairn regarding internal objects.

Following Edith Jacobson, Kernberg (1976) emphasized a developmental view of the self and object representations, beginning with a state of undifferentiation between self and object representations (stages 1 and 2). During this early period of development,[37] experience is organized into aggregates of good and bad (that is, pleasurable and unpleasurable) experiences, at a stage at which the infant cannot distinguish between self and object representations within these aggregates. This 'undifferentiation' is equivalent in Kernberg's theory to Edith Jacobson's theory of the fusion of self and object representations. Undifferentiation, or fusion, is considered to account for defective reality-testing, and fixation or regression to this stage is considered to characterize psychotic states.

The role of the object representations in development becomes an issue in Kernberg's theory only in the process of the differentiation of self and object representations. Kernberg presents two views regarding this process of differentiation, without commenting on the relationship between them. These two views seem to correspond clearly to his two theoretical frameworks – the ego psychology framework (following Jacobson), stressing structural aspects, and the Kleinian framework, stressing the dynamics of experience. In accordance with the ego psychology framework he proposes that differentiation proceeds under the influence of 'primary autonomous ego functions such as perception and memory and by cognitive developments occurring in the context of the infant–mother relationship' (Kernberg 1976: 63). He has discussed various aspects of this process (ibid.; 1984), but basically this view implies that the early development of perception and cognition takes place without the object representation playing any specific role.

The situation is very different in regard to Kernberg's views of the contributions of the dynamics of experience to the process of differentiation. Here he has repeatedly (for example, Kernberg 1966: 244; 1976: 63–4; 1984: 15–16) emphasized the idea that the wish to escape from bad experiences leads to an 'expelling of the "bad" self-object-representation to the "periphery" of psychic experience', thereby contributing to the establishment of a sense of 'not-me' as opposed to 'me'.[38] In Kernberg's theory this process becomes especially important in the discussion of the narcissistic personality. Kernberg considers that at the deepest level of the narcissistic personality lies 'the image of a hungry, enraged, empty self, full of impotent anger at being frustrated, and fearful of a world which seems as hateful and revengeful as the patient himself' (1975: 233). Although he does not mention the Kleinian paranoid–schizoid position, it is clear that this is what he is referring to (his reference to the findings of 'British psychoanalysts' makes this almost explicit).[39] Another aspect of the close connection between narcissistic pathology and the projection of bad internal objects is Kernberg's emphasis on the narcissistic patients' devaluation of his objects. This devaluation constitutes a central feature of narcissistic symptomatology, and is seen by Kernberg as a result of the fusion of ideal self, ideal object and actual self-images into a grandiose self. Due to this fusion, the bad aspects of the self and the object are all relegated to the external world.[40]

Both these aspects of Kernberg's theory of pathological narcissism point to the central role of the narcissist's technique of defending against a bad internal object. Here we may see the close connection with the ideas of Melanie Klein and Fairbairn. Both emphasized the elaborate and pathological defensive processes set into operation in order to deal with a bad internal object. As we have seen, Klein and Fairbairn differed radically as to the ultimate origin of this bad internal object. Whereas Klein saw the bad object as representative of the death instinct – that is, of the individual's own badness – Fairbairn emphasized that the bad internal object reflected the bad aspect of the real external object (namely, the mother). Kernberg does not take a clear-cut stance on this question, often mentioning that both constitutional factors (over-strong aggressive drive or lack of anxiety tolerance – the Kleinian view)[41] or frustration in the interaction with the mother (Fairbairn's view) could determine such pathological development (see, for example, Kernberg 1975: 234).

To summarize: Kernberg uses the concept of representation to denote both structural and experiential characteristics. His emphasis on an ego psychology view of the differentiation of self and object representations relegates these representations to a passive role in the process of differentiation which occurs with the maturation of cognitive capacities. In contrast, his Kleinian-oriented view of the dynamics of experience emphasizes the central role of the bad internal object in both normal development and in pathological narcissism. This mixture of the two different aspects of the concept of object representation, although sometimes giving rise to confusion between them, is what gives Kernberg's theory its special place in the development of an ego psychology view of object-relations development.

Stierlin

One of the recent attempts to develop a more modern perspective on the various phenomena related to mental objects is that of Helm Stierlin. Stierlin (1970) proposed to do for 'inner-objects' what Hartmann had done for 'ego'; that is, give a definition and conduct an exploration in terms of 'functions'. Thus, rather than defining what inner objects *are*, Stierlin suggests a definition in terms of the various *functions* that inner objects fulfil. In this fashion he sidesteps the tendency to reify mental structures and succeeds in focusing on pathology in terms of the various *disturbances* of different inner-object functions. He also includes in his paper a discussion of Fairbairn's theory of object relations, showing where Fairbairn's insights find a place within his own function-orientated framework.

Stierlin proposed three functions of inner objects: (1) a referent function; (2) a steering (or 'gyroscopic') function; and (3) an autonomy-furthering function. The referent function refers to the cognitive representation of external objects in the mind. This is similar to the cognitive, reality-orientated aspect of the object representation concept as defined by the representational theorists (Sandler, Novey and Beres).[42]

The 'gyroscopic' function refers to the 'steering' of the subject in his task of choosing an object for a relationship. Freud mentioned this function in one of his earliest discussion of 'object-choice' (1905d: 228) when he postulated that 'A man, especially, looks for someone who can represent his picture of his mother'.

The third function is probably the most interesting of the three in terms of the discussions extant in the psychoanalytic literature. This function includes the 'inner dialogues' and 'internal relationships' which are the subject of most of the literature, from Freud's 'superego', Melanie Klein's and Fairbairn's 'internal objects' to concepts of object constancy. In his

108

discussion of possible disturbances of the various functions, Stierlin considers the disturbance of the 'autonomy-furthering function' to consist of an over-investment of the internal dialogue (or 'drama', as Stierlin refers to it),[43] leading to a 'detached and often schizoid stance towards the world of real people and relations' (Stierlin 1970: 324). This fits in well with his discussion of Fairbairn's theory, which focused especially on such 'schizoid' phenomena.

Stierlin's proposals do not seem to have had (as yet) a real influence on the psychoanalytic literature. This may be because Stierlin himself has not developed these ideas further,[44] so that it is not clear what it is that they add to existing concepts. While the literature has not developed an exclusively function-orientated definition of inner objects as proposed by Stierlin, there is no doubt a great deal of interest in the functions of such psychic structures. One of the (probable) reasons why Stierlin's approach has not received more attention is the difficulty in distinguishing between such inner-object functions as he proposes and ego functions. Stierlin himself is aware that the functions he has enumerated are no different from various well-known ego functions (for example, the referent function is closely connected with the ego's cognitive mastery of reality). His argument in favour of his approach is that the perspective suggested by viewing certain functions in relation to inner objects adds to the present ego-orientated view, aspects that are not sufficiently emphasized in the present view. This argument would (probably) have to be considerably elaborated before it could have much influence on the literature.[45]

Object constancy

The concept of object constancy was first discussed as such by Heinz Hartmann (1952, 1953). Hartmann emphasized the development of 'satisfactory object relations that includes object constancy' from a previous stage at which 'the object exists only as long as it is need satisfying' (1952: 163). He considered this process to depend on neutralization of libidinal and aggressive drives, an aspect of ego development. That is, as the ego gains the capacity to neutralize drive energies, the original drive-dominated, need-satisfying relationship with the object can develop into 'satisfactory object relations'. The same idea had been described by Kris (1950), as the development from 'anaclitic needs' to 'the more integrated relationship to a permanent personalized love object that can no longer easily be replaced' (p. 33). Hartmann (1952: 173; 1953: 187–8) considered the cognitive development of the capacity to recognize 'things' as separate from the child's activity (Piaget), to be 'partly traceable' to the development of the capacity to neutralize drive energy as described above. This connection between the drive aspect of the relationship to the object and cognitive development is of crucial importance for understanding later confusions regarding the concept of object constancy, as we will see in what follows.

Anna Freud (1952), in her discussion of Hartmann's (1952) idea of the development of object constancy, related this idea to that of Hoffer (1952) regarding the development of the 'psychological object' and to that of Melanie Klein on the development from part-object to whole-object relationships. Her approach, similar to that of Hartmann, emphasized changes in the intensity of the drives as the necessary process that permits the development of the capacity to retain libidinal cathexis to absent love-objects. Anna Freud emphasized in a panel discussion (Panel 1968) that she did not use the concept of object constancy to refer to the (cognitive) 'capacity to keep an inner image of the object in the absence of the object in the external world'. In contrast, she reiterated her definition of object constancy as the capacity 'to retain attachment even when the person is unsatisfactory' (pp. 506–7). She did concede that the (cognitive) capacity to retain an inner image preceded object constancy.

Another psychoanalyst whose work contributed to the development of the concept of object constancy was Rene Spitz. In his observational studies on infants, Spitz described the development of the capacity to recognize the love-object. Before the development of that capacity the infant was at a pre-object stage, a stage during which objects were interchangeable for the infant, who was conceived of as responding to a *Gestalt* rather than to a specific love-object (that is, a specific person). Spitz (1950) considered 8-month stranger anxiety to be indicative of this capacity, and considered that to be the starting point of the infant's capacity to form a relationship with the 'libidinal object'. He later (1966) related this finding with Hartmann's concept of object constancy. Spitz's approach is of special interest because of his integration of cognitive and emotional aspects of the relationship with the object, and his view that progress in emotional development (the relationship with the libidinal object) is shown to be dependent on progress in cognitive development. Although Spitz's conclusions have been criticized for not distinguishing between different sub-levels of both cognitive and emotional development, thereby attributing later capacities to an earlier developmental stage (Fraiberg 1969), his view that emotional development takes place on the basis of the development of cognitive capacities has become widely accepted.

The theoretician whose formulations have had a decisive influence on the modern use of the concept of object constancy is Margaret Mahler. As she shifted her interest from infantile psychosis and the stages of autism and symbiosis to an elaborate exploration of the separation-individuation phase, she adopted the concept of object constancy to signify the process of conclusion of this phase.

Mahler was careful to stress the difference between her understanding of the 'availability' of the mental representation of the object, and Piaget's concept of object permanence (Mahler 1967; McDevitt and Mahler 1980). She stated that while the cognitive capacity for retaining an image of an absent object is necessarily preliminary to libidinal object constancy, they are not complementary aspects of a single process. The fact that the child has attained cognitive object permanence does not mean that he or she has attained libidinal object constancy. The latter is the outcome of the successful resolution of the previous sub-phases of separation-individuation, and especially of the integration of good and bad aspects of the object representation into a single representation. As a result of the complex emotional processes of the separation–individuation phase,

> there now exists a maternal representation which is invested predominantly with libidinal as opposed to aggressive cathexis. Disappointment and rage become tempered and are tolerated better since they are now counteracted to a greater degree by memories of the mother's loving as well as frustrating behaviour.
>
> (McDevitt and Mahler 1980: 408–9)

This difference between the cognitive and the emotional achievements is reflected in the differences between Piaget and Mahler in regard to the age at which they consider these (respective) capacities to be achieved. While Piaget places attainment of cognitive object permanence at 18 months, Mahler considers libidinal object constancy to begin in the third year of life.

At this point it is worthwhile to distinguish between different aspects in the different conceptualizations of object constancy. The first relates to the quality of the relationship with the object. According to this approach there is a development in the quality of the child's emotional attitude towards other people. Younger children relate to people (the mother) as need-satisfying objects, and the ability to relate to others as *people* ('love-objects') develops gradually. This is the main idea of Hartmann's and Anna Freud's use of the concept of object constancy, and it is closely related to Freud's (1915c: 138–9) conception of development from (autoerotic) 'organ pleasure' to love for the object. Sandler and Joffe (1966) have emphasized that this conception implies the development of 'non-sensual love' on the part of the ego; that is, the emotional attitude to the object takes on a new dimension. Anna Freud referred to this (Panel 1968) as the development from the stage at which the object is 'an object for the id, to being an object for the ego' (p. 507).

A different conceptualization (although the two are often combined) refers to the development of internal structures related to the object. This is the conceptualization that has been emphasized by Mahler and her

111

co-workers (although it was also mentioned by Hartmann). According to this view, object constancy refers to the capacity to evoke the representation of the object in its absence. This view has led to considerable confusion because of the difficulty in separating out the cognitive and emotional aspects. Piaget's work on (cognitive) object permanence analysed the stages of the development of the child's ability to conceive of the object as autonomous from the child's own actions and perceptions. As Fraiberg (1969) has emphasized, Piaget studied the development of the child's capacity to 'evoke the image of the absent object and pursue it' (p. 31). The question posed to psychoanalytic theory is: What is the relation between the cognitive capacity and the emotional capacity to evoke the image of an absent object? One approach emphasizes the similarity of the two. According to this approach, differences in the chronological ages of the two are considered to be related to the child's greater experience (and so on) with the mother (the psychoanalytic object) than with a toy (Piaget's object) (Cobliner 1965; Gouin-Decarie 1965; Spitz 1965; Fraiberg 1969; Melito 1983; Leon 1984). Mahler's own approach (McDevitt and Mahler 1980) is that the difference between the two is not merely one of timetables, but rather a conceptual one. She explained this difference in terms of the difference between the 'representational world [which] constitutes an intrapsychic map of the external world' and the 'structural organization of the . . . intrapsychic structures themselves'. In her view, the 'gradual *internalization* of a constant, positively cathected image of the mother' constitutes a reorganization of internal structures, which is different from a change in the 'representational world'.

Mahler's distinction between representational and structural aspects is compatible with the distinctions proposed in the present study. She and others, referring to the capacity to 'evoke the image of the absent mother' so as to gain emotional sustenance from it, are not referring merely to the representational aspects of the 'image' of the mother. Rather, they are implying structural aspects, as Mahler explicitly states.

To summarize: two main conceptualizations have developed in regard to the concept of object constancy. One (A. Freud 1952; Hartmann 1952; Sandler and Joffe 1966; Burgner and Edgecumbe 1972) emphasizes the quality of the relationship with the object, and the other (Fraiberg 1969; Pine 1974; Mahler and McDevitt 1980; Solnit 1982; Melito 1983; Solnit and Neubauer 1986) emphasizes the development of mental structures in relation to the object. The latter has been considerably confused with the cognitive capacity of object permanence. Mahler's conceptualization has been particularly influential, and has been shown here to imply not only representational aspects but also structural and motivational ones.

4

Self orientations

Winnicott

Among the plethora of concepts of mental objects examined in this study, Winnicott's concept of the 'transitional object' no doubt deserves a special place. While it would seem that this concept has had even more influence outside psychoanalytic theory proper than on psychoanalytic theory itself, yet it is an important concept, one that has retained its relevance over the years.

It would seem at first glance that Winnicott's (1953) statement that 'the transitional object is *not an internal object* (which is a mental concept) – it is a possession' would place this concept outside the scope of this study, which only deals with 'mental concepts' and not with their real-life correlates in external reality. But Winnicott's position is not unequivocal. Although much of the literature on transitional objects (both the psychoanalytic and the non-psychoanalytic literature) does actually refer to the 'external thing'[1] (for example, the blanket or teddy-bear), it is obvious that Winnicott was also discussing a mental or emotional capacity – the capacity to invest such a 'thing' with certain meaning.[2]

Thus what is relevant to this study is not so much the concept of the transitional object itself, but rather what Winnicott (1953) called the 'intermediate area of experience' between the 'subjective object' and the 'object objectively perceived'. In order better to understand Winnicott's ideas regarding these concepts I will just present a short sketch of certain lines of thought unique to Winnicott's work.

Winnicott's work began under the influence of Melanie Klein's ideas, as he had been in supervision with Melanie Klein and had undergone a second personal analysis with Joan Riviere (Winnicott 1962: 173).[3] His first psychoanalytic paper, on the manic defence (1935), illustrates his deep interest in Melanie Klein's concepts, both the more specific concepts of the manic defence and depressive position, and the wider idea of inner reality. In this paper Winnicott described the 'gradual deepening of my appreciation of inner reality'. He reported his move from the use of 'phantasy' as the opposing pole to 'reality', to the juxtaposition of 'inner reality' with 'external reality'. In his following papers on early emotional development (such as Winnicott 1945, 1948), he explored the gradual development of the infant's capacity to perceive external reality objectively. This was very similar to Melanie Klein's view of the development of the depressive position and of the capacity to relate to the whole-object, and gradually withdraw the projections of the paranoid-schizoid position. But while for Melanie Klein the inner world remained of prime importance, even in the depressive position, for Winnicott the issue of paramount importance was the actual interactions of the infant with its environment, and the infant's experience of those interactions. Viewing the infant's actual interaction with its environment from the perspective of the dichotomy of inner reality/external reality, Winnicott distinguished between the 'subjective object' and the 'objectively perceived object' (1945). The first referred to an attitude towards the object in which the individual was predominantly under the impression of his own inner reality, in spite of the fact that he was interacting with another person. An interesting application of this idea is in Winnicott's discussion of the fact that some children brought to him for consultation had dreamed of him the night before the actual meeting. In Winnicott's view, this placed him in 'the role of subjective object, which rarely outlasts the first or first few interviews' (1971b: 4); that is, he was not being perceived by the child realistically but rather as a reflection of the child's inner reality.

But this dichotomy was not sufficient for Winnicott's purposes. The 'subjective object' was a concept that was closely related to Melanie Klein's concept of the internal object, and as such was 'projective entity' (Winnicott 1969: 89); namely, a product of the projections of the individual, rather than a realistic perception of, and experience of, another person. What Winnicott was striving to explore was the *transition* from a relationship with a subjective object, to a relationship in which the individual recognizes and relates to the object as an 'other-than-me' entity.[4] He considered the pathology of the borderline patient to be related to the breakdown of this process of transition (Winnicott 1969). He also considered cultural activity – art, religion and so on – to be related to an intermediate area between subjective and objective reality. He emphasized that what is involved in this intermediate area is an experience of 'illusion' which is not yet a symbol. Transitional phenomena constitute the 'root of symbolism' (Winnicott 1953: 234), without achieving the level of symbolism proper. Whereas symbolism implies the capacity to distinguish 'between fact and phantasy, between inner objects and external objects, between primary creativity and perception' (ibid.: 233), transitional phenomena constitute the beginning of the development of this capacity.

114

— subj obj
— obj: objectively perceived
+O - not me, but belongs to me

If we pause at this point we will notice that Winnicott conceived of the transitional object as being 'transitional' in a process that has two aspects. One aspect relates to the individual's capacity to begin conceiving of the external world as external; that is, outside of the subject. From this point of view, the nature of the transitional object as a 'first possession' (which Winnicott emphasized) refers to the idea that this object is no longer a *part* of the individual, although it still 'belongs' to him.[5] The transitional object is thus considered to play an important role in the development of the capacity to recognize the existence of external reality which the individual accepts as 'not-me'.

The second aspect relates to the infant's relationship to his mother and the process of separating from her. In this context, Winnicott's statement, 'The transitional object stands for the breast' (1953: 236), is of importance. Winnicott emphasized the crucial necessity of 'good-enough mothering' if a successful transition from a subjective object type of relationship, to the achievement of the capacity for a relationship with an objectively perceived object is to take place. 'Good-enough mothering' provides the infant with a feeling that the 'good breast' is part of itself (that is, a good internal object). It is this feeling of its own 'goodness' (good internal object) which Winnicott considers to be the basis of the infant's capacity to endow a 'thing' (blanket, teddy-bear and so forth) with the qualities of a transitional object.

Taking these two aspects together we might say that Winnicott was discussing the infant's transition from a relationship with the mother-not-yet-differentiated-from-the-self to a relationship with an object already differentiated from the self. One of the important aspects of this transition (for Winnicott) is that in it there is a need for a 'letting go' (of the mother-not-yet-differentiated-from-the-self) which is also a 'holding on'. The transitional object provides this need by being a 'not-mother', 'not-me' object (thus allowing a 'letting go'), which is yet related to the 'mother-which-is-part-of-me' (thus allowing a 'holding on').

In a later contribution to the study of the transitional process (which was one of his last published papers before his death), Winnicott (1969) added an important aspect to the concept of transitional phenomena, an aspect that may be seen as constituting a Winnicottian version of one of Melanie Klein's central ideas. While Melanie Klein emphasized that the capacity to relate to external reality in the depressive position was closely connected with the aggressive impulses towards the object, Winnicott, in his 1953 paper on transitional objects, seems to have ignored this aspect. For Winnicott, the Kleinian view of inborn aggression was problematic (he rejected out and out the concept of the death instinct – Winnicott 1962: 177). In a paper given in 1950 (Winnicott 1950–55) he had formulated the idea that there is a necessary connection between aggression and the capacity to experience an 'external object' (that is, an object experienced by the infant as existing externally to himself). He considered aggression to be the product of the meeting point of impulsivity and opposition.[6] Rather than a reaction to the frustration of wishes and impulses (which he considered to be a much later development), Winnicott described how the impulse itself, the life-force of even a foetus, is experienced as aggression as it meets an environment which serves as an opposition to its movement – 'I am suggesting: it is this impulsiveness and the aggression that develops out of it that makes the infant need an external object, and not merely a satisfying object' (Winnicott 1950–55: 217).[7]

This formulation, although connecting aggression and (the experience of) the 'external object', did not tie in specifically to the process of transition. Winnicott (1969) finally did complete this tie-in in his later paper on 'The use of an object'. There he reformulated his earlier distinction between subjective object and objectively perceived object in new terms – object-relating in contrast with object-usage. While traditionally object-relating implied a cathexis of, or an emotional investment in, the object, Winnicott considered it to be 'an experience of the subject that can be described in terms of the subject as an isolate' (ibid.: 88); that is, no actual object need be present. Thus object-relating corresponded with his conception of the subjective object. Object-usage, on the other hand, entailed 'the subject's placing the object outside the area of the subject's omnipotent control' (ibid.: 89). This, in Winnicott's opinion, entails destruction – 'it is the destruction of the object that places the object outside the area of the subject's omnipotent control' (ibid.: 90). It is only after the object has survived the subject's destructiveness that it is experienced as being more than a projection of a part of the self, more than a subjective object. Thus the transition from subjective object to objectively perceived object entails the ongoing destruction (in phantasy) and consequent survival of the object. With this formulation Winnicott completed his version of the Kleinian concept of the depressive position.

It is difficult to summarize Winnicott's contribution regarding transitional objects and phenomena, and the intermediate area of 'potential space'. Winnicott's style is more epigrammatic than a comprehensive statement of theory and his ideas are difficult to pinpoint, although very evocative. It is not the aim of this study to add to the criticism of Winnicott's work on this account (for example, Flew 1978; Brody 1980). Nor is it necessary to 'pinpoint' the details of Winnicott's concepts and attempt to build them into a strict theory (which might be like trying to force a square peg into a round hole). Rather, I would like to note what seems to be the thrust of Winnicott's work on this subject, which distinguishes his work from that of the Kleinians on the one hand, and from ego psychology (including the representational theorists) on the other.

116

In his 1953 paper on transitional objects and phenomena, after presenting the basic idea of the 'first possession', Winnicott proceeded with a section on 'Inadequacy of usual statement of human nature' (pp. 2–3).[8] In this section he stated his position, that it is not enough to describe human nature in terms of interpersonal relationships or in terms of 'inner reality'. He then put forward his claim for the need to postulate 'an intermediate area of experiencing to which inner reality and external life both contribute' (ibid.: 2). It was the development of this 'intermediate area' that Winnicott sought to explore, and he considered this development in the life of the infant to be related to the development of the infant's capacity to recognize the 'not-me'. But he did not think of this as a stage to be passed through and done with. Rather, he considered all of creative life, including therapy, to belong to this 'intermediate area'. In fact, the further this aspect of his thought is pursued, it becomes questionable whether any healthy aspect of living does not belong to this area![9]

This thrust differs from the two major trends mentioned earlier. The difference from the Kleinian approach is explicit: the Kleinian emphasis on the 'internal world' is its hallmark, and it was specifically in regard to the Kleinian approach that Winnicott felt there to be an inadequacy. In relation to ego psychology and the representational theorists discussed above, the difference is more subtle. Many analysts adhering to these trends have adopted Winnicott's concepts of transitional objects and phenomena.[10]

However, in spite of the popularity of Winnicott's concepts in these circles, there does seem to be an interesting difference of nuance involved. Much of the work within the framework of modern ego psychology follows a (somewhat) linear approach to development. Jacobson (and following her, Kernberg) described the linear differentiation of self and object representations out of a state of confusion of self and object images. Mahler described the phase-after-phase development from autism and symbiosis through the sub-phases of separation-individuation to the attainment of 'object constancy'. A paper of Kestenberg's (1971) may serve as a good example of the use of Winnicott's concept of transitional object within an ego psychology framework. According to this approach premature stages are passed through on the way to maturity. Although they may be considered to 'persist' as potentials for regression, even in terms of momentary regression in the dynamic emotional flow, the mature state is considered to be normative and, in health, predominant. Winnicott's orientation is very different, as becomes clear in his paper on 'The location of cultural experience' (1967). There it becomes clear that for Winnicott the 'intermediate area' and the 'potential space of play' are not merely (transitional) 'stages' in a linear progression. Rather, they are what life, creative living, is all about. This different perspective of Winnicott's, a sensibility regarding 'what life is all about', is difficult to integrate within the theoretical framework of ego psychology. Winnicott's radical statement that psychoanalytic theory 'seldom reach[es] the point at which we can start to describe what life is like apart from illness or absence of illness' (ibid.: 98) and his contention that his 'third area of play' begins to deal with 'the question of what life is about' (ibid.) is a pithy expression of the difference in perspective of these approaches.[11]

Kohut

One of the most influential, and controversial, figures in psychoanalysis in the last two decades is Heinz Kohut. His studies of narcissism and narcissistic personality disorders have led him gradually to reject many of the accepted tenets of psychoanalytic thought and propose new concepts, ideas and theories. His work has awakened much admiration and agreement on the one hand and much disagreement on the other, leading to the establishment of a new 'school' of psychoanalysis – 'self psychology'. This development is of relevance to the subject of the present study, especially because of one of the central concepts in Kohut's thought – the 'selfobject'.

Kohut's first monograph, *The Analysis of the Self* (1971), in which he introduced the concept of the 'selfobject',[12] presented a new approach to the understanding and treatment of narcissistic disorders. That work was couched in language compatible with traditional psychoanalytic theory, especially ego psychology, in spite of introducing new ideas regarding the place of narcissism in development.

In his second book, *The Restoration of the Self* (1977), Kohut changed his emphasis while retaining his main idea. He no longer attempted to present his ideas within the framework of ego psychology; rather, he considered the implications of his previous work to be that a new psychoanalytic psychology needed to be formulated, a 'psychology of the self'. He viewed the difference between his 1971 approach and his 1977 approach thus:

> Formerly, although the psychology of the self in the broad sense of the term was implicit in all my writings on the subject of narcissism, I defined the self exclusively in what I now call the psychology of the self in the narrow sense of the term, i.e. a psychology in which the self is a content of the mental apparatus. The additional conceptualizations of the psychology of the self in the broad sense of the term, i.e. a psychology in whose theoretical framework the self occupies a central position, is spelled out consistently for the first time in the present work.
>
> (1977: 207, n. 15)

118

With this shift in mind we will now turn to an examination of Kohut's concept of selfobject and its place in his general theoretical framework.

Kohut's perspective on narcissism began with his realization that his narcissistic patients were relating to him in an essentially different fashion from that described by traditional psychoanalysis regarding neurotic patients. Rather than reviving object-related wishes within the transference situation and directing them towards the analyst, Kohut found that narcissistic patients experienced a narcissistic transference. He specified two types of narcissistic transference – the idealizing transference and the mirroring transference. These differed from neurotic transferences in an important way: the analyst was not experienced (by the patient) as an object towards whom wishes were felt but rather as an (auxiliary) aspect, an extension, of the patient's self. Kohut termed this narcissistic experience of the object 'selfobject' – that is, the object is not experienced as a separate, autonomous individual, but rather as an anonymous function, fulfilling certain narcissistic needs (namely, mirroring and idealization) of the patient. Kohut noted the similarity of this concept to Anna Freud's (1952) concept of the 'need–satisfying' object. His view differed from that of Anna Freud in his emphasis on the function of the selfobject, not only to fulfil the subject's (narcissistic) needs, but also to allow the patient to acquire those 'narcissism–providing functions' as structures of his own self (via optimal frustration and 'transmuting internalization'). In other words, Kohut conceived of his patient's self as deficient in structure, and of the analyst's (selfobject) function as providing that structure.

Here a word is in order regarding Kohut's use of the concept of structure. Whereas generally in the psychoanalytic literature structure refers to some aspect of the mental apparatus, Kohut's use of the term is much more specific. In Kohut's writings structure refers to 'self-structure', to the person's capacity to maintain a satisfactory level of self-esteem in relation to his ambitions and ideals. Thus, the selfobject's function is to help the subject maintain his self-esteem inasmuch as he cannot do so by himself or inasmuch as his self is still lacking in structure.

Originally, Kohut (1971) considered this function of the selfobject to be a transitory function; in other words, as the self gained in structure it would no longer be in need of selfobjects to provide narcissistic needs. According to this view the selfobject was part of a developmental line leading to the 'true object': the young child first needs his objects to fulfil narcissistic functions he himself cannot fulfil before he is able to relate to them as separate individuals. This view provided a conception of the development of the self and of the corollary relationship between the developmental state of self-structure and the developmental stage of the relationship with the object (selfobject or true object).

In 1977 Kohut changed his view of this developmental scheme.[13]

Rather than viewing the selfobject experience as an early stage of development, Kohut emphasized that selfobject experiences continue throughout life; a person is always in need of selfobjects which he can experience as supporting his self in various ways. Eventually Kohut (1984: 52) distinguished three distinct aspects of selfobject functions: the selfobject as joyfully responding to the person (mirroring); available as a source of strength and calmness (idealizing); and 'being silently present but in essence like him' (twinship). A person is in need of selfobjects to provide these functions throughout life. Whereas in 1971 development was conceived as progress from selfobject to 'true object' relationships, later Kohut considered development to occur on a line from archaic selfobject to mature selfobject (1977: 188, n. 8; 1984: 70).

This distinction is less clear than the earlier one, for the simple reason that Kohut did not define what constitutes an archaic selfobject as opposed to a mature selfobject. Wolf (1980: 127) has stated that 'selfobject needs and relations do not disappear with maturation and development; they become more diffuse and less intense'.[14] One specific aspect that does seem to be implied as characteristic of archaic rather than mature selfobjects is what Kohut called 'merging'. Kohut used this term in 1971 to refer to a specific characteristic of the selfobject experience: the selfobject is experienced as part of the self rather than as a separate object. He considered this to be especially relevant in regard to the most archaic of the three forms of the grandiose self-transference ('merger through the extension of the grandiose self', 'twinship', and 'mirror' transferences). In 'merger through the extension of the grandiose self' there is no experience of a separate object; rather, the object (analyst) is experienced as an extension of the (grandiose) self. Of this transference Kohut states:

> Since, in this revival of the early state of primary identity with the object, the analyst is experienced as a part of the self, the analysand – within the sector of the specific, therapeutically mobilized regression – expects unquestioned dominance over him. The target of this archaic mode of narcissistic libidinal investment – in the analytic situation: the analyst – experiences this relationship in general as oppressive and he tends to rebel against the unquestioning absolutarianism and tyranny with which the patient expects to control him.
> (1971: 115)[15]

It would seem that merging continued to be considered by Kohut a central characteristic of archaic selfobject experiences as opposed to mature ones.

With this major change in Kohut's view of the place of selfobject experiences in development, there is implied a change in the concept itself (although no such change has been explicitly defined by Kohut). Originally (Kohut 1971) the concept of selfobject implied a primitive, preobject relationship, one in which the object was not related to as a separate, autonomous person. It referred to a level of relating, with the implication that any relationship could be either of a selfobject nature, or a true-object relationship. As such, it also implied a disturbance of a developmental capacity of the individual – a person could attain or not attain the capacity for true-object relationships; that is, could be fixated at (or regress to) the selfobject level.

In contradistinction with this concept of the selfobject as a developmental capacity, Kohut's later (1977) view has very different implications. The selfobject experience is viewed not as a definitive phase or capacity, but rather as an aspect of every relationship. Every relationship may affect the self (or, as Kohut termed it in 1977, the 'bipolar self'), playing some role in regard to the subject's ambitions, goals or skills, influencing his self-esteem. And, conversely, the self is continuously in need of relationships which will bolster its self-esteem in various ways (by mirroring, idealization or twinship). Thus selfobject experiences are no longer seen as being so distinctive and primitive as they originally were, but are rather an ongoing aspect of all interpersonal relationships (Kohut 1977: 187).

With this change in Kohut's conception of the selfobject, the difference between his general theory of personality and that of such theorists as Mahler and Kernberg becomes clear. Kohut contended that this concept of selfobject is diametrically opposed to concepts of 'separation of self and object' as definitive of normal development. Kohut considered the latter to be a 'value-laden demand for psychological independence' (1983: 452) – a demand which he vociferously rejected. He emphasized that mature development is not characterized by independence from selfobjects, but rather by mature self-selfobject relationships. He also emphasized that these mature self-selfobject relationships need not necessarily comply with what we would often consider to be a 'mature' relationship, as long as that relationship provides the psychological milieu in which the self can fulfil its creative goals. His example of Eugene O'Neill's relationship with his third wife highlights the difference of value-judgement between Kohut's view and the more traditional psychoanalytic views (1983: 454).[16]

The change in Kohut's conception of the selfobject is also very much in line with the change in his conception of his psychology of the self as mentioned above. In Kohut's narrow sense of the psychology of the self there was room for the concept of selfobject as a primitive stage of object representation. Kohut's broad sense of self-psychology does not view the mind as a mental apparatus with mental structures that represent external objects (mental representations of objects). Rather, it is the self – its ambitions, goals and skills – that is the basic conceptual framework, and it is questionable whether such a restructuring of the basic psychoanalytic conceptual framework leaves room for concepts of mental objects. Actually, the later concept of 'selfobject' is used in an ambiguous manner, by not defining the 'inner experience' as opposed to the actual person who is related to as a selfobject.[17] Thus Friedman, in his incisive review of Kohut's work, states unequivocally that 'the selfobject and its subdivisions are interpersonal terms and their intrapsychic correlates are defects, not structures' (1980b: 396).

Kohut's position is not as clear-cut as Friedman presents it, and in later papers Kohut makes an effort to state explicitly that 'Selfobjects . . . are inner experiences' (1983: 390–5; 1984: 49–53). Kohut thereby admitted the relevance of the 'age-old puzzle . . . [of] the "inside vs. outside" question' to his work (1983: 390), a puzzle he had hoped to avoid. It goes without saying that he did not solve this puzzle. His theory has been roundly criticized for emphasizing interpersonal interactions at the expense of intrapsychic processes, as determinants of the personality. The absence of concepts referring to intrapsychic structures related to (outside) persons (those concepts which have been termed mental objects in the present study) is another aspect of this bias of Kohut's theory.

In summary, Kohut's work has contributed two different concepts under the term 'selfobject'. Common to both is the emphasis on the functions of the object *vis-à-vis* the narcissistic needs of the subject. The crux of this concept is that there is an essential difference between relationships with objects that function as narcissistic supports and relationships in which the object is related to as an autonomous person towards whom the subject experiences (libidinal or aggressive) wishes. Unique to Kohut's conception is his emphasis on the narcissistic functions that the (self)object fulfils for the self. Later (1977), Kohut extended his view of the selfobject beyond a specific developmental phase, so that selfobject relationships could be considered as continuing throughout life. In so doing, Kohut seems to have removed the concept of selfobject from that group of concepts we have called 'mental objects' in the present study, referring to an aspect of interpersonal relationships, rather than to mental structures and processes.

PART TWO

Major theoretical issues

The historical survey above described the development of the wealth of concepts and ideas related to mental objects in the psychoanalytic literature, and the various theoretical contexts within which they developed. But beyond the various specific concepts that different authors have developed and proposed, it seems that there are a number of conceptual issues central to many of these concepts. It would seem that these conceptual issues, regarding which there are widely differing opinions in the psychoanalytic literature, contribute greatly to the diversity of concepts and ideas. In order to understand the diversity of concepts in the literature, these conceptual issues need to be delineated. In this part of the book I will present a delineation of those conceptual issues that I have found have played a central part in the development of the plethora of concepts described above.

This delineation of central conceptual issues related to the various concepts of mental objects also provides us with a map of the major dimensions of meaning that these concepts have occupied. As Sandler (1983) noted, psychoanalytic concepts have a tendency to expand and contract and acquire a variety of meanings and uses over the years. The delineation of a number of central conceptual issues which underlie the diversity of concepts provides us with a conceptual map of the different dimensions of meaning which these concepts have acquired. As Sandler noted, such a map is of use in our attempts to understand correctly the different meanings that concepts take on in different contexts. This conceptual map will also serve as a preliminary to a refocusing in the following chapter on the three central concepts of mental objects that I see as basic to psychoanalytic theory today.

The major issues that have come into focus are:

- origins of the mental object – internal or external;
- status of the mental object – experiential or non-experiential;
- the mental object and motivation;

- the mental object as a developmental capacity; and
- the position of the mental object *vis-à-vis* the self.

In addition, I will discuss a clinical issue – an issue I will call the 'division of responsibility' within the therapeutic setting – which brings together many of the elements of the theoretical issues presented here.

5

Origins of the mental object – internal or external

One of the basic dilemmas that has accompanied psychoanalytic theory from its very origin is that of the relative influence of internal versus external factors on the development of the personality. Undoubtedly, this issue is not dichotomous, and what is at issue is not a question of either/or. Recently, Mitchell (1988b) distinguished between four distinct aspects, or versions, of this issue.[1] Without going into the details of Mitchell's distinctions, I think that in many ways, and at many levels, the various different versions tend to boil down to their common denominator – internal versus external – and that it is fruitful to look at the concepts of mental objects as they relate to this issue.

Early in Freud's writings the issue of real early childhood seductions operating as traumata leading to the development of neurosis, versus wishful phantasies originating in inborn drives as the neurosogenic factor, arose. Following Freud's abandonment of his earlier view of the influence of real traumatic experiences (external) in favour of internally determined drives and phantasies,[2] the question of the relative influence of internal versus external factors remained a central one in psychoanalytic theory. Freud himself continued to wrestle with it in various contexts – for example, the case of the Wolf-man (1918b – especially in the context of the concept of the superego (1923b, 1924c, 1930a). In this context Freud deliberated on how it came to be that the superego was so much more severe than the actual parental behaviour on which it was supposedly based. It was this question which gradually led him to view the superego as heavily influenced by the subject's own drives (especially the aggressive drives) and not simply as a realistic 'introjection' of the parental figures (Freud 1930a).

As described above in the historical survey, this question regarding the origins of the superego, internal versus external, became one of the major points of divergence between the Kleinian view and that of Anna Freud and the Freudians in the 'Controversial Discussions' in the British Psycho-Analytical Society during the 1940s. While Melanie Klein and her followers developed a theory of personality that tended to view 'internal objects' (Melanie Klein did not distinguish between phantasies of objects and realistic object images) as reflecting (primarily) the drives, Anna Freud and the Freudians were careful to distinguish between the reality-orientated images of objects and those originating primarily from phantasy (for example, Glover 1945).

This same issue may also be seen to be related to a basic difference of psychoanalytic views regarding the relationship between phantasying and (what we may call) reality perception. Freud's (1911b) original position regarding these was that they originated in the two regulatory principles of mental functioning – the pleasure and reality principles. According to Freud, these two principles constitute two alternatives; mental life can be guided by one or by the other, or by various admixtures of them. After the reality principle had developed in infancy and childhood, phantasying was regarded as a regression to an earlier mode of operation, due to frustration of the drives in reality. This view, of phantasy as an alternative to reality perception, reflected Freud's tendency to a (rather) naïve view of perception as a direct process.[3] In correspondence with this view, Freud considered the ego to be the 'perceiving organ' of the mental apparatus (1923b). Hartmann (for example, 1956) and others continued this tendency to contrast phantasying with reality perception. An opposing tendency may be seen in the theoretical approach of Melanie Klein and her followers. Their view of phantasying is not as an alternative to reality perception, but rather as an ongoing (and underlying) process that exerts an ongoing influence on our perception of reality (Isaacs 1945, 1952). In fact, phantasying received such emphasis in Kleinian theory that the Kleinians were accused of ignoring the influence of real events on the lives of their patients (for instance, Grosskurth 1987). Be that as it may, Melanie Klein's theory of phantasy helped develop a slightly different view regarding Freud's distinction between two realms of reality – psychic and material (Freud 1900a)[4] – from that described above (that is, as alternatives).

These two views, that of ego psychology on the one hand and of Kleinian psychology on the other, are reflected in the concepts of mental objects formulated in each of these frameworks. Melanie Klein's concept of internal objects emphasized the degree to which underlying phantasies, internally derived from the life and death instincts, are considered to influence the perception of external objects. In the paranoid-schizoid position, projection of hate and envy into the breast are considered to be a basic process whereby the infant attempts to cope with the death instinct, which threatens his existence from within. But, while this process is considered to be necessary for the infant's continued mental existence, its influence on his perception of reality is such as to justify the use of the term 'paranoid'. The internal objects fostered by the dynamics of love and hate

126

in the infant's mind, according to Melanie Klein's theory, may be seen as an extreme example of the view that an individual's mental objects originate from within.[5]

In contrast, the concept of representation, as used in the writings of analysts orientated towards ego psychology such as Novey, Beres and Joseph, and Sandler and his co-workers, provides a different view regarding the internal versus external origins of mental objects. Hartmann's (1939) emphasis on the adaptive point of view led to Rapaport and Gill's (1959) inclusion of the adaptive point of view as one of the five basic points of view of psychoanalytic metapsychology. Their exposition of the adaptive point of view emphasized the centrality of the human posture *vis-à-vis* the environment 'at every point of life', not only as a tendency that develops during childhood (as may be implied in the concept of the reality principle).

In addition, a growing interest in the interpersonal relationships of early childhood and their influence on ego development (Kris 1950) contributed to the need for a concept that would convey the idea that the interactions with, and personalities of, emotionally significant people in the child's environment leave their imprint on the child's personality. Of course, such a concept already existed in psychoanalytic theory – the concept of identification. Freud's (1923b) view of the formation of the superego via identification (or introjection)[6] set the foundation for much of the later work on the ways in which the personalities of the parents influence the development of the child's personality, whether via the superego or directly via the development of the ego.[7] However, the concept of identification as an influence in the development of the child's personality covered only certain aspects of the influence of the parents' personalities on the child. Furthermore, conceptualization in terms of the developments of the ego and of the superego tended to focus consequent discussion on the drive-defence model. Following the growth of interest in the development and influences of the object on the personality, especially in the works of the Kleinians and object-relations theorists, there was a prominent need (in ego psychology-orientated theory) for conceptualization of the influences of the parents' personalities on the ways in which the child experienced his objects in later life. The concept which had served Freud so well to express the influence of the infantile in later life – the drives – had become too restricted. A concept was needed to bridge the gap between past and present, and between drives and reality (internal and external). The concept of representation came to be used to bridge that gap, implying a reality-orientated image of the object, while leaving room for the possibility of the influence of the drives on the 'shape' (or content) of the representation. Different analysts may be seen to emphasize to differing extents the influences of reality and of the drives, but the concept of representation itself seems to have been accepted as providing for both.

In accordance with this developing complexity embodied in the concept of representation, recent views, such as those presented by Sandler (Sandler and Joffe 1969; Sandler and Sandler 1986), Arlow (1969, 1985) and Wallerstein (1973, 1985), reflect a more complex view of reality perception and its relation to phantasying. According to these views, perception of reality is not a direct process, but rather is always influenced by 'a continuous stream of phantasy thinking, which is a persistent concomitant of all mental activity and which exerts an unending influence on how reality is perceived and responded to' (Arlow 1969: 29).

These views give expression to the progress made in psychoanalytic theory beyond a simplistic internal/external dichotomy towards a more complex conceptualization. This progress was nicely reflected in a recent conference on 'The intrapsychic and interpersonal dimensions: an unresolved dilemma' (Levi and Scharff 1988). In that conference the issue of intrapsychic and interpersonal dimensions was addressed in a global way, and only some of those presenting related specifically to the implications for concepts of mental objects. It seemed apparent that this issue has lost a good deal of its 'heat' (for example, Lichtenberg 1988; Mitchell 1988; Scharff 1988), while it could still be seen as underlying some of the interesting differences of opinion (for instance, Abend 1988; Gedo 1988; Mitchell 1988b; Stern 1988).[8]

In order further to exemplify the continuing, though attenuated, effects of the issue of internal versus external origin of mental objects, I will compare two papers advocating the use of the cognitive concept 'schema' in psychoanalytic theory (Wachtel 1980; Slap and Saykin 1983).[9] Both papers note Freud's tendency to view perception as a direct process, analogous to photography, and both propose that the concept of schema can help to correct this naïve deficiency in psychoanalytic theory. But while both are very similar in regard to the problem being addressed and the concepts proposed to deal with this problem, when inspected more carefully it may be seen that there is a wide difference between these two papers in regard to their views on the process of the perception of reality, especially in regard to the clinical implications of the use of the concept of schema in this context.

Slap and Saykin emphasize the role of (what they term) the 'pathological schema' in the context of the transference, as an explanation of the patient's difficulty in correctly perceiving reality. This pathological schema, built on conflictual infantile phantasies and memories, prevents the patient from correctly perceiving reality, by persistently assimilating a (possibly) more benign reality to its pathological aspects. Accommodation is considered to occur as a *Gestalt* of the working through process in the therapy, whereby the pathological aspects of the schema may be changed and adapted to reality.

In contrast, Wachtel emphasizes that both assimilation and accommodation are ongoing processes, and that the concept of schema may be applied to all processes of interpersonal perception (not only to pathological aspects). Especially of interest is Wachtel's emphasis on Piaget's view of schema as a reality-orientated structure, the function of which is to promote reality perception; at the same time he uses it to account for deficiencies in reality perception.

Slap and Saykin's view regarding a clear division between reality perception and distortion is very similar to the traditional view regarding the clear-cut division between reality perception and phantasy mentioned above. In contrast, Wachtel's view regarding the ubiquity of schemas as a basic structure underlying all perception of reality, both distorted and not, proposes a view whereby even distortion of reality is viewed in the framework of the individual's orientation towards reality, which may not always be successful in accurately perceiving reality. Distortions of reality perception are viewed not simply as internally determined (as in Slap and Saykin's view), but rather as involving the interaction of (external) reality and (internal) schemas, both seen as contributing to the final form of the percept. Wachtel's emphasis on the ongoing interaction between the internal factor (schema) and external reality leads him to a reappraisal of technique in regard to the relative contributions of internal and external factors in the transference. The connection between the conceptual issue regarding the (internal versus external) origin of the mental object and the clinical issue regarding the role of the analyst in the formation of the transference will be further discussed in Chapter 10.

Suffice it to state here that the subtle difference between the views of Slap and Saykin on the one hand, and Wachtel on the other, regarding the conceptual issue of the relative influence of internal and external factors in the formation of the mental object (in this case referred to as 'schema') lead them to far-reaching differences in clinical technique.

This example of the role of internal versus external factors in relation to mental objects bears witness to the subtleties and intricacies of the interweaving of internal and external factors in the formation of the individual's understanding of, and response to, the world. As we have noted, psychoanalytic theory has come a great distance, even from Freud's already complex views regarding the influence of motivation on such mental processes as memory and symbolization. In spite of the distance travelled, and the complexities recognized, on this path, there is still a need to point to the conceptual implications of our terminological baggage, to remain aware that the different terms used are often invested with certain implications regarding the (simplistically termed) internal/external reality issue. Part Three will attempt to delineate some of the concepts on this dimension.

6

Status of the mental object – experiential or non-experiential

As Sandler and Joffe (1969) have stated, much confusion in regard to psychoanalytic concepts may be avoided by clarifying whether a concept under discussion belongs to the experiential or non-experiential realm. This distinction is especially important in psychoanalytic theory because many concepts refer to unconscious experiences. However, not every aspect of mental functioning inaccessible to consciousness should be considered 'unconscious'. The term 'unconscious' should be reserved for experiences which are not conscious for dynamic or other reasons, and which could conceivably attain consciousness, as during an analysis or otherwise. Concepts such as structures (id, ego and superego), defence mechanisms, ego functions and so on do not refer to experiences which may be brought to consciousness. Rather, they refer to hypothetical aspects of the 'mental apparatus', a theory of the structure and modes of functioning of the personality. This has been compared with the area of linguistics, for instance, where, although our use of language is considered to be regulated by the rules of syntax, these rules do not refer to the experiential realm; that is, they are not considered to be 'known' to the speaker, whether consciously or otherwise. More recently, Sandler (1990a) has further explained this distinction as referring to the notion that the analyst makes use of constructs to organize their understanding of the patient.

Historically, this distinction played an important part in the theoretical debates in the British Society during the 1940s regarding Melanie Klein concept of 'internal objects'. That concept especially was seen as embedded in conceptual confusion in relation to the realm of discourse being employed (A. Strachey 1941; Brierley 1942, 1944; Glover 1945). This confusion was especially prominent in connection with the concept of the superego as used by the Kleinians in contrast to the Freudians. Melanie Klein used the concept of superego almost synonymously with that of the internal object, referring to a phantasy,[1] while the Freudians emphasized the superego as a structure (for example, Glover 1945: 84–5; 1947: 498–9).

130

For the Freudians this implied a process of development in which what had previously been an object-image developed into a depersonalized structure.[2] Susan Isaacs (1945, 1952) rejected the criticism on behalf of the Kleinians, formulating the Kleinian view that theory has to adhere closely to subjective experience, and that the concepts used regarding the operation of the mental realm all have their origin in the primitive sensual 'phantasies' of the infant. This approach continues to guide the thinking of Kleinian psychoanalysts to the present time (for instance, Segal 1978), and continues to be the source of much criticism of the Kleinian approach (for example, Kernberg 1969).[3] An extreme expression of this view may be found in Bion's theory, according to which functions of the personality (perceptual functions, memory, judgement and so on) may be experienced as dangerous and may be evicted from the personality by way of projective processes, leading to actual disturbances in those functions. This notion clearly places phantasy images and ego functions at the same level of discourse with no distinction between them, an unacceptable approach from the ego psychology point of view.[4]

To a large extent, the distinction between experiential and non-experiential parallels Hartmann's (1939) and Rapaport's (1967) distinction between the 'inner' (experiential) and 'internal' (non-experiential) worlds. Schafer (1968) followed this distinction in regard to 'introjects' and what he calls 'primary process presences', which he considers refer to subjective experience, on the one hand, and representations and their cathexes, which refer to 'metapsychological' (that is, theoretical, non-experiential) realms of discourse, on the other. Wallerstein (1976), using Sandler's distinction, further analysed concepts related to 'defence' and defence mechanisms to distinguish between concepts referring to the experiential realm from the more hypothetical, mechanistic concepts. In his attempt to outline the basis for a non-metapsychological theory of psychoanalysis, Rubinstein (1976) made a similar distinction between 'experiential' and 'inferred' mental processes.

This distinction, between concepts referring to the experiential and non-experiential realms, is of general importance within psychoanalytic theory for a basic understanding regarding the universe of meaning of psychoanalytic concepts, which by their nature remain imprecisely defined as to their referents. This is due, of course, to the fact that the referents of psychoanalytic concepts are of a highly private and introspective nature, not given to measurement by objective methods (in spite of various attempts by psychoanalytic researchers to the contrary). Following Freud's tendency to anthropomorphize his pseudo-physical concepts (Grossman and Simon 1969), psychoanalytic concepts came to be too distended in both directions, a tendency which led, during the 1970s, to a 'revolt' against metapsychology in general (for example, Gill and Holzman 1976;

G. Klein 1976). Sandler's distinction between the two different kinds of psychoanalytic concepts provides a much-needed tool to regain a measure of conceptual clarity. In regard to the group of concepts under study here, this distinction is definitely of importance, and will play a central role in the delineation of basic concepts in Part Three.

7

The mental object and motivation

Ever since Freud placed the drives at the centre of his theory of neurosis, motivation has been a primary concern of psychoanalytic theory. So too in therapy, where the classical aim of analysis has been seen as the revealing of hidden (unconscious) motives, which have largely been conceptualized as wishes. The central position of motivation in psychoanalytic theory is also reflected in the fact that various alternatives have been proposed over the years for Freud's original conceptualization of motivation, replacing Freud's concept of the drives with other concepts, such as love–hate (Melanie Klein), object–libido (Fairbairn), merger–separation (Mahler), feeling of safety (Sandler), stability of self (Kohut) – but always retaining the cent- rality of motivation in both theory and therapy.[1]

The question of the nature of mental objects *vis-à-vis* motivation is thus an important one in psychoanalytic theory. Fairbairn (1944: 132) debated whether his concept of internal objects should be used to refer to a source of motivation, tending to restrict motivation to 'ego–structures' and not to attribute motivation to 'internal objects'. Similarly, those theoreticians making use of the concept 'mental representation' tend to oppose strongly attributing motivation to the referents of this concept (for example, Schafer 1968).[2] In contrast, Melanie Klein emphasized the view that internal objects are sources of motivation, being, in her view, direct expressions of the instincts.

One way of looking at this issue is in the context of our conception of the mind. The Kleinians have proposed a view of the mind divided in itself, with different 'parts' of it interacting with, and often warring against, each other.[3] This view has been referred to as a dramatic frame of reference (Bianchedi *et al.* 1984), and has been adopted by others who portray the mind as a theatre within which different parts are acted out, all being 'parts' of the mind (for example, Fairbairn 1952; McDougall 1985). In this view of 'mind', an individual's feelings, actions, reactions, thoughts and so on are all considered to express or reflect these internal, interacting parts (or aspects) of the self, all of which are viewed as having motivational status.

In contrast, other theoreticians consider the Kleinian view to be too concrete, mistaking subjective experience for theory. (This, of course, returns us to the issue discussed above – the experiential/non-experiential status of mental objects.) While a person may experience themselves as made up of different 'parts' interacting between themselves, and while it may be effective to use such concrete language in the clinical situation with a patient,[4] 'theory' demands a higher level of abstraction, a view of the person from the 'outside' and not simply a restatement of their subjective experience, argue the critics (for instance, Glover 1945; Brierley 1951; Schafer 1968, 1976; Kernberg 1969). According to this view, it is the function of theory to explain, and not merely to describe. Thus, distinction must be made between those factors that motivate behaviour, and the various 'materials' upon which the motivating factors operate. The paradigm for this view in psychoanalytic theory is Freud's distinction between 'energy' (libido) and 'idea' in his theory of the drives. In more recent formulations other constructs have come to replace Freud's hypothetical 'psychic energy', due to widespread criticism of the inadequacy and the mechanistic nature of that concept (for example, Rosenblatt and Thickstun 1970; G. Klein 1976; Sandler and Sandler 1978; Gill 1983a). However, whatever the specific motivating factor, most psychoanalytic views deem it of importance to distinguish, at the level of theory, between what is and what is not a source of motivation.

Despite this clear-cut distinction between Kleinian and related views on the one hand, and the more orthodox view on the other, intermediate positions also exist, bearing witness to the complexity of the issue. I mentioned above Fairbairn's hesitations regarding the motivational nature of 'internalized objects', not wanting to follow Melanie Klein in the direction of equal status for all players in the theatre of the mind, in spite of the fact that in his analysis of the dream as reflecting the 'state of self' he did just that (Fairbairn 1944). Similar difficulties have been encountered by Sandler (1990a), who has recently reiterated his view that internal objects are not to be considered 'active agents' within the personality, but rather as reflections of, or depositories for, the individual's own wishes and feelings. Although this statement is in accord with the more accepted view of what does and what does not constitute motivation in psychoanalytic theory, it does not sit well with Sandler's view of internal objects as providing a 'feeling of safety', which Sandler does consider to be a motivational factor (Sandler 1985: 241).

Meissner (1981), who has emphasized the introjects as a very central aspect of the personality, has also encountered this difficulty in regard to their motivational nature (for example, Meissner 1976). Recently, Pine (1988, 1989) has elaborated a 'four-fold' view of the various psychologies of psychoanalysis (drive, ego, object-relations and self), each with its own

134

view of motivation. It is of interest in this context that, in regard to motivation in the object-relations frame of reference, Pine considers object representations to play a major role in the 'tendency to repeat old object relations'. Although he does not view the object representations themselves as motivating forces, it becomes clear that at the clinical level these object representations are viewed as tending to perpetuate experience in accordance with them and draw the individual to seek out repetitions of previous experiences. Thus Pine continues in the direction developed by Fairbairn, making the concept of mental object a major determiner of behaviour (feelings, thoughts and so on), without designating it as a source of motivation. Critics of this point of view tend to find fault with it for replacing the traditional concepts of motivation (instinctual wishes) with object-related concepts as sources of motivation (for example, Gedo 1979; Kanzer 1979; Rangell 1985). Thus the issue of the nature of concepts of mental objects regarding motivation remains a thorny one in psychoanalytic theory.

8

The mental object as a developmental capacity

Another major issue that needs clarification regarding the various concepts related to mental objects is that related to the 'developmental' frame of reference and the development of various 'capacities' of the individual. Freud expressed interest in the idea that different psychopathologies were related to different periods in the child's life even before he arrived at the conclusion that children were sexual beings (for example, Freud 1950a: Letter 46). His original ideas were related to the conjecture that differences in types of psychopathology could be traced to differences in the age at which the child underwent the traumatic seduction. Later, after he developed the theory of infantile sexuality (1905d), and gradually sketched out the different stages of the development of the libido, he remained interested in the possibility of specifying different pathologies as related to different libidinal stages (for instance, 1908b, 1913i, 1914c). Furthermore, he extended this approach to include different character traits, and eventually also a view of different character types, all on the basis of different levels of libido corresponding to the different libidinal phases (1931a).

Freud's views on development received considerable elaboration due to Karl Abraham's contributions. Especially relevant to the subject under study here is Abraham's (1924) proposal of a theory of the development of the stages of object-love, parallel to the stages of the development of libidinal organization. This proposal laid the groundwork for many of the ideas and concepts regarding mental objects that have been put forward in psychoanalytic theory. But in addition to the many specific ideas related to Abraham's theory of the development of object-love, Abraham's proposal contributed by extending the developmental approach to other areas of mental life in addition to the libidinal stages. This extension of the psychoanalytic theory of development of other areas was further taken up by the ego psychology approach, especially in relation to child analysis (see Kris's 1950 and 1951 reviews of the development of ego psychology and child analysis). This direction of interest included both childhood development and disturbances in such development, on the one hand, and, from

136

the clinical side, the 'widening scope' of psychoanalytic treatment on the other (for instance, as described by Settlage 1980).

The psychoanalytic view regarding developmental capacities and their disturbances is related to the encounter between psychoanalytic developmental theory and the widening scope of treatment. As psychoanalytic therapy was offered to a growing range of pathological conditions, interest in the early developmental disturbances that were considered to have produced this pathology increased. The growing psychoanalytic interest in the severe pathologies, in their diagnosis and treatment, led psychoanalysts to attempt to conceptualize these pathologies in terms related to early developmental disturbances.[1]

One of the issues that is under debate in connection with the present emphasis on what may be called the 'developmental point of view' may be seen in the contrast with what, till recently, has been referred to as the 'genetic point of view' (Hartmann and Kris 1945; Rapaport and Gill 1959).[2] While the psychoanalytic 'genetic point of view' was, presumably, the basis for psychoanalytic developmental psychology (for example, Rapaport 1960), the subtle but definite difference between them remains an important issue in psychoanalytic theory today. The genetic point of view may be described as a theory of the pathogenesis of neurotic symptoms, which are considered to be formed on the basis of the continuing influence of infantile wishful phantasies. As such, it relies on after-the-fact explanations, largely (though not exclusively) in the framework of reconstruction in adult analysis. In contrast, the developmental point of view has been described as a theory of the growth and development of personality as a whole, which takes into consideration both phantasy and interpersonal interactions in its exploration of the origins of defects and disturbances in the personality (Kennedy 1971; Abrams 1977, 1978; Settlage 1980).

Another recent definition of this difference (Shane and Shane 1989) has been formulated in terms of the contrast between a view according to which maturation ends at a certain age, maturity being a non-developmental state, and the view that development is an ongoing, lifelong process. According to the first, more traditional, view, the surfacing of pre-maturity issues constitutes regression, which is often viewed as a defensive process. According to the second view, developmental issues originating in childhood continue to be central in all of later life. At the clinical level, this has been seen to be related to the issue of the role of the analyst as (only) a screen for projections and transference, versus the view of the patient's need for a 'new object experience' (Shane and Shane 1989: 333–9) and the 'real relationship' with the analyst (Greenson 1971).

Another difference that should be noted in relation to the difference between the genetic and the developmental points of view is related to the conflict/defect issue. The genetic point of view placed almost exclusive emphasis on conflict and compromise formation as the basic concepts of analytic understanding, emphasizing the role of repressed childhood wishes and their concomitant defensive formations as the 'codetermine[rs of] all subsequent psychological phenomena' (Rapaport and Gill 1959: 806). In contrast, the developmental point of view emphasizes, to a great extent, the concept of defect as of major explanatory value. Defects in self–object differentiation, in object constancy and self constancy and so on, are used, in this frame of reference, to explain data formerly viewed as related to conflict (for example, London 1973; Pine 1985).[3]

This difference in view leads to differences in the use of these concepts by the various authors, and also to differences in the clinical technique adopted. Views emphasizing conflict emphasize the importance of interpretation as the major therapeutic intervention, whereas views emphasizing defect of developmental capacities tend to more non-interpretative interventions. This difference of opinion is especially prominent in relation to the therapy of psychotics – for example, Arlow and Brenner (1969), on the one hand, and Wexler (1971) and London (1973), on the other – but may also be seen to be of increasing importance in regard to analysis in general (Friedman 1978). Similarly Kohut's (1984) emphasis on the 'understanding' aspect of therapy as opposed to the 'explaining' aspect, may be seen to be related to his view of developmental defect, as opposed to conflict, as the major pathogenic factor.

It is here that concepts of mental objects become involved in the growing developmental point of view. Whereas Freud's concept of the 'mnemic image' of the object was sufficient for a conflict theory, based on the repression of infantile wishes and phantasies, this idea was too limited for the developmental point of view. The exploration of the origins (in developmental defects) of adult psychopathology went together with concepts of mental objects that were viewed as developmental capacities (and not as static structures). The view that differentiated self and object representations are a developmental achievement, one which may also not be achieved, added a new dimension to the concept of representation. The same is true of the concept of object constancy, which added the quality of integratedness as a developmental achievement *vis-à-vis* representations. Under the influence of these concepts, the concept of the mature (that is, differentiated and integrated) representation came to be viewed as a basic structure – as it were, a building block – of the mature personality, in the theories of Jacobson, Mahler and Kernberg. In the last part of this book, 'A conceptual analysis', I will further discuss the implications and changes involved in this added dimension of meaning.

9

The position of the mental object
vis-à-vis the self

Even more so than other concepts discussed here the concept of 'self' in psychoanalytic theory is one regarding which there is little, if any, consensus. It is far beyond the scope of this study to undertake a systematic and comprehensive review of the vicissitudes of meaning of that concept within psychoanalytic theory, but because of the close connection between concepts of mental objects and that of the self, some comment must be made regarding the influence of the variety of issues regarding the concept of self on the various concepts of mental objects. In order to do so, I will first describe the two major directions that have developed regarding the concept of self in the psychoanalytic literature to date.

As noted by Strachey, as editor of the Standard Edition, translation of the German word '*Ich*' in Freud's writings presented a problem, and the choice to use the Latin term '*ego*' rather than the term 'self' was not a wholesale solution (Editor's introduction to 'The ego and the id', in *SE* 19: 7–8). But it was not until Hartmann (1950) pointed the way to a systematic distinction between the concepts of ego and self that the concept of self could be extracted from the widely used concept of the ego. Looking back, of course, we can point to analysts whose use of the term 'ego' was much closer to that later reserved for self (for example, Federn, Melanie Klein and Fairbairn). Actually, Hartmann did not discuss the concept of self, but rather that of self-representation. In this manner, Hartmann defined a strict distinction between the ego as a structure – non-experiential, in Sandler and Joffe's (1969) terms – and the self-representation, as an image one has of oneself. Edith Jacobson, in many of her writings, greatly elaborated on Hartmann's use of self-representation, which took on distinct structural connotations, as I have described above in the historical survey. But, even as extended by her, and further by Mahler and by Kernberg, the concept remained restricted to a representation, and did not further develop to a theory of self.

The two theoreticians who did use the concept of self as a distinct and autonomous idea were Winnicott and Kohut. Their uses of the concept of

139

self, while differing one from the other, have in common the idea that this concept refers to a (or, the) basic aspect of the individual, related to the sense of self, to which motivation is attributed. This 'sense of self' or 'self-feeling' must, according to these views, be protected and allowed to develop and grow, and all (or much) of an individual's behaviour may be seen as related to or serving such processes of protection and growth. In this manner the self becomes a major explanatory construct, replacing those formerly used, such as drives and defences, wished-for relationships with objects, feeling states and so on. More recently, more traditional theoreticians, such as Modell (1990), Meissner (1981) and Lichtenberg (1983), have adopted views approaching those of Winnicott and Kohut in regard to the concept of self, attempting to integrate them with the traditional concepts of ego and drives.

Returning to the issue of the place of mental objects *vis-à-vis* the self, we must take into consideration what concept of self is being used. Following the distinction drawn above, between concepts of self-representation and concepts of self, we may see the different issues engendered in relation to each. In relation to concepts of self-representation, issues regarding the ways in which the self-representation is changed, under the influence of the object and in relation to it (including the various processes described under the headings of projection, internalization, introjection and so on), are of major importance. Much effort has been invested in the psycho-analytic literature in attempts to unravel these concepts from one another, especially those related to processes of internalization (incorporation, introjection, identification and their various aspects). Hartmann and Loewenstein (1962), Loewald (1962), Schafer (1968), Kernberg (1976) and Meissner (1981) all tended to distinguish among the various processes of internalization (and especially between introjection and identification) on the basis of the degree of integration into the ego. Identification was considered to lead to a greater degree of integration into the ego, while introjection was considered to lead to a condition in which the new structure is not completely integrated into the ego and retains a degree of 'otherness'. These theoreticians all discuss these processes in relation to the ego, but it is not difficult to see that in the same way these processes differ in their influence on the self-representation. In fact, the distinction be-tween the concept of self-representation and that of object representation relates to such differences regarding the degree of internalization (the degree of 'selfness' versus 'otherness'). This is borne out in Sandler's (1960) definition of identification as the modification of the self-representation on the basis of the object representation.

Another question of interest in relation to the concept of self-representation is that of the relative distinction or differentiation between self-representation and object representation and the concomitant question of their merger, or fusion. The exploration of these processes (for example, by Jacobson, Mahler, Searles and others) has constituted a major break-through in the psychoanalytic work with deeper pathology compared with the neurotic level which had earlier been considered analysable. It is of interest to note that Freud (1930a: 64–73) expressed his own personal alienation from these phenomena, in the context of a discussion of an 'oceanic feeling' as part of religious experience, which Freud understood in terms of an ego feeling predating the boundaries of the ego (or self)[1] *vis-à-vis* the world. It is also of interest to note that the implications of such phenomena for therapeutic technique, especially[2] in regard to the therapy of choice for psychosis, remains a major area of debate.

In relation to concepts of self, on the other hand, different issues seem to be of primary importance. Thus we see both Winnicott and Kohut, separately but similarly interested primarily in the actual roles played by the emotionally important people surrounding the individual, and their influence on the development of the self. This emphasis on the 'actual' behaviour of the surrounding objects – that is, on interpersonal relationships rather than intrapsychic processes – is not, of course, a clear-cut matter. Both groups of theoreticians, those stressing concepts of self-representation and those stressing concepts of self, are interested in both interpersonal and intrapsychic processes.[3] But it does seem that there is a (general) correlation between the use of certain concepts of self (and self-representation) and the use of certain concepts of mental objects. In relation to this I would also mention Kohut's gradual move from the use of the concept 'self-object' to refer to a specific (intrapsychic) attitude on the part of the individual towards others (namely, a specific kind of object representation) in his first book (Kohut 1971), and his later emphasis on 'self–selfobject relations', in which 'selfobject' seems to refer (to a much greater extent, if not entirely) to the other person (that is, the external object).[4]

10

Responsibility – the clinical issue

As a summary of the theoretical and conceptual issues discussed above, I would like to discuss the clinical issue of responsibility, which is a meeting point for some, if not all, of the above issues. By 'responsibility' (or ownership) I refer to the acknowledgement of various wishes, desires, thoughts, feelings, behaviours and so on, as one's own (Loewald 1979) and the recognition of how one brings about certain of the situations and conditions in which one finds oneself (Gill 1977). (This, of course, does not imply legal responsibility, which is a different issue.) Freud (1925i) discussed the question of the 'moral responsibility' of the dreamer for his dream (although here I will not enter into the 'moral' aspects of responsibility, which may be viewed as a specific and restricted area of responsibility in general). For Freud this was intimately connected with his view of the therapeutic process, whereby those aspects of the personality experienced as 'not belonging' – 'the it' (the id) – are accepted as part of the patient's 'I' (ego) – 'where id was there ego shall be' (Freud 1933a).

Loewald (1971) has noted that responsibility for wishes and desires is also implied in the therapeutic process of bringing unconscious wishes and desires to consciousness, with consciousness implying that aspect of 'self-responsibility' that is so crucial for the success of psychoanalytic treatment (p. 63). This process, of owning up to one's wishes and desires rather than attributing them to external situations and forces, may be the process that Freud himself underwent (or traversed) in his rejection of his theory of childhood seduction in favour of a theory of drives and wishes. This process, of acceptance of responsibility or ownership, may be seen to lie at the basis of the therapeutic quest according to many of the trends of thought in psychoanalytic theory, whether the originally 'disowned' aspects be Oedipal or pre-Oedipal drives, wishes and defences, or whether they be 'parts' of the self projected 'into' objects (both external and internal), and so forth. Schafer's (1976) 'action language' is an exemplar of this approach, viewing all thoughts, feelings and so on as 'actions' on the part of the person, actions to which the person must own up.[1]

Whereas Freud focused on the id–ego axis in regard to the question of responsibility and ownership (an intrapsychic emphasis), later theorists emphasized the axis of self–other. We have seen how, with the introduction of the concept of projective identification as a central process both in the development of personality and in therapy (first in the Kleinian tradition and gradually in other related approaches), the question of what we may call the 'division of responsibility' between the patient and the therapist became a central one. The Kleinian view has been regarded as the extreme view in psychoanalytic theory, considering the individual responsible not only for their own feelings, thoughts and so on, but also responsible, via processes of projective identification, for the feelings and thoughts of their objects. In this approach, it is only the 'inner world' of the individual that is of importance, with reality functioning mainly as a 'container' for the projected aspects of the individual's inner world.

Melanie Klein's approach set the scene for a shift regarding the issue of responsibility and ownership from the id–ego axis to that of the self–other. Following Klein, Fairbairn and Winnicott (and, of course, others) took up the same questions regarding this axis, differing from Klein on how the responsibility and ownership between self and other were to be divided. In the United States, Edith Jacobson and Margaret Mahler too accepted Klein's designation of the axis self–other as that of basic interest, but again, as with Fairbairn and Winnicott, differing from Klein in regard to the division of responsibility. Interestingly, Jacobson and Mahler especially emphasized a developmental approach, stating the problem in terms of the development of the individual's capacity to distinguish consistently between self and other in a realistic manner.

The contrasting position regarding the division of responsibility between self and other is that proposed by Kohut. While Kohut's self psychology began (1971) with a theory in which the individual's emotional attitude towards others (that is, the narcissistic attitude towards the other as 'self-object') was the 'responsibility' of the individual (in other words, was emphasized as specifically *their* attitude, an expression of a specific dynamic of that individual's personality), this view was soon to change. Via a theory emphasizing the centrality of 'self structure', with other people seen mainly as functioning to promote or detract from the healthy development of the self, Kohut (1984) eventually came to emphasize the actual responsibility of 'others' for the cohesion of the individual's self structure.

This issue, of the division of responsibility or ownership between self and other at the clinical level, has recently become the object of major interest in discussions between the proponents of the various different psychoanalytic trends. The boom of interest in the concept of empathy, especially emphasizing (following Kohut) the *analyst's* empathy, has focused attention on many aspects of the analytic relationship as 'belonging to', or the responsibility of, the analyst, under the label of failures of empathy on his part. Formerly, or according to the view of more orthodox analysts, these aspects have been attributed to resistance or transference on the part of the patient.[2] Thus, by taking what may be considered to be a radical stance on this issue, Kohut has thrown into doubt the previously accepted division of responsibility between self and other (patient and analyst).

Another interesting example of the growing interest in this issue is the work of Gill (1982, 1983b; Gill and Hoffman 1982) on the analysis of transference. While Gill's interest and emphasis on the analysis of transference are certainly well within the scope of the ego psychology tradition of which Gill was originally a major proponent (together with Rapaport, Schafer and Holt), his view on the role of what he calls the 'actual analytic situation' in the transference is, as he recognizes, a radical shift in emphasis. This shift may be seen in relation to the issue of the division of responsibility between patient and analyst, with Gill adopting a view that calls for a greater extent of acceptance of responsibility on the part of the analyst for the patient's reactions. Arguing that 'no matter how much the analyst may limit the range and intensity of his behaviour the analytic situation remains an interpersonal one' (Gill 1982: 107), Gill calls for analysts to examine, to a greater extent than had previously been thought proper, the influence of their own behaviours, both active and passive, on the patient's reactions. He considers it to be a necessary part of the resolution of the transference to discover what behaviour on the part of the analyst had triggered the patient's reaction, and to understand the plausibility of the patient's interpretation of that behaviour. Thus the division of responsibility within the here-and-now situation is changed, with the analyst called upon to take a greater share of the responsibility.

Gill does not follow Kohut to the extent of accepting the patient's interpretation of the meaning of the analyst's behaviour as necessarily 'correct', or of accepting the fact of there having been a failure of empathy on the part of the analyst just on the basis of the patient's having felt such. Rather, Gill considers the patient's subjective experience and interpretation of the analyst's behaviour to be but one of several possible reactions and interpretations. Patient and analyst together may then explore why the patient tends to react or interpret in the way he does, returning us to the more traditional approach. But, in spite of this, Gill's view does advocate an important shift in the division of responsibility between patient and analyst, though one more moderate than that suggested by Kohut.[3]

Viewed in terms of the subject of this study, the clinical issue of responsibility may be viewed in terms of the concepts different theoreticians apply to it. Here enter, to a great extent, the conceptual issues discussed above, especially regarding the issues of the internal versus external origin of mental objects, their motivational status and their position *vis-à-vis* the self. It may be seen in the literature that certain tendencies regarding these conceptual issues are conducive to a more radical view regarding the clinical issue of responsibility (that is, an emphasis on the analyst's responsibility). Thus a tendency to use concepts of mental objects to refer to structures that are considered to originate in, and reflect, the external world, rather than the self and internal motivation, is more conducive to the view allowing for a greater degree of responsibility of the analyst for aspects of the analyst–patient relationship.

Kohut's later use of the concept of 'selfobject' in the context of 'self–selfobject relationship' as referring to the actual behaviour of the other *vis-à-vis* the self (as opposed to his earlier use of 'self-object' as an intrapsychic concept), is conducive to his position calling for increased responsibility on the part of the analyst, via the notion of 'failures of empathy'. Similarly, Gill's emphasis on the influence of input from the 'actual analytic situation' – namely, the external origin of the patient's mental objects – leads to his position calling for a lessening of the one-sidedness of the traditional division of responsibility between patient and analyst. Thus we see the close (though not definitive) connection between the conceptual issues dealt with above and the clinical issue of division of responsibility.

PART THREE

A conceptual analysis

Following the discussion of theoretical and clinical issues presented above, I shall present a delineation of the three concepts that focus the central meanings regarding mental objects in the psychoanalytic literature today. This proposal does not purport to solve the many questions that remain regarding the various concepts of mental objects. Rather, it is presented as a conceptual map of the central meanings that have developed in the psychoanalytic literature, integrating the different issues discussed above.

The three major concepts of mental objects which I shall present are:

- mental objects as representations (or schemas);
- mental objects as phantasies; and
- mental objects as basic structures of the personality (or developmental capacities).

11

Mental objects as representations (or schemas)

Ever since Freud's statement that 'Hysterics suffer mainly from reminiscences' (Freud and Breuer 1895: 7), psychoanalytic theory has been interested in the influence of past memories on the present. But both Freud's theory of perception and his theory of memory appear naïve to the modern reader – his theory of perception as being one of 'direct' or 'photographic' perception (Wallerstein 1973; Schimek 1975; Wachtel 1980), and his theory of memory as a trace theory (Paul 1967), according to which memories are stored as distinct memory traces which may be later 'cathected' or 'innervated'. As Rapaport (Levy and Rapaport 1944) stated regarding Freud's theory of memory: 'The psychoanalytic theory of memory is based on the view that memory traces are used by psychic forces which find expression through them' (p. 152).

As psychoanalytic theory developed from a theory of the drives to a more general ego psychology, the influence of the past on the present came to be seen in terms of the formative influences on the development of the ego. This shift in perspective granted greater emphasis to the role of the environment in the child's development, and within this context, of course, to the influence of early object relations (Kris 1950). As the relationship with the emotionally significant others of childhood came into focus as a whole, rather than specific drives and wishes and the defensive reactions to them, the concept of object took on a more inclusive meaning than that implied by the concept of the 'drive object'.[1] It was under the influence of this shift in emphasis in psychoanalytic theory that the concept of the mental representation of the object came to assume a significance beyond that of a 'memory trace' in the service of instinctual wishes.

Thus 'object representations' were not considered to be only specific 'images' of objects revived in response to the awakening of various wishes (although they are considered to provide the basis upon which such images are based), but also the amalgamation of all the experiences the individual has of his objects, including his actual interactions with them and their emotional meanings, as well as the distortions of realistic aspects under the

149

influence of drives and phantasies. As such a mental representation of an object refers to a 'schema'[2] which, on the basis of past experience (not necessarily realistic), organizes present experience and provides a context for both present perceptions and for the recall of past memories.

This broadened conception of mental representation is, of course, not unique to the representational theorists (Sandler, Novey and Beres) whom I have surveyed in the present study. As noted by Paul (1967) and in a different context by Compton (1986), Freud too implied a concept of the mental representation of objects, as, of course, did many others, before the elaboration of this concept in the 1960s by the representational theorists reviewed here.[3] The contribution of these theorists was not in the innovation of a new concept, but in focusing, defining and elaborating the implications of the concept of mental representation. The central idea implied by this concept is that perception is not a passive process in which impressions of reality are in some way received and stored. Rather, perception is an active process, a 'constructing' of present experience, which (to a certain extent) is organized on the basis of past experience. In the process of interacting with others, representations of them are constructed, including cognitive, perceptual and emotional aspects, which later serve as an 'anticipatory set' for future interactions (which are real or phantasied).[4]

A comment should be added here regarding the issue of the status of the mental representation as belonging to the experiential or non-experiential realms (see Chapter 6). As noted above, the view of representation presented here is that of an anticipatory set, or schema. As such, it is a theoretical construct that aids us in building a viable theory. It is not considered to be an experience in itself, as an image, a thought, a percept or a phantasy. A person does not 'experience his representations' any more than they can experience their cognitive style or their defence mechanisms, these being theoretical abstractions that serve theoretical (and, in the case of psychoanalysis, clinical) understanding, rather than describe aspects of experience. This may be compared to linguistics; although our use of language is considered to be regulated by the rules of syntax, these 'rules' are not considered to be experiential; that is, they are not 'known' to the speaker, either consciously or otherwise (unless, by chance, he or she is a professional linguist). It is important to note that Kleinian theory basically rejects this distinction between the experiential and nonexperiential realms, which is one of the reasons why the concept of mental representation has had so little influence on the writings of this group. We shall see in the chapter on phantasies how this issue (experiential/ non-experiential) enters into the distinction between the two concepts.[5]

In order further to clarify the psychoanalytic concept of representation, a discussion of the differences between the psychoanalytic concept of representation and the concept of representation as it is used in other areas of psychology is in order. I will devote an extended discussion to the comparison of Piaget's concepts to those of psychoanalysis because of the influence that Piaget's concepts have had on the development of psychoanalytic concepts and the confusions that have arisen regarding the two. In contrast, cognitive science has had little (if any) influence on psychoanalytic concepts. Cognitive science has been especially interested in the question, what particular format of representation would account (most parsimoniously) for the performance (especially the inadequate performance) of certain cognitive tasks? As noted recently by Scholnick (1983) in her discussion of some recent trends in cognitive science and their challenge to Piaget's theory of representation, the formats of representation proposed by the different theories are often closely related to the characteristics of the cognitive *tasks* under study. Thus, one of the reasons why psychoanalytic and cognitive science concepts have so little in common lies in the vastly different domains being studied by each. In fact, the question of the 'format' of representation is one that psychoanalytic theory has found little use for, being more interested in the contents relevant to different individuals rather than the specifics of the (hypothetical) underlying structures common to all thought processes.

Proceeding to the comparison with Piaget, it should be noted that his concept of representation has caused confusion in regard to the use of the concept of representation in psychoanalytic theory. Two important distinctions must be emphasized between these two concepts, one related to a major difference between the two theoretical frameworks and the other related to the specific use of the term 'representation'. In regard to the two theoretical frameworks (Piagetian psychology and psychoanalysis), it is clear that there is a vast difference in the realms of phenomena which each theory addresses. Whereas Piaget's theory addresses the realm of cognitive development, psychoanalytic theory emphasizes the realm of the emotions as its major focus, with cognitive aspects often appearing in relation to the emotional dynamics. Thus Piaget's objects are (by and large) toys, and the objects of psychoanalysis are (by and large) emotionally significant people (especially the mother!).[6] Piaget was interested in the development of mental structures (schemas, representations) which represent reality in a mature fashion, whereas psychoanalysis is mainly interested in those specific aspects of emotionally relating and reacting to other people that a person develops early in life and repeats (in unending variations) throughout life. This drastic difference in the general universe of phenomena being addressed by the two theories makes any comparison, and especially an attempt to translate from one area to the other, very tricky.

In regard to the specific concept of representation, further difficulties arise. In Piagetian psychology, representation is used to refer to a level of thought beyond the sensorimotor level. It implies the capacity to operate on signifiers in the absence of their significates, a capacity which the child in the sensorimotor period does not possess (Flavell 1963: 151–2). The transition from sensorimotor to preoperational thought is defined in terms of the capacity to 'represent'. Especially relevant to the interface with psychoanalytic theory is Piaget's emphasis on what he referred to as the 'narrow sense of representation' – 'the symbolic evocation of absent realities' (Piaget, quoted in Furth 1968: 79). Piaget considered that this capacity to 're-present' (that is, mentally to make present something not present) via symbolic evocation is necessary for the development of pre-operational knowledge, for in this way the child is freed from his direct dependence on external action for knowing.[7] Thus the term 'representation' is used in the context of a theory of the developmental stages of thought to refer to a specific level of development.

As described above, the context of the psychoanalytic concept of 'presentation', from which the concept of 'representation' gradually developed, originally had no such developmental implications. Rather, as mentioned above, it was used to refer to a 'memory trace' of external objects (Paul 1967). For a long time, no consideration was taken in psychoanalytic theory of the possibility that the 'capacity to represent' was something that had to develop and was not present at birth. In fact, one of the great difficulties of psychoanalytic theory in its meeting with Piagetian psychology resides in Freud's postulation of the hallucinatory image of the wished-for object (wish-fulfilment) as the 'primary model of thought' (Rapaport 1960; Fraiberg 1969). Thus, it was not a matter of simply ignoring developmental subtleties that led psychoanalytic theory to a different concept of representation from that of Piaget. Rather, the developmental implications of Piaget's concept were actually inimical to the trend of thought of (early) psychoanalytic theory (Fraiberg 1969).

With the elaboration of a psychoanalytic theory of development based on an ego psychology approach (especially by Anna Freud, Rene Spitz and Margaret Mahler) and a concomitant interest in the disturbances of various areas of ego functioning, the implications of the developmental level of the attitude towards the object began to be discussed in the psychoanalytic literature. These discussions focused on the concept of object constancy, as I have reviewed above in the historical survey of this concept. A disturbance in this area of ego functioning was considered to contribute to a specific type of pathology (Mahler 1968; Kernberg 1975).

The psychoanalytic idea of object constancy was undoubtedly influenced by Piaget's concepts, and it is here that much confusion arises in regard to the differences between Piaget's concepts of representation and object permanence, and the psychoanalytic concepts of object representation and object constancy. Piaget's concepts are closely related, object permanence being one aspect (among many) of the achievement of the representational level of thought. In psychoanalytic theory the connection between the concepts (object) representation and object constancy is somewhat different; here it is the concept of object constancy that expresses the idea that the capacity to re-present the (absent) object is a developmental capacity not to be taken for granted, and lacking in certain kinds of pathology. Psychoanalytic theory is not, by and large, interested in the other types of 'permanence' which Piaget discussed. Thus the idea of a developmental capacity to re-present came to focus, in psychoanalytic theory, on the concept of object constancy (although in Piagetian theory it implies much more). The psychoanalytic concept of (object) representation, therefore, was not drawn into the discussion of developmental capacities, and continued to refer to the emotional and cognitive 'set' (or schema) which determines an individual's later reactions to objects, a concept very central to the domain of phenomena discussed by psychoanalytic theory (but one of relatively little specific meaning in the domain discussed by Piaget).[8]

In summary, the psychoanalytic concept of mental representation (schemas) may be defined as an amalgamation of past experiences with the object which provides an emotional and cognitive anticipatory set for future interactions (either interpersonal or phantasied). In contrast with phantasies, representations are not considered to be, in themselves, experiences. Rather, they are theoretical constructs referring to experiential tendencies. In contrast with the 'representations' of Piagetian psychology, the psychoanalytic concept of representation does not refer exclusively to the cognitive representation of reality. Rather, it includes both emotional aspects of relationships and the influences of non-realistic factors such as the drives, wishes and phantasies which are all considered to influence the 'shape' (content) of the representations. In addition, in contrast with the Piagetian concept of representation, the psychoanalytic concept does not refer to the capacity to 're-present',[9] which in psychoanalytic theory is related to the concept of object constancy. Rather, it can also be used to refer to sensorimotor schemata, which in Piagetian concepts would be considered to be 'pre-representational'.

12

Mental objects as phantasies

In distinction from the use of concepts of mental objects to refer to mental representations (or schemas), they are often used to refer to *phantasies* regarding objects (other people, or things which symbolize other people). Although the distinction between representations and phantasies is not strictly adhered to in the psychoanalytic literature (and is expressly rejected by some, such as the Kleinians), for the purposes of a conceptual analysis, this distinction is of importance. Especially, two implications of the concept of phantasy in contrast to that of representation should be noted.

The concept of phantasy, as generally used in the psychoanalytic literature, refers to a subjectively experienced phenomenon – whether conscious or unconscious. Opinions may differ as to whether certain processes should be considered to be phantasies (implying that they are considered to be experiential) or mechanisms (implying that they are considered to be non-experiential).[1] For example, projection may be used to refer to a phantasy of something being ejected from the individual's body. In contrast to phantasy, representations (schemas) have been defined here as anticipatory sets which organize experience, not as experiences in themselves. Thus, we do not 'experience our representations', just as we do not experience our mental structures (for example, id, ego, superego) or our defence mechanisms.

An important correlate of this distinction between phantasy as experience and representation as schema is related to the issue of motivation. Phantasying is considered in psychoanalytic theory to be motivated behaviour, and one of the aims in uncovering unconscious phantasies in therapy is to understand the motives involved. By and large, phantasying has been considered to be related to wish-fulfilment. Different approaches have emphasized different motives (such as sexual and aggressive drives, object-related needs, narcissistic needs and so on), but phantasies have largely been considered to play a role in attaining the wished-for state, whether as a 'plan' for realization, or as an emotionally satisfying experience in itself. Because this emphasis on the gratifying function of phantasy has been so prominent in psychoanalytic theory, much interest has been directed to the question of the motives for painful phantasies, a phenomenon seemingly in contradiction to the view that phantasy is wish-fulfilling. It was in this context that Freud (1933a: 27–8) explored the motives for punishment dreams. This question especially interested Fairbairn (1943, 1944), who emphasized the issue of the motives for the retention of (phantasies of) hostile objects. His view that bad (internal) objects are better than no objects has had widespread influence in the psychoanalytic litera- ture – for instance, Sandler (1960, 1981) and Meissner (1981) have come to similar conclusions without rejecting the Freudian drive theory as did Fairbairn.

In contrast, representations (schemas) are not considered to be motivated. Regarding representations the relevant question is not 'What motivates the retention of such a representation?' as it is regarding (for example) introjects. Rather, the relevant question is: 'What factors (such as the characteristics of the external object, the phantasies of the individual regarding the object) contributed to the specific 'shape' (or contents) of the representations?' The function of representation is not considered to be that of (disguised) wish-fulfilment as is the function of phantasy. As has been noted above, Sandler and Rosenblatt (1962) relegated the formation of representations to a general 'organizational activity' of the ego (follow-ing Hartmann 1939). In contrast, Beres and Joseph (1970) considered it as related to processes of delay of discharge (that is, of the transition from primary to secondary processes). This distinction is important in the context of the shift in psychoanalytic theory from a drive (or drive-defence) psychology (Beres and Joseph), to a more general emphasis on object-relationships as having a formative influence on the organization of personality (Sandler).

Having distinguished between representation and phantasy, I would like to discuss two different approaches to phantasy (in relation to concepts of mental objects). Melanie Klein's seminal concept of internal objects pro-vided a major impetus for the development of the various concepts of mental objects. Klein's concept of internal objects has been discussed at length in the historical survey, but two points are of importance here:

1 Melanie Klein conceived of internal objects as *expressions* of the instincts.
2 She conceived of personality in terms of the interactions of the internal objects among themselves and with the ego.

Regarding the first, Klein considered phantasies of objects (especially part-objects) to be the psychological manifestations of the life and death instincts. In Klein's view, internal objects (namely, phantasies) are the medium whereby the life and death instincts are experienced. In connection with this view, her conception of personality as consisting of the (phantasied) interactions of such objects between themselves, and with the 'ego',[2] is of major importance. Her portrayal of an inner reality (of phantasy) which determines the individual's feelings and behaviour gave phantasy a central role, crucial for the understanding of personality. In fact, one of the criticisms directed at Kleinian theory is that it ignores 'outside' reality – that is, an individual's interpersonal relationships – in favour of an (almost) exclusive focus on internal reality.[3]

A different approach to phantasy and the function of 'internal objects' is that advanced by Fairbairn. As described in the historical survey above, Melanie Klein's concept of an inner reality had an important influence on Fairbairn's theory of the 'basic schizoid position of the psyche' (Fairbairn 1940: 8). Fairbairn considered one of the basic characteristics of the schizoid posture to be a preoccupation with inner reality. In Fairbairn's view, what is internalized is the bad or frustrating object, so that what an individual[4] is occupied with in his inner reality is phantasies regarding those objects which he experienced as 'bad' in his relationships with them. This preoccupation in phantasy is part of an attempt to control the 'bad' objects and force them to be 'good' (in phantasy). This attempt, of course, cannot succeed, but the child is compelled to cling to his phantasies of his objects because of his intense *need* for his objects (Fairbairn 1943: 65–8). Guntrip (1961) added to Fairbairn's formulations regarding the motives for the ongoing preoccupation with phantasies of (bad) objects, the idea that without these phantasies the (schizoid) individual 'risks the total loss of all objects and therewith the loss of his own ego as well' (p. 56).

These formulations lead to a different view of internal objects (phantasy) from that suggested by Melanie Klein. While Melanie Klein considered phantasies regarding objects to represent the instincts, Fairbairn considered them to serve as a necessary substitute for frustrating interpersonal relationships (although continuing to reflect the 'bad' nature of those relationships). Although Klein did recognize the influence of interpersonal relationships on the dynamics of the internal world (of phantasy), that internal world is primarily considered to be an expression of the instincts. In contrast, Fairbairn considered the internal world to reflect the (frustrating but needed) external world, which is considered to play an important role in the emotional economy of the individual. While both approaches emphasize an internal reality (of phantasy), Klein's emphasizes internal reality as the matrix of motivation in the personality whereas Fairbairn's emphasizes the function of internal reality *vis-à-vis* external reality. It has been noted in the literature that these diverging approaches are repeated in the works of later theoreticians – for example, the divergence between Kernberg and Kohut (Robbins 1980; Mitchell 1981).

Returning to the distinction between representation and phantasy, we may now see some of the complexities of the issue. Representation (as

156

defined here) neither serves as a 'representative of the instincts' (as do the phantasied 'internal objects' of Kleinian theory) nor as an emotional substitute for frustrating interpersonal relationships (as in Fairbairn's concept of 'internalized objects'). Furthermore, representations are not considered to be motivating factors in the personality. Rather, represent-ations are an organizing system, a matrix of meaning, guiding, limiting and (to varying extents) distorting the individual's subjective experience. In Melanie Klein's and Fairbairn's theories there is little room for such a concept separate from the elaborate inner worlds of phantasy which they emphasize. Both may consider the internal motivational matrix as pro-viding a basis for the organization of experience. In fact, Fairbairn's theory has been translated into representational terms (Rinsley 1982), emphasizing the function of his concept of internalized objects as organizers of experience.[5] But while the concept of representation may be incorporated into the more powerful concept of phantasy in theories such as those of Melanie Klein and Fairbairn, there is a need to distinguish between the two in the framework of an overview of concepts of mental objects in psycho-analytic theory.[6]

Another important concept that should be discussed in terms of the distinction between representation and phantasy proposed here is Schafer's (1968) concept of representation. In contrast with the definition of repre-sentation proposed here, which emphasizes its non-experiential nature, Schafer conceived of representation as experiential, both at unconscious and conscious levels. Furthermore, he tended to use representation and phantasy almost interchangeably (as in regard to his concept of primary-process presences). For Schafer, the important distinction was between representations (and phantasies) and motives. As described in the historical survey, his emphasis on motives may be viewed against the background of Hartmann's version of ego psychology. In contrast to Hartmann's emphasis on the adaptive point of view, Schafer emphasized the dynamic point of view, and his monograph on internalization (Schafer 1968) was no less a study, and renovation, of the psychoanalytic theory of motivation. In addition, Schafer's study on internalization may be seen as an attempt to provide ego psychology with concepts to deal with the Kleinian descrip-tions of the dynamics of internal objects. An earlier ego psychology version of the dynamics of internal objects had been provided by Jacobson, but Schafer seems to have found Jacobson's theories too close to the 'demonology' described in Melanie Klein's writings. His answer to that was an even stricter divorce between representations and phantasies on the one hand and motives on the other, than that presented by Jacobson. But while perhaps succeeding in that venture, Schafer ignored the thrust of the developmental point of view with its emphasis on the influence of environment on the formation of the personality of the child. This may be ironical in regard to a major study of 'aspects of internalization', but the fact remains that Schafer's study contains little if any discussion of either developmental processes or of the interplay between the interpersonal and the intrapsychic. His almost exclusive emphasis on intrapsychic motivation left little room for the kind of issues discussed above in regard to the origin of mental objects, and as such provides concepts that are too limited to deal with the great variety of concepts of mental objects we have encountered in the psychoanalytic literature.

To summarize: the concept of phantasy has often been confused with the two other concepts here being delineated – representation and (developmental) capacity. It is here proposed to distinguish between concepts of mental objects referring to phantasies, and those referring to representations or to capacities. Phantasies refer to the experiential realm, whether of a conscious or an unconscious nature. Furthermore, they are considered to be motivated, and (possibly) motivating. It is common in the literature to use the terms 'introject', 'internal object' or 'psychic presence' to refer to such phantasies, in contrast to the terms 'object representation' or 'schema', on the one hand, and 'object constancy' as a capacity, on the other.

13

Mental objects as developmental capacities

The concepts of mental objects presented above – representation (schema) and phantasy – do not carry developmental implications. As defined here, representation refers not to a developmental level (as in Piaget's theory, which is a theory of the development of mental structures) but rather to an organization of meanings which serves to organize and filter ongoing experience (and also, retrospectively, memory). While such organizations are assumed to develop throughout childhood and later life, such development involves the content of the representations and not their structure. This concept does not carry any assumptions about the structural differences between representations at different ages, although, of course, the content, both ideational and emotional, is considered to undergo dramatic changes during the different stages of childhood.

This state of (conceptual) affairs is compatible with a clinical approach that sees conflict as the primary objective of therapy. This approach does not need concepts that will distinguish between different levels of representation because the clinical approach will be basically the same – interpretation of the underlying conflict. Of course this clinical approach will be interested in the changing contents of the representations as these developed throughout childhood and later, and will be especially interested in uncovering underlying representations. But the basic clinical approach to whatever is uncovered will be the same within the therapeutic framework – interpretation, insight and working through.

The developmental point of view has had an interesting effect on the concepts of mental objects because it has led to distinctions not only between different contents but to distinctions between different levels of structure of mental objects. A prime example of this is the evolution of a developmental theory of representations in the work of Jacobson, Mahler and Kernberg. Following Jacobson, study has been devoted to the structural changes of representations during development (and, of course, in pathology). Two axes of structural development have been described: differentiatedness (of self and object representations from each other) and integratedness (of each).

159

This view of representations as structures with different levels of development has had far-reaching implications in Kernberg's theory of levels of personality organization. According to this theory it is the structural characteristics of an individual's representations that determine the level of their personality organization. The lowest level of personality organization, the psychotic level, is characterized by representations that are defective in their differentiatedness, leading to a tendency for the merging of self and object representations and a concomitant confusion between self and other, inside and outside, phantasy and reality. At the next level, the borderline personality organization, representations are differentiated but are not integrated. Accordingly, such people will succeed in retaining reality testing but will suffer from a tendency towards a splitting of their experience of others as an outcome of the split in their representations.[1] The highest level of personality organization is that at which the individual's representations have achieved their full structural development and they are both differentiated and integrated.

This view adds a new dimension to the concept of representation as it was defined above, and with this addition the concept of representation takes on meaning as a developmental capacity. When using this concept of representation, specification must be made as to what level of representation is being discussed; that is, the developmental level. The concept of representation is thus being used to refer to developmental capacities and defects – the capacity to differentiate between self and object, and the capacity to experience (others and self) in an integrated way. This developmental approach to the structural level of representations has been the basis for the work of a research team at Yale University (Blatt and Lerner 1983). The findings of that team have provided empirical support for this concept of representation, especially in correlation with different levels of pathology.

The reason why it is important to distinguish the use of concepts of mental objects in reference to developmental capacities from the concept of representation as defined above is that not all theoreticians have followed Jacobson, Mahler and Kernberg in this shift of meaning regarding representations. As mentioned above, the more traditional view of personality and treatment, one emphasizing conflict as the ubiquitous cause of psychopathology, does not have a need for the distinctions between different levels of developmental capacities regarding representation and does not have a tendency to view psychopathology and treatment in those terms.

This becomes very clear in a fascinating clinical-theoretical study of borderline patients by members of the Kris Study Group of the New York Psychoanalytic Institute (Abend *et al.* 1983). The aim of this study was to examine various theoretical and clinical approaches to borderline patients

160

in conjunction with the study of material from the ongoing analysis of a number of borderline patients. Kernberg's theories regarding the borderline personality organization were prominent among those studied by the participants and compared with the actual case material at hand. It is very interesting to see how the conclusions of this group of analysts orientated towards ego psychology remain well within the tradition of an ego psychology approach, both in regard to their understanding of the pathology of the patients and in regard to treatment. Kernberg's views regarding the centrality of splitting, both as a clinical phenomenon and as a basic explanatory construct, were clearly rejected (1983: 158–73).

While Abend *et al.* did report evidence of splitting on the part of their patients, they considered this concept to be 'simply a phenomenological description which has different implications for different authors . . . [stating their own view that] splitting does not represent an immutable fixation which persists unchanged into adult mental life' (p. 165). Concomitantly they rejected Kernberg's recommendations for the interpretation of splitting as an important therapeutic tool (pp. 193–7). This does not mean that this group does not refer to such disturbances as the fusion of self and object representations – they do (p. 236). But, unlike Kernberg who considers such fusion to be a developmental defect in the structure of representations, Abend *et al.* consider it to be a defensive phenomenon in the context of a conflict model and not a developmental defect. This difference of opinions regarding the role of developmental defects in borderline patients was clearly a major subject of debate in the issue of *Psychoanalytic Inquiry* devoted to 'Commentaries on Abend, Porder and Willick's *Borderline Patients: Psychoanalytic Perspectives*' (Bornstein 1988).

Thus, note must be made of the different meanings of the term 'representation', distinguishing between representation as an organization of meanings, as defined here, and the use of the term to refer to levels of developmental capacities, as in the theories of Jacobson and Kernberg. These different meanings differ not only at a theoretical level, but often also tend to have implications for treatment. Friedman, an advocate of the traditional view and critic of various new 'trends' in psychoanalytic theory and treatment (1978, 1980b, 1982), pithily noted this tendency for concepts of developmental defects to have treatment implications: 'We cannot ask [why the patient chooses to see only in straight lines and not around corners] . . . expecting to hear a wish or a concealment confess itself' (Friedman 1988: 357).

Thus, while the classical Freudian model of treatment emphasizes conflict and consequently choice and responsibility – of the patient! (Friedman 1988) – the developmental point of view, in emphasizing developmental deficits and disturbances, shifts this emphasis.[2] This tendency can also be seen in connection with Mahler's use of the concept of object constancy as a central developmental achievement, with the corollary for pathology regarding the role of the disturbance of this capacity. Although Mahler herself did not (to the best of my knowledge) suggest in what way this concept might influence the treatment of patients suffering from such a disturbance, other analysts (Fleming 1975; Adler and Buie 1979; Buie and Adler 1982–83; Pine 1985, 1990; Adler 1988) have done so, suggesting various degrees of adjustment of technique to deal with the developmental defect. The same may be said regarding Kohut's earlier work (Kohut 1971), which sought to extract treatment implications from a developmental approach to the concept of mental object he called the self-object (later Kohut evolved a completely new theory of personality, doing away with the need for concepts of mental objects, as I described in the historical survey). Gedo (1988), whose work might be considered a continuation of Kohut's earlier approach, has also specified how his understanding of the developmental defect involved in serious pathology has affected his technique *vis-à-vis* patients with such pathology.

Another example of the difference between approaches which use the concept of representation to imply a developmental capacity (which may be disturbed) and one which does not carry such developmental implications, may be seen in the ongoing debate in the psychoanalytic literature regarding the theory of psychosis. This debate, which has been summarized in London (1973) and in Pao (1979), involves the general question whether psychosis should be understood in terms of conflict – for example, Arlow and Brenner (1969) – or in terms of deficit – as in London (1973) and Wexler (1971). In more specific terms, London (1973) suggests that the deficit in schizophrenia may be seen specifically to involve the deterioration of the representations (both self and object). According to this view, these representations constitute basic structures which may be intact or not. In contrast, those who consider conflict to be at the heart of psychosis do not view representations as basic structures which may be defective as a result of disturbances in development, but rather as schemas, the content of which may be distorted *vis-à-vis* reality to a greater or lesser degree, depending on the influence of intrapsychic conflict.

Thus, these two differing understandings of the concepts of representation are closely related to diverging views regarding both pathology and treatment. Other examples of divergent theories related to differences regarding the question whether developmental deficits of the self and object representations may be considered to stand at the basis of pathological phenomena may be seen in various discussions – for instance, Singer (1977), regarding feelings of emptiness; Pine (1985), regarding separation anxiety and other phenomena.

The above discussion emphasizes the differences between concepts of representation on the one hand and concepts of developmental capacity and defect on the other. The other category which must be distinguished from that of developmental capacity and defect is the concept of phantasy. Here there is less overlap than between representation and developmental capacity. As discussed above (in Chapter 12), phantasy involves the experiential realm, in contrast to both representation and developmental capacity, which refer to the non-experiential realm. An example of confusion between the two is discussed in Pine (1979) in regard to merging and fusion. Pine emphasizes that not every phantasy of merging is to be taken as evidence for a process of the fusion of self and object representations. The latter refers to the disturbance of a developmental capacity, related to the process of separation-individuation, a disturbance that has widespread implications for the functioning of the personality. A phantasy of merging, or a wish for merger, may occur without there being a disturbance of the developmental capacity to distinguish between self and other, and may be related to much higher-level conflicts than those involved in the process of separation-individuation. Thus, processes of phantasy and processes related to disturbances of developmental capacities should not be confused.

Another concept which is used to refer both to aspects of phantasy and to developmental aspects is that of 'part-objects'. Here, following Abraham and Melanie Klein, the view developed that the content of the phantasy (whether the image of the object in phantasy was an image of the whole object or of a part of the object) reflected the developmental level involved (Wisdom 1961, 1962). The concept of part-object as a level of relationship with the object, and concomitantly an aspect of the level of organization of the personality as a whole (at the paranoid-schizoid or at the depressive position), carries far-reaching implications, and the content of the phantasy serves, according to this view, as an indicator of the developmental level involved. This distinction is important because, while the concept of part-object, as a level of relationship with the object, has been adopted by many non-Kleinian analysts (for example, A. Freud 1965), the view that the phantasy image necessarily reflects this developmental level has not been widely accepted. Thus, in order to understand the differences between Kleinian and non-Kleinian usages of the same concept, the distinction between part-object as an aspect of a phantasy and part-object as a developmental level needs to be made.

To summarize: in addition to the two aspects of concepts of mental objects discussed above, representation and phantasy, there is a need to distinguish a third aspect — that related to developmental capacity and deficit. This aspect has structural implications not necessarily implied by the concept of representation as defined in the present study (as schema), although the term 'representation' has often been used in the psychoanalytic literature to refer to the developmental and structural aspects, leading to some difficulty in distinguishing between them. A number of examples were discussed to show the importance of this distinction for an understanding of the differences of opinion in the psychoanalytic literature on various subjects. Furthermore, the concepts of developmental capacities and deficits were also seen to differ from concepts of phantasy in regard to the realm of discussion (experiential versus non-experiential), and the relevance of this distinction, and examples of it, were discussed.

14

Conclusion

The differences between the three main concepts of mental objects extant in the psychoanalytic literature parallel some of the major theoretical trends in the literature, without there being a strict one-to-one relationship between concepts and trends. We have seen how the emergence of psychoanalytic theory from the id psychology of its beginnings towards a more developmentally orientated approach was accompanied by shifts from Freud's concept of 'object presentation' as an aspect of the drives, to a concept of object representation which encompasses and shapes experience. We have distinguished between this concept and a more active concept of mental object as phantasy. The latter has been seen to be characteristic of those psychoanalytic theories which emphasize the inner world of phantasy as the stage on which internal dramas are worked out, determining the emotional life of the individual and their behaviour. Lastly, we have discussed the concept of developmental capacities and defects in relation to concepts of mental objects, and have seen how these concepts carry implications beyond those of representation and phantasy, implications employed especially by those trends in psychoanalytic theory that explore personality development in terms of capacities achieved and impaired (rather than a strictly conflict-orientated model of development).

The aim of this delineation, and of the historical survey and the discussion of theoretical issues that led up to it, is to further our understanding of the plethora of terms and concepts that have developed in the psychoanalytic literature to describe and explain the ways in which the mind structures its interactions with people. No attempt was made to prefer one approach to another, the manifest aim being a mapping of the different ideas and the ties and differences between them.

Notes

Introduction

1 See also Mitchell (1988a).
2 While I personally prefer to refer to people as people rather than as objects, this is not always convenient when discussing psychoanalytic concepts. This is especially so in the context of the present study in which it is not people who are being discussed, but rather people as the objects of the individual's interest. Therefore I have allowed myself to continue using the psychoanalytic term 'object' to refer to the above.

Chapter 1 Freud and his associates

1 See Paul (1967) for a detailed discussion of Freud's 'trace' theory of memory, which Paul contrasts with a 'schema' theory. The latter is, of course, the kind of theory implied in the concept of representation as it is being used in the present study. For a discussion of Freud's tendency to conceive of perception as a 'direct' process, see Wachtel (1980).
2 The influences of Herbart's psychology on Freud have been discussed by Jones (1953) and Ellenberger (1970).
3 *Vorstellung*, in Locke's sense, refers to both perceptions and ideas.
4 The parallel to this in Freud's terminology would be 'ego', as Freud used the term in his early writings.
5 See Editor's footnote in Freud (1915e: 174).
6 See Editor's introduction to Freud and Breuer (1895).
7 Freud did not conceive of the investment of energy in the mental image of the seduction scene to be a straightforward process. At the time at which the seduction occurred the child did not experience the full affect, which was awoken at a later date after the child had attained sexual maturation. Freud (1896b) called this the 'delayed effects' of the traumatic experience, and although this is an important point in Freud's thinking at the time, it is not specifically relevant to the ideas under discussion here.
8 *Affektbetrag* – translated as 'quota of affect'; see Appendix to Freud (1894a).

166

9 Although Freud (1906a) abandoned his theory of childhood seduction as the major pathogenic factor in neurosis in favour of a theory of pathogenesis based on drives, wishes and phantasy, he did not completely abandon the view that discrete memory traces may serve as pathogenic factors (e.g., Freud 1918b).

10 These have been discussed by Compton (1985a, 1985b, 1986). In the present chapter I have not entered into the intricacies of the differences between the eight different object concepts which Compton delineated. It is the aim of this chapter to point to a line of thought developing in Freud's writings over the years, from a conception of a passive, externally derived image of the object to a conception of an image of object (introject) that plays an active role in the mental economy. To the development of this line of thought, Compton's detailed delineations are not, in my opinion, necessarily relevant.

11 See Editor's footnote 2 in Freud (1905d: 217). As mentioned in note 10, Compton (1985a, 1985b, 1986) discusses this point comprehensively.

12 Due to the extensive revisions of this paper (Freud 1905d), it is sometimes difficult to determine what parts are of the original and what are later additions.

13 At the time of the introduction of the concepts introversion and narcissism there was much confusion between them, related to the fact that both processes are considered to involve a withdrawal of libido from external objects and a turning of that libido inwards. At the clinical level the distinction between the two was considered by Freud to involve the distinction between the neuroses (especially hysteria) and the psychoses (paranoia and schizophrenia, or paraphrenia, as Freud (1911c: 76) preferred to call it). It was not clear to Freud to what extent Jung restricted his concept of introversion to schizophrenia or extended it to the neuroses (Freud 1912b: 102, n.1; McGuire 1974: 486). Freud, at this point, was distinguishing between the processes of withdrawal to phantasies and withdrawal to the ego (or self). In the former, relationships with the object were considered to be retained, although at the level of phantasy. (Here we see an instance of the advantage of using the term 'object' to refer to both the external object and its mental image.) Jung's confusion may be illustrated in his criticism of Freud's explanation of the loss of reality in schizophrenia as a result of libidinal decathexis. Jung (1913, quoted in Freud 1914c: 80) argued that such a decathexis 'would result in the psychology of an ascetic anchorite, not in a dementia praecox'. This view of Jung's confuses the withdrawal of libido from external objects (which, according to Freud's view might result in an anchorite) with the withdrawal of libido from the mental images of objects, which in Freud's view is a very different process (Freud 1914c: 74–81; 1917: 250).

14 Although published in 1917, 'Mourning and melancholia' (Freud 1917e) was originally written in 1915 (Editor's note to Freud 1917e).

15 See Editor's note to Freud (1917e) for a short history of related ideas of Freud's before eventually presenting his final theory of melancholia in Freud (1917e).

16 Meissner (1970) and Compton (1985a, 1985b, 1986) have both carefully traced the developments of the concept of identification in Freud's theories. Compton (1985b) seems to have missed the Ferenczi's (1949) correspondence with Freud that sheds important light on Freud's adoption of the concept of introjection. This will be further discussed in the chapter on Ferenczi.

17 Compton (1986) considers such formulations 'untenable' and leading to 'an absurdity'. This is the result of the circular explanation engendered by such formulations – 'If we have the constructs relating to one another as if they were people, we have not advanced the cause of explanation at all' (1986: 578). I do not believe this to be so, and I think that Sandler's (1990a) reformulation of concepts of internal object relations may prove acceptable even to such ego psychology orientated theoreticians as Compton. Be that as it may, Compton is left with the onus of finding a rationale for a large portion of psychoanalytic theory that takes just such formulations for a starting point (as Compton himself recognizes), unless he simply wishes to ignore all of object-relations theory. It is not by chance that an important part of his critique begins, 'If the universe of discourse is to consist of four constructs – ego, id, superego and reality . . .' (1986: 585). This, in my opinion, is a rather restricted universe, one plagued by conceptual difficulties no less serious than those of the theory he is attacking.

18 See Furer (1972) for a review of the main points of Freud's theory.

19 Such identifications were not all that constituted the superego in Freud's view. Another important component was considered to be the reaction formation to the Oedipal wishes (Freud 1923b: 34).

20 Freud explicitly mentions this difficulty – 'These identifications are not what we should have expected [from the previous account (p. 29)], since they do not introduce the abandoned object into the ego' (Freud 1923b: 32). His solution at this point is very incomplete, merely stating that 'this alternative outcome may also occur' (ibid.), and introducing the responsibility that a girl will identify with her father. Only in subsequent papers (Freud 1924c, 1924d) did Freud propose a more general solution to this difficulty.

21 This is not to say that only such observations led to this formulation. See Sandler *et al.* 1978.

22 This idea of Freud's was not presented specifically in the context of the question of the origin of the superego's severity, but it does seem relevant to it.

23 For a comprehensive definition of the basic points of view of psychoanalytic theory, of which the economic point of view is one, see Rapaport and Gill (1959).

24 Although both here ('The ego and the id' – Freud 1923b) and in 'The economic problem of masochism' (Freud 1924c), discussed above, reference is made to the process of desexualization as connected with the fact of the superego's severity, the two explanations are not identical. They do appear compatible, but Freud did not attempt to integrate them into one theory and eventually developed a different approach in *Civilization and its Discontents* (Freud 1930a).

25 We should note that Freud did not consider these approaches to be contradictory. In spite of this it seems clear, at least in retrospect, that the two do lead in different directions.

26 Ferenczi (1933) expressly referred to his return to Freud's earlier views as 'a regression in technique (and partly also in the theory) of the neuroses'.

27 Ferenczi's view was not a simplistic one, and he expressly took internal factors into consideration, especially as regards individual differences regarding

sensitivity to parental behaviour, on the basis of different intensities of the need for love in different individuals (Grosskurth 1987: 189).

28 The use of the term 'Kleinian' here is, of course, facetious – at the time under discussion there was as yet no 'Kleinian' view in the meaning we would attach to that term today.

29 It is interesting to note that Freud did not mention his 1930 solution in his 1933 lecture on the superego, where he discussed his earlier views and their problematics (Freud 1933a: 62). He did mention the 1930 solution later on in the lectures, in one sentence at the end of the lecture on anxiety (ibid.: 109). It would probably be in order to note here Grosskurth's (1987) discussions of the tension between Anna Freud and Melanie Klein in regard to their opinions regarding this and other issues, and Freud's place in regard to these tensions.

30 Also in Freud 1924d: 176; 1925j: 257.

31 This will be further discussed in Part Three, 'A conceptual analysis', in connection with the distinction between the dimension of phantasy and those of representation and developmental capacity.

32 The concepts of experiential and non-experiential realms will be further discussed in Part Two, 'Major theoretical issues'.

33 There are two indirect references to the idea of the regression of the superego in Freud's writings (1923b: 55; 1926d: 115–16). It seems clear, though, that Freud viewed regression mainly as regression of libido, and considered the superego to be affected by this, rather than viewing superego regression as an autonomous process, or even as a distinct concept, in its own regard.

34 One topic to which this developmental concept was applied by Freud was the question of the difference between the male and female superego. Regarding this Freud (1925j) wrote: 'Their [women's] superego is never so inexorable, so impersonal, so independent of its personal origins' as that of the male (p. 257). In spite of the fact that this statement seems directly relevant to the developmental concept of the superego discussed in the text above, it is not clear from Freud's context whether he was not discussing a difference in the process of the formation of the male and female superego, rather than a difference in its later development.

35 This aspect received emphasis in the title of Schafer's well-known paper (1960), 'The loving and beloved superego'.

36 The ego's response to superego attacks was also emphasized by Freud (1924c) as a distinguishing feature between unconscious moral inhibition and moral masochism. Whereas in the case of the former the ego simply submits to the superego's sadistic attacks, in the latter the ego actively, masochistically seeks punishment from the superego (or from other parent-substitutes in the external world).

37 This tendency has been noted by Zetzel (1956), Rapaport (1958) and Apfelbaum (1965, 1966).

38 This tendency is closely related to what Sandler (1960) has called the 'conceptual dissolution' of the concept of the superego.

39 Compton's (1986) fierce criticism of the idea of an intrapsychic relationship between 'parts' of the mind is a good example of the difficulty in integrating these two models.

40 Greenberg and Mitchell (1983) have discussed this development in psycho-analytic theories at length in terms of the contrast between drive models and relational models.

41 It would be of interest to explore the connection between these early differences of view between Freud and Ferenczi, and Ferenczi's later 'deviations' regarding theory and technique. Thus, Ferenczi's later views emphasizing the 'real perceptions' and 'objective reality' in paranoiac delusions (Dupont 1988: 57–60) appear to be highly compatible with his earlier view of paranoia as originating in the reality-orientated (projection) stage of development.

42 According to Ferenczi's letter (of 25 Feb. 1915, in Ferenczi 1949), Freud's original wording seems to have been 'the projection of the shadow of the object on the ego'.

43 They were finally translated for the *International Journal of Psycho-Analysis* in 1949 by Balint; see his comments in Balint (1949b). This is not surprising, considering that Jones (who was editor of the *International Journal of Psycho-Analysis*) was of the opinion that Ferenczi was suffering from 'latent psychotic trends' at the time (Jones 1957: 176). (See Young-Bruehl 1988: 194, and n.24 regarding the possible inaccuracy of this remark of Jones.)

44 Ferenczi (1933) himself referred to this return to Freud's earlier views as 'a *regression* in technique (and partly also in the theory) of the neuroses' (emphasis mine).

45 The concept of identification with the aggressor was shortly thereafter to be presented and elaborated by Anna Freud in her book *The Ego and the Mechanisms of Defence* (A. Freud 1936), and is widely considered to be her own original contribution (Young-Bruehl 1988: 210). The fact that Ferenczi did mention this concept in his 1932 paper is an interesting historical coincidence, but there is no reason to think that this mention in Ferenczi's paper had any influence, either on A. Freud or on almost anyone else, for the reasons mentioned above.

In addition, it should be noted that although the concept is the same, the gist of A. Freud's use of the concept is very different from that of Ferenczi. For while Ferenczi was seeking to give expression to the ways in which a traumatic interaction with a parent leads to a compliant, guilt-ridden personality of the child, A. Freud was tracing the origins of the child's aggression (possibly as an alternative to M. Klein's emphasis on the death instinct – Young-Bruehl 1988: 212–15).

46 Recently, Modell (1990) traced the divergence between the classical theory of treatment on the one hand, and object-relations and self psychology theories of treatment on the other, to the controversy between Freud and Ferenczi.

47 Freud (1921c) later adopted the term suggested by Ferenczi – 'introjection' – (see 'Ferenczi's concept of introjection' page 23 above).

Chapter 2 Object-related orientations

1 Some prominent exceptions, e.g., Bychowski, Kernberg, Grotstein and others will be reviewed separately.

2 This approach of Melanie Klein's to the origins of the severity of the superego, according to which the superego's aggression drew on the individual's original aggressive wishes towards his objects, was further developed in subsequent papers. It was this approach which Freud finally adopted in *Civilization and its Discontents* (1930a) as a solution to the disparity between superego and 'real' parental behaviour. See Chapter 1, 'Freud and his associates'.

3 In later writings she tended to use the term 'internal objects' more often than 'superego'. Even later she distinguished between the normal early superego and terrifying internal objects which are not part of the superego, but are rather split off from the ego and 'relegated to the deeper layers of the unconscious' (M. Klein 1958: 241).

4 According to the editors of Melanie Klein's *Writings*, this is, historically, the first published report of an analysis of a psychotic child.

5 Freud himself was, of course, not alive at this time, and the taking of the label 'Freudian' by the non-Kleinian camp was seriously disputed by the Kleinians.

6 The four papers presented at the Discussion were later revised and expanded, and included in the book *Developments in Psycho-Analysis* (Klein 1952). All references here will be to the original unpublished papers and comments, unless otherwise noted.

7 20 Oct. 1943, in discussion of Paula Heimann's paper.

8 In the 1952 version: 'world of desire and emotions'.

9 1952: believed to be.

10 Freud (1930: 130, n.1).

11 Earlier in this passage, Melanie Klein stated her conclusion that 'the phase in which sadism is at its zenith. . . precedes the earlier anal stage', i.e., oral sadism.

12 This is especially prominent in the case of John (Klein 1931).

13 Or as some have called it, the 'dramatics' (Bianchedi *et al.* 1984).

14 This idea was mentioned by Freud (1905d) and elaborated by Abraham (1924). It seems to have been accepted as a common-sense theory of perceptual development.

15 Melanie Klein used the term 'part-object' in a manner similar to her use of the concept internal object. It referred to both a specific phantasy of the part of the object's body being physically present within the individual and to all cognitive and instinctual phenomena related to the *level* of part-object.

16 It would seem that Melanie Klein was straining to express in the language of metapsychology the intuition that there is a difference between 'real love' and some 'lesser' attitude, and that depression is a result of the former only. She eventually (Klein 1948) abandoned this idea, stating that depression could occur in relation to a part-object, too.

17 Mention of this idea is made by Brierley (1939), who points to the tension between the concept of internalized objects as foreign bodies, and the tendency of the ego to synthesis. There, she suggests that the experience of internalized objects as foreign bodies within the individual is a pathological process, in patients whose ego-synthesis is defective. Matte-Blanco (1941) devoted a whole paper to the processes of the absorption of the introjected objects into the ego. He referred to Heimann's (1942b) paper and seems to have further developed her original idea.

18 This idea was present in Melanie Klein's writings from the time she began using the concepts of the life/death instincts in 1932.

19 Grotstein (1981) has traced the precursors of the concept of projective identification both in Melanie Klein's earlier writings, and in the work of Freud and Victor Tausk. The idea under discussion here does not appear in Freud's and Melanie Klein's writings, although it does appear in Tausk's (1919).

20 Melanie Klein admittedly uses the terms 'ego' and 'self' interchangeably.

21 The extent to which this was so led to the need for a special paper on 'Regression' in the Controversial Discussions (Heimann and Isaacs 1952), due to criticism by 'Freudians' that the Kleinians had abandoned that concept altogether.

22 Fairbairn (1940) considered the schizoid position to be even more basic than the depressive position presented by M. Klein a few years earlier (M. Klein 1935). When Klein proposed the concept of a paranoid position prior to the depressive position (1946), she felt it to be basically similar to Fairbairn's concept of the schizoid position, and consequently, in a later version of the paper (1952), renamed it 'the paranoid-schizoid position', acknowledging Fairbairn's contribution. See M. Klein (1946: 2, n.1).

23 Fairbairn himself considered the difference in the type of pathology on which his and Freud's respective theories were based to account to a large degree for the differences between them.

24 Guntrip (1961) described in detail the many different interactions possible between these various internal structures, and the personality types produced by such interactions.

25 This, in spite of the fact that various theorists describing Fairbairn's theories do translate his concept of internal objects as representations; e.g., Rinsley (1982). This, of course, also depends on the definition of 'representation', which is discussed at length in Chapter 11 on 'Mental objects as representations'.

26 We have seen above, in the historical surveys of Freud and of Melanie Klein, that Klein's view of the matter did eventually influence Freud's own opinion.

27 This approach of analysing processes in terms of their function within an interpersonal context, rather than within an intrapsychic context, has been termed 'two-person psychology' as opposed to the traditional 'one-person' context of psychoanalytic theory (e.g., Ghent 1989; Modell 1990).

28 Guntrip (1961: 429–33) interpreted this concept of 'loss of ego' as signifying the experience of depersonalization. Although Fairbairn (1940: 5) did mention depersonalization as a symptom of the schizoid category, he did not, to the best of my knowledge, refer to it in relation to the ultimate psychic disaster of 'loss of ego'. Whether Guntrip's interpretation was based on personal knowledge of Fairbairn's views (as often seems to have been the case) or whether this is his own contribution is difficult to determine. It is of interest to note the similarity of Fairbairn's concept of 'loss of ego' and Kohut's later concept of 'disintegration anxiety'.

29 See Fairbairn (1943: 75–6).

30 In addition, the individual will also experience himself in accordance with the nature (i.e. badness) of his internal objects, viewing himself as bad, and

establishing internal structures of the ego (= self) in accordance. This process has also been called 'identification with the introjects' (Sandler 1960).

31 Even Meltzer, a close associate of Bion's and an important expounder of Bion's ideas, complained extensively about Bion's whole attempt to provide psychoanalysis with a mathematics-like system of notation (Meltzer 1978). Wisdom (1981), also, criticized Bion's investment in the development of a system of notation, hinting that Bion himself 'had second thoughts' on this (p. 611, n.).

32 And of the present writer.

33 *Vorstellung.*

34 I have not found Bion to have referred to this idea of Freud's as influencing his own ideas.

35 Among the Kleinians, Meltzer has been cited as presenting an extreme position on this issue (Spillius 1983).

36 Although in the 1959 paper it was cited that Bion made a direct statement on this, he had already been implying it in his first paper on schizophrenia (Bion 1954).

37 In a recent attempt to accommodate psychoanalytic and Piagetian theories regarding the development of the capacity to experience the (human) object in the first year of life (Leon 1984), the concept of 'action object' was proposed as a characterization of the schemata of objects at the sensorimotor level. Although Leon himself did not discuss Kleinian concepts, the notion of a schema lacking the capacity to integrate various aspects of the object may probably also be applied to the Kleinian concept of part-objects.

38 Here the obvious question would be: 'parts' of what? For an answer, we must recall the dual nature of internal objects in Melanie Klein's theory, experienced as both self and object.

39 It is important to note that Bion considered the capacity to bear anxiety and frustration to be an individual, and presumably inborn, factor, differing from one infant to another. We shall return to this issue shortly.

40 Bion's use of the concept of function, especially as elaborated in Bion (1962b), is more complex than the general use of that concept in ego psychology (e.g., Hartmann 1939). But, because Bion's use is so wide it clearly includes also the many ego functions discussed in ego psychology. Some of these – perception, judgement, verbal thought – are explicitly mentioned by Bion.

41 Sandler (1987a) has traced the development of the concept of projective identification from Melanie Klein's use, in reference to a phantasy, through two more stages of which Bion's use was the last. While, as Sandler has shown, it may not be exact to attribute to Bion the introduction of the interpersonal aspect, he undoubtedly added much to it and greatly elaborated the concept, as will be shown.

42 It is interesting, for example, to compare two statements made by Rosenfeld over a span of ten years, regarding the role of the mother in the development of schizophrenia. In a comment on the North American view of the 'schizophrenogenic mother', Rosenfeld (1952) warned against 'accept[ing] uncritically the patient's attempt to blame the external environment for his illness' (p. 74, n.1). In contrast, he referred in a later paper (Rosenfeld 1963)

to Bion's views regarding the pathogenic effect of the mother's 'diminished tolerance towards the projections of the infant', and stated that 'when we consider the question of disturbed mother–infant relationship in the first year of life it is important to consider not only the influence of the mother on the child but the reaction of the mother to a particularly difficult schizoid infant' (p.168). This shift in emphasis in Rosenfeld's writings may be taken as a clear indication of the influence of Bion's views on his Kleinian contemporaries.

43 This does not refer to technique, but rather to a theory of personality that accounts not only for pathology but also provides a rationale for the manner in which the technique achieves change in the personality. Lack of such a theory of therapy in Kleinian theory is prominent, as may be seen in two important Kleinian surveys of Kleinian theory – Segal (1978) and Spillius (1983). Both discuss technique, but not a theory of therapy.

44 The reference section of Grotstein's latest series (Grotstein 1980, 1983, 1984) encompasses more than 350 items!

45 This solution bears, of course, great similarity to Kohut's solution of the narcissism/object-love question.

46 Grotstein does not explicitly discuss the question of the very different time-tables of Mahler and of Melanie Klein in his correlation of the two models. Elsewhere (Grotstein 1982–83: 519–20), he discusses the distinction between 'early' processes and 'deep' processes, criticizing ego psychology for its emphasis on a chronological ordering of experience. Grotstein himself prefers the Kleinian approach according to which psychic organization is not necessarily chronologically ordered. This preference would probably account for his disregard of the question of Mahler's and Melanie Klein's differing timetables.

47 Grotstein, following Isaacs (1952), rejects the classical distinction between 'structure' and 'phantasy' (experience).

48 Grotstein emphasizes the literal meaning of 'representation' as a 're-presentation'; i.e., as an image that can be evoked in the absence of the object.

49 The six 'invariant' internal objects that Grotstein suggests are: (1) the background subject-object of primary identification: (2) the self as 'I's' first object choice; (3) the object of the future; (4) the interpersonal selfobject; (5) the caretaking environment; (6) the stranger.

Chapter 3 Orientations in ego psychology

1 Jacobson often used the term 'image' interchangeably with 'representation', although she usually attempted to reserve 'image' for reference to the products of regressive deterioration of representations. This, in accordance with her view of the developmental progression from primitive to structurally cohesive structures.

2 In Schafer's (1968) criticism of Jacobson's formulations regarding cathected representations he hints at the affinity between Jacobson's concepts and those of Melanie Klein.

3 I have not seen this fact – the relegation of the concepts of self and object

representations and the fluctuations between them (including projection and introjection) to the area of psychotic phenomena – mentioned in descriptions of Jacobson's theories. Nor have other theoreticians who have drawn on Jacobson's work (e.g., M. Mahler, Kernberg) followed here in this. I think it is an interesting peculiarity related to the specifically structural meaning that Jacobson attributed to the concepts of representation.

4   This approach, equating wishes with structural processes, has been seen, more recently, to have its drawbacks. Not all wishes for merger or unity with the object can be conceived as involving (structural) fusion of self and object representations, with its concomitant weakening of ego functioning, as Pine (1979) has demonstrated.

5   This is not the same as the difference between the need-satisfying object versus object-constancy (e.g., Burgner and Edgecumbe 1972). Jacobson maintained that even after the need-satisfying stage, 'the baby is still mainly concerned with his own precious self' and does not yet have fully differentiated representations. This conception may be seen as a forerunner of Kohut's concept of self-object.

6   In her later works Jacobson (1964, 1967) added 'severely narcissistic types of neurosis' to the field of pathology suffering from defects in object and self representation boundaries.

7   Searles (1965, 1966–67), too, criticized Jacobson on this issue. The interchange between them also touched on their differing clinical approaches (Jacobson 1964, 1967).

8   Jacobson (1964: 124) presented these three aspects without ordering them hierarchically. Some of her clinical examples (ibid.: 210–16) do suggest a hierarchy. Kernberg (1981) considers Jacobson's views to be basically hierarchical.

9   Searles (1965) complained that Jacobson's 'many creative insights are expressed through a Procrustean bed of technical jargon'. Friedman (1982), in turn, criticized the humanistic trend in psychoanalytic thought for trying to do away with theory altogether.

10   This point, regarding the contribution of the concept of representation to the psychoanalytic theory of perception, following Freud's rather naïve conception of perception as a 'direct' process, is further discussed in the final chapters of this study.

11   This conceptualization of the pathology of borderline patients is remarkably similar to that proposed by Adler and Buie (1979). The latter formulate this pathology in terms of the defect of the borderline's introjects rather than in terms of defects of representation.

12   Because of Novey's death at the age of 56 in 1967 (Loewald 1967), we do not know in what direction he would have further developed his views.

13   For a short list of some of the concepts discussed in papers coming out of the Hampstead Clinic Index project, see Sandler's preface to Sandler (1987b). Of course, in addition to the papers on theory and concepts, there are a plethora of clinical papers making use of the concepts discussed in the theoretical papers.

14   This idea is closely related to Hartmann's (1947) concept of the ego's 'organizing function', a term which Hartmann suggested instead of the term 'synthetic function'. While the 'synthetic function' carried libidinal connotations, the 'organizing function' was more clearly a term referring to the ego.

15 This idea is further elaborated in Sandler (1976).

16 Boesky (1983) criticized Sandler for not adhering to the idea that mental representations were not active agents, stating that Sandler and Rosenblatt 'seem to have it both ways. The mental representation cannot be an active agent but yet it has structure, function and guiding capacities'. Sandler's views on this are more clearly spelled out in his discussion of the 'experiential and non-experiential realms' in Sandler and Joffe (1969). This question is further discussed in relation to the issue of the nature of mental objects as motivated or non-motivated, in Part Two, 'Major theoretical issues'.

17 This function of mental representations as 'guiding' the mental apparatus is prominent in a series of papers on the ego ideal and the ideal self (Sandler *et al.* 1963) and on pain and depression (Joffe and Sandler 1965; Sandler and Joffe 1965).

18 Sandler did not explicitly repeat his earlier (1960) account of how this takes place but presumably his views on this remain unchanged.

19 This may be seen as Sandler's solution to the one-person-psychology/two-person-psychology dilemma, a solution whereby two-person dynamics may be translated back into one-person-psychology terms.

20 All three of the representational theorists discussed here cite Piaget in relation to the concept of representation. Fraiberg (1969) presents the most detailed comparison of the two concepts. In my opinion Fraiberg's comparison brings the psychoanalytic concept of representation too close to the Piagetian one, not sufficiently emphasizing the deep gap between them, as I have attempted to do in the present study.

21 A defence of the concept of mental representation was devoted specifically to show that it could be used without abandoning the structural theory (id, ego and superego) of ego psychology (J. Jacobson 1983a and 1983b).

22 The one paper of Rapaport's in which concepts related to internalization were discussed at any length, 'A theoretical discussion of the superego concept', was not finished by Rapaport, but rather was edited and published posthumously (Gill 1967).

23 A relatively large portion of the book deals with questions related to concepts of psychic energy and the economic point of view (chaps 3 and 7). Schafer seems to have been striving to reformulate the whole economic point of view, an effort that was soon to become obsolete, with the widespread rejection of that point of view in the psychoanalytic literature of the 1970s.

24 The concept of incorporation, while included among the 'principal terms of the discussion' in Schafer's preliminary definitions (chap. 1), does not receive much discussion in the study itself. Incorporation refers to a specific group of phantasies (Schafer prefers 'ideas') regarding the taking-in of another person (whole or part, creature or thing) into oneself corporeally. This group of phantasies, while much emphasized in the earlier psychoanalytic literature when drive psychology was prominent, plays a limited role in the ego psychology discussion of concepts of internalization.

25 All references are to Schafer (1968).

26 Schafer also discussed the concepts of self and object representations in Schafer (1967). There is little to add here from that discussion.

27 Friedman (1980a) considers Schafer's attempt to avoid attributing motivation

to representations as unsuccessful, and is of the opinion that Schafer, too, subtly allowed representations to acquire motivational status. I tend to agree with Friedman on this point, but am less disturbed by his divergence from a strictly ego psychology orientated, drive-defence view. See the summary of criticisms of the concept of representation at the end of the chapter on the representational theorists.

28 Schafer (1967) distinguished between realistic aspects of self and object representations ('experienced representations') and between ideal representations. While he did discuss processes of the distortion of the realistic aspects (idealization and depreciation), there too he seems to have considered the realistic aspects to be the basis for the processes of distortion.

29 Of course the concept of splitting existed in the psychoanalytic literature before Kernberg's discussions of it, but in Kernberg's theory it acquired a very special implication, as we shall see in this chapter.

30 Freud's (1927e, 1940e) concept of 'splitting' was considerably different from Fairbairn's, emphasizing a split between conscious and unconscious attitudes of the ego. Kernberg (1967) was specifically searching for a concept that would allow for alternating attitudes to be present in consciousness, rather than one being conscious and the other unconscious. Interestingly, one of Kernberg's earliest published papers (1963) deals with Sutherland's (1963) summary of Fairbairn's views.

31 Gradually Kernberg (1976, 1982) would come to emphasize the affective states rather than the drives as the primary organizing factor of mental life.

32 Fairbairn's analysand and student, Guntrip, devoted extensive discussions to the comparison of Fairbairn's concept of ego with that of Hartmann, rejecting Hartmann's 'system-ego' in favour of Fairbairn's 'person-ego' (Guntrip 1969, 1971). Guntrip (1975) also mentioned that Fairbairn agreed with him regarding the appropriateness of using the term 'self' in place of 'ego'.

33 Although Kernberg embraced Hartmann's elaboration of the structural concept of the ego, he did not accept Hartmann's strict distinction between ego and self. Rather, he considered the two to be closely interrelated – Kernberg (1982).

34 Kernberg (1966: 240) noted this disagreement on his part with Melanie Klein's views.

35 Regarding the relationship between self and self-representation, Kernberg (1982) defined the self as 'the sum total of self representations'.

36 Kernberg is very critical of the Kleinian understanding of internal objects as phantasies and of the consequence that 'If internal objects are phantasies and the structure of the personality is largely determined by phantasies which the ego has about itself and its internal objects, structure in this sense seems to imply largely phantasies about phantasies' (Kernberg 1969: 322).

37 Kernberg (1966) originally considered this period to end at about three months. Later (Kernberg 1976), he revised this view to bring his theory into concordance with Mahler's findings on the phases of symbiosis and differentiation.

38 An earlier version of this idea had already been discussed by Freud (1915c). Recently, Kernberg (1984) has discussed this process as an early manifestation of projective identification.

39 Kernberg recently devoted a special discussion to the subject of 'paranoid regression and malignant narcissism', further emphasizing his view on the close connection between the two (Kernberg 1984: chap. 19).

40 Kernberg often seems to use the terms 'object images' or 'representations' to refer to the Kleinian 'internal object', distinguishing between these and 'external objects', by which he means mental representations of external objects (e.g., Kernberg 1966: 244–5; 1975: 241; 1982: 902).

41 Kernberg (1976) strenuously rejects the Kleinian concept of a death instinct.

42 As noted in the discussion of these theorists, they also made considerable attempts to integrate the affective aspect of the concept into their theories.

43 It is interesting that this emphasis on 'drama' is considered by a group of Kleinians to be one of the metapsychological points of view in Melanie Klein's theory (Bianchedi *et al.* 1984).

44 A later paper of his (Stierlin 1973) emphasizes interpersonal rather than intrapsychic aspects of internalizations or inner objects.

45 Another possible reason for the lack of influence Stierlin's ideas have had on the psychoanalytic literature is that the ego psychology, function-orientated approach (which Stierlin is suggesting be adopted to the area of inner objects) has itself been losing in popularity recently, as may be seen from the recent series of papers in honour of Hartmann's 1939 book, *Ego Psychology and the Problem of Adaptation* (in the 1989 volume of *Psychoanalytic Quarterly*).

Chapter 4 Self orientations

1 The transitional object is not necessarily, or even commonly, a person. Therefore it is not an 'object' as this term has commonly been used in the psychoanalytic literature to refer to a person.

2 In spite of Goldberg's recent argument against 'translating' Winnicott's concept of transitional objects into intrapsychic terms (Goldberg 1984–5: 126), it is my contention that an important aspect of the concept of the transitional object in the context within which Winnicott used it had to do with the mental capacities of the infant. In Winnicott's words: 'It is not the object, of course that is transitional. The object represents the infant's transition from a state of being merged with the mother to a state of being in relation to the mother as something outside and separate' (1953: 14–15).

3 Grosskurth (1987) brings material eloquently describing Winnicott's deep sorrow and hurt as Melanie Klein gradually withdrew her support for Winnicott's ideas.

4 It should be noted that Winnicott is here identifying two aspects that could conceivably be distinguished: (1) the capacity to relate to another person realistically; (2) the subjective experience of the individual regarding another person. The former refers to what might be considered to be an ego function, one which might be objectively assessed and rated on a scale from 'poor' to 'good'. The latter refers to subjective experience, which is not 'done better or worse'. Winnicott's primary interest is in the subjective experience that accompanies the objective capacity. See note 5.

5 Abraham (1924) discussed a similar idea, regarding the anal object as a possession belonging to the individual, but no longer part of him. He even mentioned in this context 'how a child will take an object that is especially dear to him to bed with him at night and will lie on top of it' (p. 492). Winnicott's emphasis differs from Abraham's. Winnicott is specifically emphasizing the attitude to an actual object (or thing), and not a phantasy. It is here that Winnicott's uniqueness in exploring the development of the individual's capacity to relate to reality stands out. Whereas Abraham discussed the development of inner experiences by themselves (drives and phantasies), Winnicott emphasized the subjective experience involved in the capacity to relate to the reality of the object. See note 4.

6 In this context it is worth noting that the etymology of the word 'object' implies being 'thrown in the way' or 'thrown against'.

7 Winnicott explained that he contrasted 'external object' with 'satisfying object' because the satisfying object will tend to be experienced as 'internal', there being no reason to 'place' it 'outside' of the self.

8 In the original 1953 paper in the *International Journal of Psycho-Analysis* this section is titled 'Inadequacy of usual statement'.

9 Winnicott (1967) himself took up this elaboration when he stated that what is involved in the intermediate area is 'what life itself is about'.

10 Grolnick and Barkin (1978) present a representative anthology of these.

11 It is fascinating to note that in the middle of this paper (Winnicott 1967: 10) Winnicott reaches the sudden realization, 'I can see that I am in the territory of Fairbairn's (1941) concept of "object-seeking" (as opposed to "satisfaction-seeking")'. This is especially interesting because Winnicott had strongly criticized Fairbairn in regard to his attempt to 'supplant' Freud's theory of the drives (which is based on the idea of 'satisfaction-seeking') with an alternative theory of motivation, in a review of the latter's work (Winnicott and Khan 1953). It would seem that his 1953 criticism of Fairbairn would now be very close to home.

12 Kohut (1977) later abandoned the use of the hyphen in the term 'self-object'. This change may be taken to reflect the changing meaning of this term for Kohut, as will be described below.

13 More recently (1983), Kohut stated that the differences between his 1971 and 1977 books were not as great as his critics implied. In spite of this later tendency to emphasize the similarities between his 1971 and 1977 views, certain differences do remain, such as that discussed above.

14 In a later paper Wolf (1983) refers to Kohut's metaphor of 'empathic resonance' as relevant to development: 'The analysand's seeking of archaic mergers is replaced by empathic resonating' (p. 214).

15 It is of interest to note the similarity of this concept with that of projective identification, even down to the emphasis on the 'oppressive control' the analyst feels that the patient is exerting on him.

16 I am, of course, implying that Kohut has not achieved a 'value-free' judgement, but rather has replaced one value judgement for another.

17 It is interesting to note that just this ambiguity in Freud's use of the term 'object' between the external object and its mental representation was one of

the factors that led to the development of concepts of mental representation in the generation after.

Chapter 5 Origins of the mental object – internal or external

1 Mitchell's (1988b) four dichotomies are: phantasy versus perception, psychic reality versus actuality, inner world versus outer world, and drive theory versus a theory of environmental interaction.

2 Recently Schimek (1987) has reviewed the vicissitudes of Freud's seduction theory, reaching the conclusion that the change in Freud's views was not so clear-cut as is often described. This revision does not detract from the importance of the issue of internal versus external factors; in fact, it may be seen, in Schimek's paper, to enhance it.

3 This criticism of Freud's theory of perception does not detract from the fact that it is undoubtedly to Freud that we owe so much for showing the great complexities of the processes of mental functioning – see, e.g., Paul (1967); Wallerstein (1985).

4 Also see Editor's footnote to Freud (1900: 620), regarding different versions of this formulation.

5 E. Jaques (1981), in a discussion of the aims of psychoanalytic treatment from a Kleinian point of view, referred to the anxieties described by Melanie Klein (both persecutory and depressive) as 'delusional'. Presumably, the objects infused with such anxieties would be considered similarly.

6 As noted in the chapter on Freud, Freud did not tend to distinguish between identification and introjection.

7 See, e.g., A. Freud's (1965) frequent references to the process of identification in her discussion of the development of the child's personality.

8 I would like to note that the crux of the clinical (as opposed to theoretical) aspect of the intrapsych/interpersonal issue seems to have been absent from the clinical discussions of this conference – the countertransference as noted by Scharff (1988: 600–1). I shall discuss the relevance of this clinical aspect in the section on 'Division of responsibility in the therapeutic setting' in Chapter 10.

9 Neither of the papers discusses the advantages of using the concept of schema over that of representation. As I have shown in the historical survey, 'representation' has been used to do much of the 'work' which they expect from 'schema', so I will not enter into the question of the possible differences between them, and will consider 'schema' as roughly equivalent to 'represent-ation'. From a strictly semantic point of view it should be noted that the term 'schema' does not present psychoanalytic theory with some of the difficulties which arise with the use of 'representation', due to the accepted definition (following Piaget) of 'representation' as referring to a more advanced structure (implying the capacity to represent an absent object). I will further discuss this issue in relation to 'representation' in Part Three, 'A conceptual analysis'.

Chapter 6 Status of the mental object – experiential or non-experiential

1 Segal (1978) explicitly refers to the superego as a 'phantasy' similar to internal objects.

2 The idea of the superego as a depersonalized structure had originally been mentioned by Freud (1926d, 1931b). Anna Freud (1928) emphasized the difference between the child's superego and that of the adult in terms of its not yet being independent of the external objects on the basis of whose images it is formed. This became an important difference between Anna Freud's and Melanie Klein's respective treatment rationales.

3 Mackay (1981) has discussed the complex and problematic interplay of mechanistic and phenomenological concepts in Melanie Klein's theory, implying that Kleinian theory would do best to stick to a purely phenomenological approach. In contrast, Kernberg (1969) has praised those Kleinians who have attempted to develop structural concepts more compatible with an ego psychology framework.

4 While Kernberg (1969) did refer to Bion as one of those Kleinians who has developed structural concepts, he also noted that Bion's understanding of structure seemed to be at variance with the concept of structure as commonly used in ego psychology!

Chapter 7 The mental object and motivation

1 Stolorow's (1978) attempt to construct a 'psychoanalytic phenomenology' without concepts of motivation is the 'abnormal' which proves the norm. I tend to agree with Friedman's (1980a) criticism that Stolorow's formulations do integrate postulates regarding motivation, but simply do not acknowledge them as such.

2 This last question, to what extent the construction of object representations is considered to be motivated, has been the subject of a detailed critique by Friedman (1980a).

3 Meltzer (1981) expressed this in an extreme manner, stating that Melanie Klein's theory may be conceived as a 'theological model of the mind' in which 'internal objects perform the functions of Gods . . . [which] do in fact perform functions in the mind'.

4 Schafer (1983) has been critical of this approach from a clinical point of view, in addition to his criticism from the point of view of theory.

Chapter 8 The mental object as a developmental capacity

1 See E. Zetzel's (1970) description of the context of her interest in developmental capacities during the 1950s, and F. Pine's (1985) description of the same during the 1970s.

2 It should be noted that when Rapaport and Gill (1959) adopted the genetic point of view as one of the five basic points of view constituting metapsychology, they also took note of Glover's (1943) similar five-point formulation, which referred to the 'developmental' rather than the 'genetic' point of view. Evidence of the non-trivial nature of the distinction between the genetic and the developmental points of view may be gained from the critical reaction to the growing emphasis on the developmental point of view, in Goodman (1977: 85–94).

3 See Frosch's (1983) discussion of the defect-defence controversy in regard to psychosis.

Chapter 9 The position of the mental object *vis-à-vis* the self

1 This (Freud 1930a: 65) was one of the few places in which Freud referred to both terms – ego and self – as synonymous. It is also of interest to note that Freud here referred to the 'certainty' of the feeling of self, which later theorists and clinicians considered to be very open to uncertainty.

2 But not only – see the very interesting interchange between Edith Jacobson (1964, 1967) and Searles (1965, 1966–67) on this question. See also Gedo (1988), in regard to his concept of therapeutic symbiosis.

3 As was borne out in the conference on 'The intrapsychic and interpersonal dimensions' (Levi and Scharff 1988), discussed above.

4 I am aware that most advocates of self psychology do not tend to view the development of Kohut's views in this way and prefer to consider Kohut as intrapsychically orientated. While I agree that Kohut may be interpreted in this way, I think that the crux of the issue is in the clinical approach, where I find Kohut's technique to be quite interpersonally orientated, as I shall show in the next chapter, 'Responsibility – the clinical issue'.

Chapter 10 Responsibility – the clinical issue

1 See Levenson's (1982) criticism of the extremeness of this aspect of Schafer's view.

2 It is of interest to note that recently Modell (1990), influenced by both Winnicott and Kohut, has stated his discontent with the concept of resistance.

3 It is interesting to note that Hoffman (1983), Gill's co-worker in his work on the analysis of transference, prefers to view Gill's position as more radical than that of Kohut. He considers Kohut's position to be basically in accordance with the traditional psychoanalytic view regarding (what I have here called) the division of responsibility between patient and analyst in the transference, in contrast to Gill's position which Hoffman considers to reflect a more truly 'social' view. It may be that Hoffman's appraisal of Kohut's position would have been different after the publication of Kohut's last (1984) book, which in my opinion brings to full realization the radical nature of Kohut's proposals.

Chapter 11 Mental objects as representations (or schemas)

1 Compton (1985a, 1986) has traced the different meanings of the term 'object' in Freud's writings.
2 On the term 'schema' in psychoanalytic theory, see Paul (1967); also Wachtel (1989); Slap and Saykin (1983). It is also of interest to note that before settling on the term 'representation' for the idea he wished to express, Sandler (1960) also used the term 'schema'.
3 In fact, the term itself, 'representation', is an alternative translation of the German *Vorstellung* that Freud used, and that Strachey translated as 'presentation', 'idea' or 'imago'. Following Hartmann (1950), the term 'representation' gained in popularity, although it had earlier been used by Sterba (1942).
4 This definition is also in accord with Friedman's (1980a) criticism of the use of the concept of representation. There Friedman accepts the use of representation to denote 'potentialities for experiences and organizations into which experiences may fit' (p. 223). But it should also be noted that Friedman in general is critical of the shift in psychoanalytic theory towards an object-relations-orientated theory (Friedman 1988), so that it is not surprising that he is wary of the concept of representation which, as I have shown, plays an important role in that shift.
5 It is also interesting to note that Schimek's (1975) suggestion that the time has come to abandon the concept of 'unconscious mental representation' is related to his understanding of this concept as referring to 'a content of experience' (p. 177, n. 4) and his preference for the concept 'schema' which does not carry, in his opinion, this 'experiential' connotation. In my opinion, Schimek adheres too closely to Freud's use of the term *Vorstellung*, which he simply translates as 'representation', without taking into consideration the far-reaching changes that have taken place in the use of the term '*re*presentation' as I have described above and in the historical survey.
6 Psychoanalytic theoreticians who have compared Piaget's findings with those of psychoanalysis have discussed this difficulty; e.g., Wolff 1960; Fraiberg 1969.
7 Furth (1969) is critical of what he considers to be a confusion regarding different meanings of the concept of representation in Piaget's writings, and he suggests restricting 'representation' to the strict sense of 'making present something not present, as in an image or symbolic play' (p. 264). It is this meaning which has become especially relevant to the various meanings of the psychoanalytic concept of object constancy.
8 The Piagetian concept which may be considered to be comparable to the psychoanalytic concept of (object) representation is that of 'schema' with an emphasis on its assimilation to the schema. Schimek (1975) and Wachtel (1980) have proposed adopting the Piagetian concept of schema for just such reasons.
9 Beres and Joseph (1970) differ on this point, defining representation as implying the capacity to re-present (an absent object) in Piaget's meaning of the term. This definition does not seem to have had much influence in the psychoanalytic literature. This is probably due to the use of the concept of object constancy for that implication, as described above.

12 Mental objects as phantasies

1 I am here referring to phantasies as experiences and not to the function of phantasying (Sandler and Nagera 1963), which as a function would be considered non-experiential.
2 The term 'ego' in Kleinian terminology is often used to refer to what we would call the self-representation.
3 Both Fairbairn and Winnicott were deeply influenced by Melanie Klein's work, and both diverged from her views most significantly in regard to her almost exclusive emphasis on internal reality (Guntrip 1971: 96–7, regarding Fairbairn; Winnicott 1962). It seems that Bowlby underwent a similar process (Grosskurth 1987).
4 It should be noted that this does not apply only to certain people with schizoid disturbances, for Fairbairn considered the schizoid position to be basic to human nature, and considered everyone to be schizoid to some degree – Fairbairn (1940: 8–9).
5 Sutherland's (1963) presentation of Fairbairn's theory also tends to emphasize the organizing functions of Fairbairn's concept of 'endopsychic structure'.
6 In fact, it is clear that Melanie Klein also felt the need for a distinction between the individual's inner world and their experience of the external world (e.g., Klein 1935). While this distinction is not the same as a distinction between representation and phantasy as proposed here, it may be construed as a step in that direction.

Chapter 13 Mental objects as developmental capacities

1 Kernberg (1975, 1976) does not view splitting as only a developmental defect but also considers it to be an active defence mechanism. This leads to his technical approach that recommends the interpretation of splitting as such.
2 Eagle (1984: 127–43), in his discussion of the tendency to view pathology in terms of developmental defect rather than in terms of dynamic conflict, criticizes the developmental approach for its shift of emphasis regarding treatment strategies and orientations. But be it for better or for worse, it is clear that such a shift in the approach to treatment is a frequent accompaniment to the developmental point of view.

Bibliography

Abend, S. (1988) 'Intrapsychic versus interpersonal: the wrong dilemma', *Psychoanalytic Inquiry*, 8: 497–504.

Abend, S., Porder, M. and Willick, M. (1983) *Borderline Patients: Psychoanalytic Perspectives*, New York: International Universities Press.

Abraham, K. (1911) 'Notes on the psychoanalytical investigation and treatment of manic-depressive insanity and allied conditions', in *Selected Papers on Psychoanalysis*, London: Maresfield Reprints, 1979, pp. 137–56.

—— (1924) 'A short study of the development of the libido viewed in the light of mental disorders', in *Selected Papers on Psychoanalysis*, London: Maresfield Reprints, 1979, pp. 418–501.

—— (1925) 'Character formation on the genital level of the libido', in *Selected Papers on Psychoanalysis*, London: Maresfield Reprints, 1979, pp. 407–17.

Abraham, H. and Freud, E. (eds) (1965) *A Psychoanalytic Dialogue: The Letters of Sigmund Freud and Karl Abraham*, New York: Basic Books.

Abrams, S. (1977) 'The genetic point of view: historical antecedents and developmental transformations', *Journal of the American Psychoanalytic Association*, 25: 417–26.

—— (1978) 'The teaching and learning of psychoanalytic developmental psychology', *Journal of the American Psychoanalytic Association*, 26: 387–406.

Adler, G. (1988) 'How useful is the borderline concept?', *Psychoanalytic Inquiry*, 8: 353–72.

Adler, G. and Buie, D. (1979) 'Aloneness and borderline psychopathology: the possible relevance of child development issues', *International Journal of Psychoanalysis*, 60: 83–96.

Apfelbaum, B. (1965) 'Ego psychology, psychic energy and the hazards of quantitative explanation in psychoanalytic theory', *International Journal of Psychoanalysis*, 46: 168–82.

—— (1966) 'On ego psychology: a critique of the structural approach to psychoanalytic theory', *International Journal of Psycho-Analysis*, 47: 451–75.

Arieti, S. (1967) *The Intrapsychic Self: Feelings, Cognition and Creativity in Health and Mental Illness*, New York: Basic Books.

Arlow, J. (1969) 'Fantasy, memory and reality testing', *Psychoanalytic Quarterly*, 38: 28–51.

—— (1985) 'The concept of psychic reality and related concepts', *Journal of the American Psychoanalytic Association*, 33: 521–35.

Arlow, J. and Brenner, C. (1969) 'The psychopathology of the psychoses: a proposed revision', *International Journal of Psycho-Analysis*, 50: 5–14.

Balint, M. (1949a) 'Early developmental states of the ego: primary object love', *International Journal of Psycho-Analysis*, 30: 265–73.

—— (1949b) 'Sandor Ferenczi, 1933', *International Journal of Psycho-Analysis*, 30: 215–19.

Barchilon, J. (1973) 'Gustav Bychowski (1895–1972)', *International Journal of Psycho-Analysis*, 54: 112–13.

Beres, D. (1960a) 'The psychoanalytic psychology of imagination', *Journal of the American Psychoanalytic Association*, 8: 252–69.

—— (1960b) 'Perception, imagination and reality', *International Journal of Psycho-analysis*, 41: 327–34.

Beres, D. and Joseph, E. (1970) 'The concept of mental representation in psycho-analysis', *International Journal of Psycho-Analysis*, 51: 1–10.

Bianchedi, E. *et al.* (1984) 'Beyond Freudian metapsychology', *International Journal of Psycho-Analysis*, 65: 389–98.

Bieber, I. (1980) *Cognitive Psychoanalysis*, New York: J. Aronson.

Bion, W. R. (1954) 'Notes on the theory of schizophrenia', in *Second Thoughts* (1967), New York: J. Aronson, pp. 23–35.

—— (1957) 'Differentiation of the psychotic from the non-psychotic personalities', in *Second Thoughts* (1967), New York: J. Aronson, pp. 43–64.

—— (1958) 'On hallucination', in *Second Thoughts* (1967), New York: J. Aronson, pp. 65–85.

—— (1959) 'Attacks on linking', in *Second Thoughts* (1967), New York: J. Aronson, pp. 93–109.

—— (1962a) 'A theory of thinking', in *Second Thoughts* (1967), New York: J. Aronson, pp. 110–19.

—— (1962b) *Learning from Experience*, London: W. Heinemann Books.

—— (1967) *Second Thoughts*, New York: J. Aronson.

Blatt, S. and Lerner, H. (1983) 'Investigations in the psychoanalytic theory of object relations and object representations', in *Empirical Studies of Psychoanalytical Theories*, ed. J. Masling, Hillsdale, NJ: Analytic Press, pp. 189–250.

Boesky, D. (1983) 'The problem of mental representation in self and object theory', *Psychoanalytic Quarterly*, 52: 564–83.

Bornstein, M. (ed.) (1988) *Commentaries on Sander Abend, Michael Porder, and Martin Willick's Borderline Patients: Psychoanalytic Perspectives*, Hillsdale, NJ: Analytic Press.

Brierley, M. (1939) 'A prefatory note on internalized objects', *International Journal of Psycho-Analysis*, 20: 241–5.

—— (1942) 'Internal objects and theory', *International Journal of Psycho-Analysis*, 23: 107–12.

—— (1943) 'Theory, practice and public relations', *International Journal of Psycho-Analysis*, 24: 119–225.

—— (1944) 'Notes on metapsychology as process theory', *International Journal of Psycho-Analysis*, 25: 97–107.

—— (1951) *Trends in Psychoanalysis*, London: Hogarth Press.

Brody, S. (1980) 'Transitional objects: idealization of a phenomenon', *Psychoanalytic Quarterly*, 49: 561–605.

Buie, D. and Adler, G. (1982–83) 'Definitive treatment of the borderline patient', *International Journal of Psychoanalysis and Psychotherapy*, 9: 51–87.

Burgner, M. and Edgecumbe, R. (1972) 'Some problems in the conceptualization of early object relationships: part 2. The concept of object constancy', *Psychoanalytic Study of the Child*, 27: 315–33.

Bychowski, G. (1952) *Psychotherapy of Psychosis*, New York: Grune & Stratton.

—— (1956a) 'The ego and the introjects', *Psychoanalytic Quarterly*, 25: 11–36.

—— (1956b) 'Central aspects and implications of introjection', *Psychoanalytic Quarterly*, 25: 530–48.

—— (1956c) 'The release of internal objects', *International Journal of Psycho-Analysis*, 37: 331–8.

—— (1958) 'The struggle against the introjects', *International Journal of Psycho-Analysis*, 39: 182–7.

Cobliner, W. (1965) 'The Geneva school of genetic psychology and psychoanalysis: parallels and counterparts', in R. Spitz (1965) *The First Year of Life*, New York: International Universities Press, pp. 301–56.

Compton, A. (1985a) 'The development of the drive object concept in Freud's work: 1905–1915', *Journal of the American Psychoanalytic Association*, 33: 93–116.

—— (1985b) 'The concept of identification in the work of Freud, Ferenczi and Abraham: a review and commentary', *Psychoanalytic Quarterly*, 54: 200–33.

—— (1986) 'Freud: objects and structure', *Journal of the American Psychoanalytic Association*, 34: 561–90.

Dupont, J. (ed.) (1988) *The Clinical Diary of Sandor Ferenczi*, Cambridge, Mass.: Harvard University Press.

Eagle, M. (1984) *Recent Developments in Psychoanalysis: A Critical Evaluation*, Cambridge, Mass.: Harvard University Press.

Ehrenwald, J. (1973) 'Gustav Bychowski: an appreciation', *American Imago*, 30: 1–7.

Ellenberger, H. (1970) *The Discovery of the Unconscious*, New York: Basic Books.

Erikson, E. (1956) 'The problem of ego identity', *Journal of the American Psychoanalytic Association*, 4: 56–121.

Fairbairn, W. R. D. (1940) Schizoid factors in the personality', in W. R. D. Fairbairn (1952), *Psychoanalytic Studies of the Personality*, London: Tavistock, pp. 3–27.

—— (1941) 'A revised psychopathology of the psychoses and psychoneuroses', in *Psychoanalytic Studies of the Personality* (1952), London: Tavistock, pp. 28–58.

—— (1943) 'The repression and return of bad objects', in *Psychoanalytic Studies of the Personality* (1952), London: Tavistock, pp. 59–81.

—— (1944) 'Endopsychic structure considered in terms of object relationships', in *Psychoanalytic Studies of the Personality* (1952), London: Tavistock, pp. 82–136.

—— (1949) 'Steps in the development of an object relations theory of the personality', in *Psychoanalytic Studies of the Personality* (1952), London: Tavistock, pp. 152–61.

—— (1951) 'A synopsis of the development of the author's views regarding the structure of the personality', in *Psychoanalytic Studies of the Personality* (1952), London: Tavistock, pp. 162–79.

—— (1952) *Psychoanalytic Studies of the Personality*, London: Tavistock.

—— (1954) 'Observations on the nature of hysterical states', *British Journal of Medical Psychology*, 27: 105–22.

—— (1955) 'Observations in defence of the object relations theory of the personality', *British Journal of Medical Psychology*, 28: 144–58.

—— (1963) 'Synopsis of an object relations theory of the personality', *International Journal of Psycho-Analysis*, 44: 224–5.

Fenichel, O. (1925) 'Introjection and the castration complex', in *The Collected Papers of Otto Fenichel*, New York: Norton (1953), pp. 39–70.

—— (1945) *The Psychoanalytic Theory of Neurosis*, New York: Norton.

Ferenczi, S. (1909) 'Introjection and transference', in *Sex and Psychoanalysis*, New York: Brunner (1950), pp. 35–93.

—— (1912) 'On the definition of introjection', in *Final Contributions to the Problems and Methods of Psychoanalysis*, London: Hogarth (1955), pp. 316–18.

—— (1913) 'Stages in the development of the sense of reality', in *Sex in Psychoanalysis*, New York: Brunner (1950), pp. 213–39.

—— (1914) 'The ontogenesis of the interest in money', in *Sex in Psychoanalysis*, New York: Brunner (1950), pp. 319–31.

—— (1922) 'Freud's "Group psychology and the analysis of the ego"', in *Final Contributions to the Problems and Methods of Psychoanalysis*, London: Hogarth (1955), pp. 371–6.

—— (1933) 'Confusion of tongues between the adults and the children', in *Final Contributions to the Problems and Methods of Psycho-Analysis*, London, Hogarth (1955), pp. 156–67.

—— (1949) 'Ten letters to Freud', *International Journal of Psycho-Analysis*, 30: 237–50.

Flavell, J. (1963) *The Developmental Psychology of Jean Piaget*. Princeton: NJ: Van Nostrand.

Fleming, J. (1975) 'Some observations on object constancy in the psychoanalysis of adults', *Journal of the American Psychoanalytic Association*, 23: 743–60.

Flew, A. (1978) 'Transitional objects and transitional phenomena: comments and interpretations', in *Between Reality and Fantasy*, eds S. Grolnick and L. Barkin, New York: J. Aronson, pp. 483–502.

Fraiberg, S. (1969) 'Libidinal object constancy and mental representation', *Psychoanalytic Study of the Child*, 24: 9–47.

Freud, A. (1928) 'The theory of child analysis', in *The Writings of Anna Freud*, vol. 1, New York: International Universities Press, pp. 162–75.

—— (1936) *The Ego and the Mechanisms of Defence* (rev. edn), New York: International Universities Press (1966).

—— (1952) 'The mutual influences in the development of ego and id: introduction to the discussion', *Psychoanalytic Study of the Child*, 7: 42–50.

—— (1965) *Normality and Pathology in Childhood*, New York: International Universities Press.

[The references to Freud's work have been arranged in accordance with the bibliographical references of the *Standard Edition of the Complete Psychological Works of Sigmund Freud*.]

Freud, S. (1984a) 'The neuro-psychoses of defence', *SE* 3.

—— (1896b) 'Further remarks on the neuro-psychoses of defence', *SE* 3.

—— (1900a) *The Interpretation of Dreams, SE* 4, 5.

—— (1901b) 'The psychopathology of everyday life', *SE* 6.

—— (1905c) 'Jokes and their relation to the unconscious', *SE* 8.

—— (1905d) *Three Essays on the Theory of Sexuality, SE* 7.

—— (1906a) 'My views on the part played by sexuality in the aetiology of the neuroses', *SE* 7.

—— (1908a) 'Hysterical phantasies and their relation to bisexuality', *SE* 9.

—— (1908b) 'Character and anal erotism', *SE* 9.

—— (1910c) 'Leonardo Da Vinci and a memory of his childhood', *SE* 11.

—— (1910h) 'A special type of choice of object made by men', *SE* 11.

—— (1910j) 'Two instances of pathogenic phantasies revealed by the patients themselves', *SE* 11.

—— (1911b) 'Formulations on the two principles of mental functioning', *SE* 12.

—— (1911c) 'Psycho-analytic notes on an autobiographical account of a case of paranoia (dementia paranoides)', *SE* 12.

—— (1912b) 'The dynamics of transference', *SE* 12.

—— (1912d) 'On the universal tendency to debasement in the sphere of love', *SE* 12.

—— (1913i) 'The predisposition to obsessional neurosis', *SE* 12.

—— (1914c) 'On narcissism: an introduction', *SE* 14.

—— (1915c) 'Instincts and their vicissitudes', *SE* 14.

—— (1915e) 'The unconscious', *SE* 14.

—— (1916x) *Introductory Lectures on Psycho-Analysis, SE* 15, 16.

—— (1917c) 'On transformations of instinct as exemplified in anal erotism', *SE* 17.

—— (1917e) 'Mourning and melancholia', *SE* 14.

—— (1918b) 'From the history of an infantile neurosis', *SE* 17.

—— (1921c) *Group Psychology and the Analysis of the Ego, SE* 18.

—— (1923b) *The Ego and the Id, SE* 19.

—— (1924c) 'The economic problem of masochism', *SE* 19.

—— (1924d) 'The dissolution of the Oedipus complex', *SE* 19.

—— (1925i) 'Some additional notes on dream-interpretation as a whole', *SE* 19.

—— (1925j) 'Some psychological consequences of the anatomical distinction between the sexes', *SE* 19.

—— (1926d) *Inhibitions, Symptoms and Anxiety, SE* 20.

—— (1927e) 'Fetishism', *SE* 21.

—— (1930a) *Civilization and its Discontents, SE* 21.

—— (1931a) 'Libidinal types', *SE* 21.

—— (1931b) 'Female sexuality', *SE* 21.

—— (1933a) *New Introductory Lectures on Psycho-Analysis, SE* 22.

—— (1940a) *An Outline of Psycho-Analysis, SE* 23.

—— (1940e) 'Splitting of the ego in the process of defence', *SE* 23.

—— (1950a) 'The origins of psychoanalysis', *SE* 1.

Freud, S. and Breuer, J. (1895) *Studies on Hysteria, SE* 2.

Friedman, L. (1978) 'Trends in psychoanalytic theory of treatment', *Psychoanalytic Quarterly*, 47: 524–67.

—— (1980a) 'The barren prospect of a representational world', *Psychoanalytic Quarterly*, 49: 215–33.

—— (1980b) 'Kohut: a book review essay', *Psychoanalytic Quarterly*, 49: 393–422.

—— (1982) 'The humanistic trend in recent psychoanalytic theory', *Psychoanalytic Quarterly*, 51: 353–71.

—— (1988) 'The clinical polarity of object relations concepts', *Psychoanalytic Quarterly*, 57: 667–91.

Frosch, J. (1983) *The Psychotic Process*, New York: International Universities Press.

Furer, M. (1972) 'A history of the superego concept in psychoanalysis: a review of the literature', in *Moral Values and the Superego Concept*, ed. S. Post, New York: International Universities Press, pp. 11–62.

Furth, H. (1968) 'The nature of representation and interiorization', in *Piaget and Knowledge*, ed. H. Furth, Englewood Cliffs, NJ: Prentice-Hall, pp. 68–82.

Gedo, J. (1979) *Beyond Interpretation: Toward a Revised Theory for Psychoanalysis*, New York: International Universities Press.

—— (1988) 'Character, dyadic enactments, and the need for symbiosis', *Psychoanalytic Inquiry*, 8: 459–71.

Ghent, E. (1989) 'Credo: the dialectics of one-person and two-person psychologies', *Contemporary Psychoanalysis*, 25: 169–211.

Gill, M. (ed.) (1967) *The Collected Papers of David Rapaport*, New York: Basic Books.

—— (1977) 'The two models of the mental health discipline', *Bulletin of the Menninger Clinic*, 41: 79–84.

—— (1982) *Analysis of Transference*, vol. 1, New York: International Universities Press.

—— (1983a) 'The point of view of psychoanalysis: energy discharge or person', *Psychoanalysis and Contemporary Thought*, 6: 523–51.

—— (1983b) 'The interpersonal paradigm and the degree of the therapist's involvement', *Contemporary Psychoanalysis*, 19: 200–37.

Gill, M. and Hoffman, I. (1982) *Analysis of Transference*, vol. 2, New York: International Universities Press.

Gill, M. and Holzman. P. (eds) (1976) *Psychology vs. Metapsychology*, New York: International Universities Press.

Gillespie, W. (1980) Book review, *International Journal of Psycho-Analysis*, 61: 85–8.

Glover, E. (1943) 'The concept of dissociation', in E. Glover, *Basic Mental Concepts* (1947) London: Imago, pp. 307–23.

—— (1945) 'Examination of the Klein system of child psychology', *Psychoanalytic Study of the Child*, 1: 75–118.

—— (1947) *Basic Mental Concepts*, London: Imago.

Goldberg, A. (1984–5) 'Translation between psychoanalytic theories', *The Annual of Psychoanalysis*, 12/13: 121–36.

Goodman, S. (ed.) (1977) *Psychoanalytic Education and Research: The Current Situation and Future Possibilities*, New York: International Universities Press.

Gouin-Decarie, T. (1965) *Intelligence and Affectivity in Early Childhood*, New York: International Universities Press.

Greenberg, J. and Mitchell, S. (1983) *Object Relations in Psychoanalytic Theory*, Cambridge, Mass.: Harvard University Press.

Greenson, R. (1971) 'The "real"relationship between the patient and the psychoanalyst', in *Explorations in Psychoanalysis*, New York: International Universities Press, pp. 425–40.

Grolnick, S. and Barkin, L. (eds) (1978) *Between Reality and Fantasy: Transitional Objects and Phenomena*, New York: J. Aronson.

Grosskurth, P. (1987) *Melanie Klein: Her World and Her Work*, Cambridge, Mass.: Harvard University Press.

Grossman, W. and Simon, B. (1969) 'Anthropomorphism: motive, meaning and causality in psychoanalytic theory', *Psychoanalytic Study of the Child*, 24: 78–111.

Grotstein, J. (1977) 'The psychoanalytic concept of schizophrenia', *International Journal of Psycho-Analysis*, 58: 403–52.

—— (1980) 'A proposed revision of the psychoanalytic concept of primitive mental states. Part 1', *Contemporary Psychoanalysis*, 16: 479–546.

—— (1980–81) 'The significance of Kleinian contributions to psychoanalysis. 1 and 2', *International Journal of Psychoanalysis and Psychotherapy*, 8: 375–428.

—— (1981) *Splitting and Projective Identification*, New York: J. Aronson.

—— (1982) 'Newer perspectives in object relations theory', *Contemporary Psychoanalysis*, 18: 43–91.

—— (1982–83) 'The significance of Kleinian contributions to psychoanalysis. 3 and 4', *International Journal of Psychoanalysis and Psychotherapy*, 9: 487–536.

—— (1983) 'A proposed revision of the psychoanalytic concept of primitive mental states. part 2', *Contemporary Psychoanalysis*, 17: 570–604.

—— (1984) 'A proposed revision of the psychoanalytic concept of primitive mental states. part 2-2, *Contemporary Psychoanalysis*, 20: 77–119.

Guntrip, H. (1961) *Personality Structure and Human Interaction*, New York: International Universities Press.

—— (1969) *Schizoid Phenomena, Object Relations and the Self*, New York: International Universities Press.

—— (1971) *Psychoanalytic Theory, Therapy and the Self*, New York: Basic Books.

—— (1975) 'My experience of analysis with Fairbairn and Winnicott', *International Review of Psycho-Analysis*, 2: 145–56.

Hartmann, H. (1939) *Ego Psychology and the Problem of Adaptation*, New York: International Universities Press, 1958.

—— (1947) 'On rational and irrational action', in *Essays on Ego Psychology: Selected Problems in Psychoanalytic Theory* (1964), New York: International Universities Press, pp. 37–68.

—— (1950) 'Comments on the psychoanalytic theory of the ego', in *Essays on Ego*

Psychology: Selected Problems in Psychoanalytic Theory (1964), New York: International Universities Press, pp. 113–41.

—— (1952) 'The mutual influences in the development of ego and id', in *Essays on Ego Psychology: Selected Problems in Psychoanalytic Theory* (1964), New York: Inter- national Universities Press, pp. 155–81.

—— (1953) 'Contributions to the metapsychology of schizophrenia', in *Essays on Ego Psychology: Selected Problems in Psychoanalytic Theory* (1964), New York: Inter- national Universities Press, pp. 182–206.

—— (1956) 'Notes on the reality principle', *Psychoanalytic Study of the Child*, 11: 31–53.

—— (1964) *Essays on Ego Psychology: Selected Problems in Psychoanalytic Theory*, New York: International Universities Press.

Hartmann, H. and Kris, E. (1945) 'The genetic approach in psychoanalysis', *Psychoanalytic Study of the Child*, 1: 11–30.

Hartmann, H. and Loewenstein, R. H. (1962) 'Notes on the superego', *Psychoanalytic Study of the Child*, 17: 42–81.

Heimann, P. (1942a) 'Some notes on the psychoanalytic concept of introjected objects', *British Journal of Medical Psychology*, 22: 8–15.

—— (1942b) 'A contribution to the problem of sublimation and its relation to processes of internalization', *International Journal of Psycho-Analysis*, 23: 8–17.

—— (1952) 'Certain functions of introjection and projection in early infancy', in *Developments in Psychoanalysis*, ed. J. Riviere (1952), London: Hogarth, pp. 122–68.

Heimann, P. and Isaacs, S. (1952) 'Regression', in *Developments in Psychoanalysis*, ed. J. Riviere (1952), London: Hogarth, pp. 169–97.

Hoffer, W. (1952) 'The mutual influences in the development of ego and id: earliest stages', *Psychoanalytic Study of the Child*, 7: 31–41.

Hoffman, I. (1983) 'The patient as interpreter of the analyst's experience', *Contemporary Psychoanalysis*, 19: 389–422.

Isaacs, S. (1945) 'Notes on metapsychology as process theory: some comments', *International Journal of Psycho-Analysis*, 26: 58–62.

—— (1952) 'The nature and function of phantasy', in *Developments in Psychoanalysis*, ed. J. Riviere (1952), London: Hogarth, pp. 67–121.

Jacobson, E. (1946) 'The effect of disappointment on ego and superego formation in normal and depressive development', *Psychoanalytic Review*, 33: 129–47.

—— (1953) 'Contributions to the metapsychology of cyclothymic depression', in *Affective Disorders*, ed. P. Greenacre, New York: International Universities Press, pp. 49–83.

—— (1954a) 'Contributions to the metapsychology of psychotic identification', *Journal of the American Psychoanalytic Association*, 2: 239–62.

—— (1954b) 'On psychotic identifications', *International Journal of Psycho-Analysis*, 35: 102–8.

—— (1954c) 'The self and the object world', *Psychoanalytic Study of the Child*, 9: 75–127.

—— (1964) *The Self and the Object World*, New York: International Universities Press.

—— (1967) *Psychotic Conflict and Reality*, New York: International Universities Press.

Jacobson, J. (1983a) 'The structural theory and the representational world', *Psychoanalytic Quarterly*, 52: 514–42.

—— (1983b) 'The structural theory and the representational world', *Psychoanalytic Quarterly*, 52: 543–63.

Jaques, E. (1981) 'The aims of psychoanalytic treatment', in *Do I Dare Disturb the Universe?* ed. J. Grotstein, Beverly Hills, Ca.: Caesura Press, pp. 417–26.

Joffe, W. (1969) 'A critical review of the status of the envy concept', *International Journal of Psycho-Analysis*, 50: 533–46.

Joffe, W. and Sandler, J. (1965) 'Notes on pain, depression and individuation', *Psychoanalytic Study of the Child*, 20: 394–424.

Jones, E. (1953) *The Life and Work of Sigmund Freud*, vol. 1, New York: Basic Books.

—— (1957) *The Life and Work of Sigmund Freud*, vol. 3, New York: Basic Books.

Jung, C. (1913) 'The theory of psychoanalysis', in *Collected Works of C. G. Jung*, vol. 4, Princeton, NJ: Princeton University Press (1970), pp. 83–226.

Kanzer, M. (1979) 'Developments in psychoanalytic technique', *Journal of the American Psychoanalytic Association*, supplement, 27: 327–74.

Kennedy, H. (1971) 'Problems in reconstruction in child analysis', *Psychoanalytic Study of the Child*, 26: 386–402.

Kernberg, O. (1963) 'Discussion of J. D. Sutherland's paper: "Object relations theory and the conceptual model of psychoanalysis"', *British Journal of Medical Psychology*, 36: 121–4.

—— (1966) 'Structural derivatives of object relationships', *International Journal of Psycho-Analysis*, 47: 236–53.

—— (1967) 'Borderline personality organization', *Journal of the American Psychoanalytic Association*, 15: 641–85.

—— (1969) 'A contribution to the ego-psychological critique of the Kleinian school', *International Journal of Psycho-Analysis*, 50: 317–34.

—— (1975) *Borderline Conditions and Pathological Narcissism*, New York: J. Aronson.

—— (1976) *Object Relations Theory and Clinical Psychoanalysis*, New York: J. Aronson.

—— (1981) 'An overview of Edith Jacobson's contributions', in *Object and Self: a Developmental Approach*, eds S. Tuttman, C. Kaye and M. Zimmerman, New York: International Universities Press, pp. 103–28.

—— (1982) 'Self, ego, affects and drives', *Journal of the American Psychoanalytic Association*, 30: 83–917.

—— (1984) *Severe Personality Disorders*, New Haven, CT: Yale University Press.

—— (1987) 'Projection and projective identification: developmental and clinical aspects', *Journal of the American Psychoanalytic Association*, 35: 795–820.

Kestenberg, J. (1971) 'From organ-object imagery to self and object representations', in *Separation–Individuation*, eds J. McDevitt and C. Settlage, New York: International Universities Press, pp. 75–99.

King, P. (1983) 'The life and work of Melanie Klein in the British Psycho-Analytical Society', *International Journal of Psycho-Analysis*, 64: 251–60.

Klein, G. (1969) 'Freud's two theories of sexuality', in G. Klein (1976) *Psycho-analytic Theory*, New York: International Universities Press, pp. 72–120.

—— (1976) *Psychoanalytic Theory: an Exploration of Essentials*, New York: International Universities Press.

Klein, M. (1926) 'The psychological principles of early analysis', in *Love, Guilt and Reparation and Other Works*, New York: Delacorte Press (1975), pp. 128–38.

—— (1927a) 'Symposium on child-analysis', in *Love, Guilt and Reparation and Other Works*, New York: Delacorte Press (1975), pp. 139–69.

—— (1927b) 'Criminal tendencies in normal children', *Love, Guilt and Reparation and Other Works*, New York: Delacorte Press (1975), pp. 170–85.

—— (1928) 'Early stages of the oedipus conflict', in *Love, Guilt and Reparation and Other Works*, New York: Delacorte Press (1975), pp. 186–98.

—— (1929a) 'Personification in the play of children', in *Love, Guilt and Reparation and Other Works*, New York: Delacorte Press (1975), pp. 199–209.

—— (1929b) 'Infantile anxiety situations reflected in a work of art and in the creative impulse', in *Love, Guilt and Reparation and Other Works*, New York: Delacorte Press (1975), pp. 210–18.

—— (1930) 'Importance of symbol formation in the development of the ego', in *Love, Guilt and Reparation and Other Works*, New York: Delacorte Press (1975), pp. 219–32.

—— (1931) 'A contribution to the theory of intellectual inhibition', in *Love, Guilt and Reparation and Other Works*, New York: Delacorte Press (1975), pp. 236–47.

—— (1932) *The Psychoanalysis of Children*, London: Hogarth Press.

—— (1935) 'A contribution to the psychogenesis of manic-depressive states', in *Love, Guilt and Reparation and Other Works*, New York: Delacorte Press (1975), pp. 262–89.

—— (1940) 'Mourning and its relation to manic-depressive states', in *Love, Guilt and Reparation and Other Works*, New York: Delacorte Press (1975), pp. 344–69.

—— (1945) 'The oedipus complex in the light of early anxieties', in *Love, Guilt and Reparation and Other Works*, New York: Delacorte Press (1975), pp. 370–419.

—— (1946) 'Notes on some schizoid mechanisms', in *Envy and Gratitude and Other Works*, New York: Delacorte Press (1975), pp. 1–24.

—— (1948) 'On the theory of anxiety and guilt', in *Envy and Gratitude and Other Works*, New York: Delacorte Press (1975), pp. 25–42.

—— (1952c) 'Some theoretical conclusions regarding the emotional life of the infant', in *Envy and Gratitude and Other Works*, New York: Delacorte Press (1975), pp. 61–93.

—— (1957) 'Envy and gratitude', in *Envy and Gratitude and Other Works*, New York: Delacorte Press (1975), pp. 176–235.

—— (1958) 'On the development of mental functioning', in *Envy and Gratitude and Other Works*, New York: Delacorte Press (1975), pp. 236–46.

—— (1975) *Envy and Gratitude and Other Works*, New York: Delacorte Press.

Kohut, H. (1971) *The Analysis of the Self*, New York: International Universities Press.

—— (1977) *The Restoration of the Self*, New York: International Universities Press.

—— (1983) 'Selected problems of self psychological theory', in *Reflections on Self Psychology*, eds J. Lichtenberg and S. Kaplan, NJ: Lawrence Erlbaum, pp. 387–416.

—— (1984) *How Does Analysis Cure?*, Chicago: Chicago University Press.

Kris, E. (1950) 'Notes on the development and of some current problems of psychoanalytic child psychology', in *The Selected Papers of Ernst Kris* (1975), New Haven, CT: Yale University Press, pp. 54–79.

—— (1951) 'The development of ego psychology', in *The Selected Papers of Ernst Kris* (1975), New Haven, CT: Yale University Press, pp. 375–89.

Leon, I. (1984) 'Psychoanalysis, Piaget and attachment: the construction of the human object in the first year of life', *International Review of Psycho-Analysis*, 11: 255–78.

Levenson, E. (1982) *The Ambiguity of Change: an Inquiry into the Nature of Psychoanalytic Reality*, New York: Basic Books.

Levi, L. and Scharff, D. (eds) (1988) *The Intrapsychic and Interpersonal Dimensions: an Unresolved Dilemma*, Hillsdale, NJ: Analytic Press.

Levy, E. and Rapaport, D. (1944) 'The psychoanalytic concept of memory and its relation to recent memory theories', in M. Gill (ed.) (1967) *The Collected Papers of David Rapaport*, New York: Basic Books, pp. 136–59.

Lichtenberg, J. (1983) *Psychoanalysis and Infant Research*, Hillsdale, NJ: Analytic Press.

—— (1988) 'Commentary', *Psychoanalytic Inquiry*, 8: 578–92.

Lichtenstein, H. (1961) 'Identity and sexuality', *Journal of the American Psychoanalytic Association*, 9: 179–260.

Loewald, H. (1962) 'Internalization, separation, mourning and the superego', *Psychoanalytic Quarterly*, 31: 483–504.

—— (1967) 'Obituary for S. Novey', *Psychoanalytic Quarterly*, 36: 590.

—— (1971) 'Some considerations on repetition and repetition compulsion', in *Papers on Psychoanalysis*, New Haven, CT: Yale University Press (1980), pp. 87–101.

—— (1979) 'The waning of the oedipus complex', in *Papers on Psychoanalysis*, New Haven, CT: Yale University Press, pp. 384–404.

London, N. (1973) 'An essay on psychoanalytic theory: two theories of schizophrenia', *International Journal of Psycho-Analysis*, 54: 169–94.

McDevitt, J. and Mahler, M. (1980) 'Object constancy, individuality and internalization', in *The Course of Life*, vol. 1, eds S. Greenspan and G. Pollock, Washington DC: US Government Printing Office, pp. 407–24.

McDougall, J. (1985) *Theaters of the Mind*, New York: Basic Books.

McGuire, W. (ed.) (1974) *The Freud/Jung Letters*, Princeton, NJ: Princeton University Press.

Mackay, N. (1981) 'Melanie Klein's metapsychology: phenomenological and mechanistic perspectives', *International Journal of Psycho-Analysis*, 62: 187–98.

Mahler, M. (1967) 'On human symbiosis and the vicissitudes of individuation', *Psychoanalytic Study of the Child*, 29: 89–106.

—— (1968) *On Human Symbiosis and the Vicissitudes of Individuation*, New York: International Universities Press.

Matte-Blanco, I. (1941) 'On introjection and the processes of psychic metabolism', *International Journal of Psycho-Analysis*, 22: 17–36.

Meissner, W. (1970) 'Notes on identification. 1. Origins in Freud', *Psychoanalytic Quarterly*, 39: 563–89.

—— (1976) 'A note on internalization as process', *Psychoanalytic Quarterly*, 45: 374–93.

——(1981) *Internalization in Psychoanalysis*, New York: International Universities Press.

Melito, R. (1983) 'Cognitive aspects of splitting and libidinal object constancy', *Journal of the American Psychoanalytic Association*, 31: 513–34.

Meltzer, D. (1967) *The Psycho-Analytical Process*, Strath Tay, Perthshire: Clunie Press.

—— (1978) *The Kleinian Development*, Part 3, Strath Tay, Perthshire: Clunie Press.

—— (1981) 'The Kleinian expansion of Freud's metapsychology', *International Journal of Psycho-Analysis*, 62: 177–85.

Michels, R. (1988) 'Commentary', *Psychoanalytic Inquiry*, 8: 568–77.

Mitchell, S. (1981) 'The origin and nature of the "object" in the theories of Klein and Fairbairn', *Contemporary Psychoanalysis*, 17: 374–98.

—— (1988a) *Relational Concepts in Psychoanalysis: an Integration*, Cambridge, Mass.: Harvard University Press.

—— (1988b) 'The intrapsychic and the interpersonal: different theories, different domains, or historical artifacts', *Psychoanalytic Inquiry*, 8: 472–96.

Modell, H. (1990) *Other Times, Other Realities: Toward a Theory of Psychoanalytic Treatment*, Cambridge, Mass.: Harvard University Press.

Novey, S. (1958) 'The meaning of the concept of mental representation of objects', *Psychoanalytic Quarterly*, 27: 57–79.

—— (1959) 'A clinical view of affect theory in psychoanalysis', *International Journal of Psycho-Analysis*, 40: 94–104.

—— (1961) 'Further considerations on affect theory in psychoanalysis', *International Journal of Psycho-Analysis*, 42: 21–31.

Panel (1968) 'Panel discussion', *International Journal of Psychoanalysis*, 49: 506–12.

Pao, P.-N. (1979) *Schizophrenic Disorders*, New York: International Universities Press.

Paul, I. (1967) 'The concept of schema in memory theory', in *Motives and Thought: Psychoanalytic Essays in Honor of David Rapaport*, ed. R. Holt, New York: International Universities Press, pp. 218–58.

Peterfreund, E. (1971) *Information, Systems and Psychoanalysis: an Evolutionary Biological Approach to Psychoanalysis*, New York: International Universities Press.

Pine, F. (1974) 'Libidinal object constancy', *Psychoanalysis and Contemporary Science*, 3: 307–13.

—— (1979) 'Pathology of the separation–individuation process as manifested in later clinical work', *International Journal of Psycho-Analysis*, 60: 225–42.

—— (1985) *Developmental Theory and Clinical Process*, New Haven, CT: Yale University Press.

—— (1988) 'The four psychologies of psychoanalysis and their place in clinical work', *Journal of the American Psychoanalytic Association*, 36: 571–96.

—— (1989) 'Motivation, personality organization and the four psychologies of psychoanalysis', *Journal of the American Psychoanalytic Association*, 37: 31–64.

—— (1990) *Drive, Ego, Object Relations and Self*, New York: Basic Books.

Rangell, L. (1985) 'On the theory of theory in psychoanalysis and the relation of theory to psychoanalytic therapy', *Journal of the American Psychoanalytic Association*, 33: 59–92.

—— (1988) 'Roots and derivatives of unconscious fantasy', in *Fantasy, Myth and Reality*, eds H. Blum, Y. Kramer, A. Richards and A. Richards, New York: International Universities Press, pp. 61–78.

Rapaport, D. (1958) 'A historical survey of psychoanalytic ego psychology', in *The Collective Papers of David Rapaport*, ed. M. Gill (1967), New York: Basic Books, pp. 745–57.

—— (1960) 'Psychoanalysis as a developmental psychology', in *The Collected Papers of David Rapaport*, New York: Basic Books, pp. 820–52.

—— (1967) 'A theoretical analysis of the superego concept', in *The Collected Papers of David Rapaport*, New York: Basic Books, pp. 685–709.

Rapaport, D. and Gill, M. (1959) 'The points of view and assumptions of metapsychology', in *The Collected Papers of David Rapaport*, New York: Basic Books, pp. 795–811.

Rinsley, D. (1982) *Borderline and Other Self Disorders*, New York: J. Aronson.

Riviere, J. (1927) 'Symposium on child analysis', *International Journal of Psycho-Analysis*, 8: 370–77.

—— (1936) 'On the genesis of psychical conflict in earliest infancy', in ed. J. Riviere (1952a) *Developments in Psychoanalysis*, London: Hogarth, pp. 37–66.

—— (ed.) (1952a) *Developments in Psychoanalysis*, London: Hogarth.

—— (1952b) 'The unconscious phantasy of an inner world reflected in examples from literature', *International Journal of Psycho-Analysis*, 33: 160–72.

Robbins, M. (1980) 'Current controversy in object relations theory as an outgrowth of a schism between Klein and Fairbairn', *International Journal of Psycho-Analysis*, 61: 477–92.

Rosenblatt, A. and Thickstun, J. (1970) 'A study of the concept of psychic energy', *International Journal of Psycho-Analysis*, 51: 265–78.

Rosenfeld, H. (1952) 'Notes on the psychoanalysis of the superego conflict in an acute schizophrenic patient', in *Psychotic States*, New York: International Universities Press (1966), pp. 63–104.

—— (1963) 'Notes on the psychopathology and psychoanalytic treatment of schizophrenia', in *Psychotic States*, New York: International Universities Press (1966), pp. 155–68.

Rubinstein, B. (1976) 'On the possibility of a strictly clinical psychoanalytic theory: an essay in the philosophy of psychoanalysis', in eds M. Gill and P. Holzman (1976) *Psychology vs. Metapsychology*, New York: International Universities Press, pp. 229–64.

Sandler, J. (1960) 'On the concept of superego', *Psychoanalytic Study of the Child*, 15: 128–62.

—— (1962) 'Psychology and psychoanalysis', in J. Sandler (1987b) *From Safety to Superego: Selected Papers of Joseph Sandler*, London: Karnac Books, pp. 45–57.

—— (1972) 'The role of affects in psychoanalytic theory', in *From Safety to Superego: Selected Papers of Joseph Sandler*, London: Karnac Books, pp. 285–97.

—— (1976) 'Dreams, unconscious fantasies and "identity of perception"', *International Review of Psycho-Analysis*, 3: 33–42.

—— (1981) 'Unconscious wishes and human relationships', *Contemporary Psychoanalysis*, 17: 180–96.

—— (1983) 'Reflections on some relations between psychoanalytic concepts and psychoanalytic practice', *International Journal of Psycho-Analysis*, 64: 35–45.

—— (1985) 'Towards a reconstruction of the psychoanalytic theory of motivation', *Bulletin of the Anna Freud Centre*, 8: 223–44.

—— (1987a) 'The concept of projective identification', in *Projection, Identification and Projective Identification*, ed. J. Sandler, Madison, CT: International Universities Press, pp. 13–26.

—— (1987b) *From Safety to Superego: Selected Papers of Joseph Sandler*, London: Karnac Books.

—— (1990a) 'Internal objects and internal object relationships', *Psychoanalytic Inquiry*, 10: 163–81.

—— (1990b) 'What do we mean by objects? Some comments', *Psychoanalysis in Europe: Bulletin of the European Psychoanalytic Federation*, 35: 13–17.

—— (1991) 'Comments on the psychodynamics of interaction', Presentation at Fall Meetings of the American Psychoanalytic Institute, New York.

—— (1993) 'On communication from patient to analyst: not everything is projective identification', *International Journal of Psycho-Analysis*, 74: 1097–1107.

Sandler, J., Dare, C. and Holder, A. (1978) 'Frames of reference in psychoanalytic psychology: 11. Limitations of the topographical model', *British Journal of Medical Psychology*, 51: 61–5.

Sandler, J., Holder, A. and Meers, P. (1963) 'The ego ideal and the ideal self', *Psychoanalytic Study of the Child*, 18: 139–58.

Sandler, J. and Joffe, W. (1965) 'Notes on childhood depression', *International Journal of Psycho-Analysis*, 46: 88–96.

—— (1966) 'On skills and sublimation', *Journal of the American Psychoanalytic Association*, 14: 335–55.

—— (1969) 'Towards a basic psychoanalytic model', *International Journal of Psycho-Analysis*, 50: 79–90.

Sandler, J. and Nagera, H. (1963) 'Aspects of the metapsychology of fantasy', *Psychoanalytic Study of the Child*, 18: 159–94.

Sandler, J. and Rosenblatt, B. (1962) 'The concept of the representational world', *Psychoanalytic Study of the Child*, 17: 128–48.

Sandler, J. and Sandler, A.-M. (1978) 'On the development of object relations and affects', *International Journal of Psycho-Analysis*, 59: 285–96.

—— (1986) 'The gyroscopic function of unconscious fantasy', in *Towards a Compre-*

hensive Model for Schizophrenic Disorders, ed. D. Feinsilver, Hillsdale, NJ: Analytic Press, pp. 109–24.

Schafer, R. (1960) 'The loving and beloved superego in Freud's structural theory', *Psychoanalytic Study of the Child*, 15: 163–88.

—— (1967) 'Ideals, the ego ideal and the ideal self', in *Motives and Thought: Psychoanalytic Essays in Memory of David Rapaport*, ed. R. Holt, New York: International Universities Press, pp. 131–74.

—— (1968) *Aspects of Internalization*, New York: International Universities Press.

—— (1970) 'The psychoanalytic vision of reality', *International Journal of Psycho-Analysis*, 51: 279–97.

—— (1972) 'Internalization: process or fantasy', *Psychoanalytic Study of the Child*, 27: 411–36.

—— (1976) *A New Language for Psychoanalysis*, London: Yale University Press.

—— (1983) *The Analytic Attitude*, New York: Basic Books.

Scharff, D. (1988) 'Epilogue: countertransference as the interface between the intrapsychic and the interpersonal', *Psychoanalytic Inquiry*, 8: 598–602.

Schimek, J. (1975) 'The interpretations of the past: childhood trauma, psychic reality and historical truth', *Journal of the American Psychoanalytic Association*, 23: 835–65.

—— (1987) 'Fact and fantasy in the seduction theory: a historical review', *Journal of the American Psychoanalytic Association*, 35: 937–66.

Scholnick, E. (1983) 'Why are new trends in conceptual representation a challenge to Piaget's theory?', in *New Trends in Conceptual Representation: Challenges to Piaget's Theory*, ed. E. Scholnick, Hillsdale, NJ: L. Erlbaum, pp. 41–70.

Searles, H. (1965) 'Identity development in Edith Jacobson's *The Self and the Object World*', *International Journal of Psycho-Analysis*, 46: 529–32.

—— (1966–67) 'Concerning the development of an identity', in *Countertransference and Related Subjects*, New York: International Universities Press, 1979, pp. 45–70.

Segal, H. (1972) 'A note on internal objects', in *The Work of Hanna Segal*, New York: J. Aronson (1981), pp. 159–64.

—— (1978) *Introduction to the Work of Melanie Klein*, London: Hogarth.

Settlage, C. (1980) 'Psychoanalytic developmental thinking in current and historical perspective', *Psychoanalysis and Contemporary Thought*, 3: 139–70.

Shane, E. and Shane, M. (eds) (1989) *The Developmental Perspective in Psycho-analysis*, Hillsdale, NJ: Analytic Press.

Singer, M. (1977) 'The experience of emptiness in narcissistic and borderline states: 1 and 2', *International Review of Psycho-Analysis*, 4: 459–80.

Slap, J. and Saykin, A. (1983) 'The schema: basic concept in a nonmeta-psychological model of the mind', *Psychoanalysis and Contemporary Thought*, 6: 305–25.

Solnit, A. (1982) 'Developmental perspectives on self and object constancy', *Psychoanalytic Study of the Child*, 37: 201–18.

Solnit, A. and Neubauer, P. (1986) 'Object constancy and early triadic relation-ships', *Journal of the American Academy of Child Psychology*, 25: 23–9.

Spillius, E. (1983) 'Some developments from the work of Melanie Klein', *International Journal of Psycho-Analysis*, 64: 321–32.

Spitz, R. (1945) 'Hospitalism: an inquiry into the genesis of psychiatric conditions in early childhood', in *Rene A. Spitz: Dialogues from Infancy*, ed. R. Emde (1983), New York: International Universities Press, pp. 5–22.

—— (1946) 'Hospitalism: a follow-up report', in *Rene A. Spitz: Dialogues from Infancy*, ed. R. Emde (1983), New York: International Universities Press, pp. 23–7.

—— (1950) 'Anxiety in infancy: a study of its manifestations in the first year of life', *International Journal of Psycho-Analysis*, 31: 138–43.

—— (1965) *The First Year of Life: a Psychoanalytic Study of Normal and Deviant Object Relations*, New York: International Universities Press.

—— (1966) 'Metapsychology and direct infant observation', in *Rene A. Spitz: Dialogues from Infancy*, ed. R. Emde (1983), New York: International Universities Press, pp. 276–86.

Sterba, R. (1942) *Introduction to the Psychoanalytic Theory of the Libido*, New York: Nervous and Mental Disease Monographs.

Stern, D. (1988) 'The dialectic between the "interpersonal" and the "intrapsychic": with particular emphasis on the role of memory and representation', *Psychoanalytic Inquiry*, 8: 505–12.

Stierlin, H. (1970) 'The function of "inner objects"', *International Journal of Psycho-Analysis*, 51: 321–30.

—— (1973) 'Interpersonal aspects of internalization', *International Journal of Psycho-Analysis*, 54: 203–24.

Stolorow, R. (1978) 'The concept of psychic structure: its metapsychological and clinical psychoanalytic meanings', *International Review of Psycho-Analysis*, 53: 313–20.

Stolorow, R. and Atwood, G. (1979) *Faces in a Cloud: Subjectivity in Personality Theory*, New York: J. Aronson.

Strachey, A. (1941) 'A note on the use of the word "internal"', *International Journal of Psycho-Analysis*, 22: 37–43.

Strachey, J. (1930) 'Some unconscious factors in reading', *International Journal of Psycho-Analysis*, 11: 322–31.

Sutherland, J. (1963) 'Object relations theory and the conceptual model of psychoanalysis', *British Journal of Medical Psychology*, 36: 109–20.

Tausk, V. (1933) 'The origin of the "influencing machine" in schizophrenia', *Psychoanalytic Quarterly*, 2: 519–56 (original German publication 1919).

Wachtel, P. (1980) 'Transference, schema and assimilation: the relevance of Piaget to the psychoanalytic theory of transference', *The Annual of Psychoanalysis*, 8: 59–76.

Wallerstein, R. (1973) 'Psychoanalytic perspectives on the problem of reality', *Journal of the American Psychoanalytic Association*, 21: 5–33.

—— (1976) 'Psychoanalysis as a science: its present status and its future', in *Psychology vs. Metapsychology*, eds M. Gill and P. Holzman, New York: International Universities Press, pp. 198–228.

—— (1985) 'The concept of psychic reality: its meaning and value', *Journal of the American Psychoanalytic Association*, 33: 555–69.

Wexler, M. (1971) 'Schizophrenia: conflict and deficiency', *Psychoanalytic Quarterly*, 40: 83–99.

Winnicott, D. (1935) 'The manic defence', in *Through Paediatrics to Psychoanalysis* (1978), London: Hogarth Press, pp. 129–45.

—— (1945) 'Primitive emotional development', in *Through Paediatrics to Psychoanalysis* (1978), London: Hogarth Press, pp. 145–56.

—— (1948) 'Paediatrics and psychiatry', in *Through Paediatrics to Psychoanalysis* (1978), London: Hogarth Press, pp. 157–73.

—— (1950–55) 'Aggression in relation to emotional development', in *Through Paediatrics to Psychoanalysis* (1978), London: Hogarth Press, pp. 204–18.

—— (1953) 'Transitional objects and transitional phenomena', in *Through Paediatrics to Psychoanalysis* (1978), London: Hogarth Press, pp. 229–42.

—— (1962) 'A personal view of the Kleinian contribution', in D. Winnicott, *The Maturational Processes and the Facilitating Environment* (1965), London: Hogarth Press, pp. 171–8.

—— (1965) *The Maturational Processes and the Facilitating Environment*, London: Hogarth Press.

—— (1967) 'The location of cultural experience', in D. Winnicott, *Playing and Reality* (1971a), London: Tavistock Publications, pp. 95–105.

—— (1969) 'The use of an object and relating through identifications', in D. Winnicott, *Playing and Reality* (1971a), London: Tavistock Publications, pp. 86–94.

—— (1971a) *Playing and Reality*, London: Tavistock Publications.

—— (1971b) *Therapeutic Consultations in Child Psychiatry*, London: Hogarth Press.

Winnicott, D. and Khan, M. (1953) Book review, *International Journal of Psycho-Analysis*, 34: 329–33.

Wisdom, J. O. (1961) 'A methodological approach to the problem of hysteria', *International Journal of Psycho-Analysis*, 42: 224–37.

—— (1962) 'Comparison and development of the psychoanalytical theories of melancholia', *International Journal of Psycho-Analysis*, 43: 113–32.

—— (1981) 'Metapsychology after forty years', in *Do I Dare Disturb the Universe?* ed. J. Grotstein, Beverly Hills, CA: Caesura Press, pp. 601–24.

Wolf, E. (1980) 'On the developmental line of selfobject relations', in *Advances of Self Psychology*, ed. A. Goldberg, New York: International Universities Press, pp. 117–32.

—— (1983) 'Discussion of papers by Drs Lichtenberg and Ornstein', in *Reflections on Self Psychology*, eds J. Lichtenberg and S. Kaplan, Hillsdale, NJ: Analytic Press, pp. 203–15.

Wolff, P. (1960) *The Developmental Psychologies of Jean Piaget and Psychoanalysis*, New York: International Universities Press.

Young-Bruehl, E. (1988) *Anna Freud*, New York: Summit Books.

Zetzel, E. (1956) 'Concept and content in psychoanalytic theory', in E. Zetzel (1970), *The Capacity for Emotional Growth*, New York: International Universities Press, pp. 115–38.

—— (1970) *The Capacity for Emotional Growth*, New York: International Universities Press.

Index

ego structure 59, 64, 133
Ehrenwald, J. 74
empathy 143–5
endopsychic structure 56, 58
Erickson, E. 104
experiential and nonexperiential
    realms 4, 20, 64, 66, 81, 92–3,
    130–2, 134, 139, 150, 154, 157–8,
    163 *see also* mental objects

Fairbairn, W. R. D. 4, 26, 54, 56–64,
    93, 103–4, 107, 133–4, 143, 155–7
Federn, P. 72
feeling states 92, 140
Fenichel, O. 3, 78
Ferenczi, S. 14, 19, 23–7, 31
Flavell, J. 152
Fleming, J. 162
Flew, A. 116
Foulkes, S. 41
Fraiberg, S. 110, 112, 152
Freud, A. 35, 39, 110–12, 119, 126,
    152, 163
Freud, S. 4, 9–35, 39, 43–5, 56–60,
    65, 72, 78, 108, 111, 125–8, 136,
    138–9, 141–3, 149–52, 155; theory
    of childhood seduction 19, 125,
    136, 142
Friedman, L. 96–8, 122, 138, 161
Furth, H. 152

Gedo, J. 128, 135, 162
Gill, M. 131, 142–5
Gillespie, W. 40
Glover, E. 32, 39, 41, 126, 130, 134
Gouin-Decarie, T. 112
grandiose self 107, 120–1
Greenberg, J. 1, 63
Greenson, R. 137
Grosskurth, P. 19, 26, 40, 59, 64, 126
Grossman, W. 131
Grotstein, J. 3, 69–71
Guntrip, H. 62–3, 156

Hartmann, H. 13, 63, 74–8, 98–9,
    104, 106, 109–10, 126, 131, 137,
    139–40, 155

Heimann, P. 31–3, 40, 42, 48, 52–4
Herbart, J.F. 10
Hoffer, W. 110

idealization 50, 119–20
identification 14–23, 25, 34, 79, 81,
    87, 91, 94, 99, 101–2, 104–5, 127,
    140; hysterical 14; narcissistic 14,
    18, 24, 27–8
identity 82–3, 104
imagination 89–90
imago 13, 33–9, 43
incorporation 29–30, 38, 40, 56, 81,
    104, 140
instincts, life and death 44–6, 49–51,
    56, 60, 65, 67–8, 88, 107, 115,
    126, 155
integration of good and bad aspects of
    object 49–50, 75–6, 105, 111, 138,
    159–60
internal objects 3, 21–3, 66, 69–71,
    108–9, 113, 134, 158; assimilation
    of 32, 52–5; Fairbairn's concept of
    57, 59–64, 107–8, 133–4, 156;
    functions of 108–9, 156; M. Klein's
    concept of 22, 31–56, 59–60, 65,
    69–71, 93, 107–8, 126, 130, 155–7
internalization 91, 98–102, 112, 140,
    157; Fairbairn's concept of 56–64
introjection 59, 65, 79, 91, 93,
    99–102, 104–5, 112, 127, 140;
    Abraham's concept of 28–30; of
    the aggressor 26; Ferenczi's concept
    of 14, 23–7; Freud's concept of
    13–21, 24–7, 34, 43, 60–1, 125;
    M. Klein's concept of 34, 36–7,
    45, 50; partial 30
introjects 3, 10, 72–4, 97, 99–101,
    131, 134, 155, 158
introversion 12–14, 22, 167
Isaacs, S. 32–3, 40–2, 45–6, 126, 131

Jacobson, E. 4, 70, 74, 76–85, 88,
    95–6, 98–9, 103–6, 117, 138–41,
    143, 157, 159–60
Joffe, W. 6, 32, 92, 97
Jones, E. 25